Pentaho Data Integration 4 Cookbook

Over 70 recipes to solve ETL problems using Pentaho Kettle

Adrián Sergio Pulvirenti

María Carina Roldán

BIRMINGHAM - MUMBAI

Pentaho Data Integration 4 Cookbook

First published: June 2011

Production Reference: 1170611

Published by Packt Publishing Ltd.
32 Lincoln Road
Olton
Birmingham, B27 6PA, UK.

ISBN 978-1-849515-24-5

www.packtpub.com

Cover Image by Ed Maclean (edmaclean@gmail.com)

Credits

Authors

Adrián Sergio Pulvirenti

María Carina Roldán

Reviewers

Jan Aertsen

Pedro Alves

Slawomir Chodnicki

Paula Clemente

Samatar Hassan

Nelson Sousa

Acquisition Editor

Usha Iyer

Development Editor

Neha Mallik

Technical Editors

Conrad Sardinha

Azharuddin Sheikh

Project Coordinator

Joel Goveya

Proofreaders

Stephen Silk

Aaron Nash

Indexer

Tejal Daruwale

Graphics

Nilesh Mohite

Production Coordinator

Kruthika Bangera

Cover Work

Kruthika Bangera

About the Authors

Adrián Sergio Pulvirenti was born in Buenos Aires, Argentina, in 1972. He earned his Bachelor's degree in Computer Sciences at UBA, one of the most prestigious universities in South America.

He has dedicated more than 15 years to developing desktop and web-based software solutions. Over the last few years he has been leading integration projects and development of BI solutions.

> I'd like to thank my lovely kids Camila and Nicolas, who understood that I couldn't share with them the usual videogame sessions during the writing process. I'd also thank my wife who introduced me to the Pentaho world.

María Carina Roldán was born in Esquel, Argentina, in 1970. She earned her Bachelors degree in Computer Science at UNLP in La Plata; after that she did a postgraduate course in Statistics at the University of Buenos Aires (UBA) in Buenos Aires city where she lives since 1994.

She has worked as a BI consultant for more than 10 years. Over the last four years, she has been dedicated full time to developing BI solutions using Pentaho Suite. Currently she works for Webdetails, one of the main Pentaho contributors.

She is the author of *Pentaho 3.2 Data Integration: Beginner's Guide* published by *Packt Publishing* in April 2010.

You can follow her on Twitter at `@mariacroldan`.

I'd like to thank those who have encouraged me to write this book: On one hand, the Pentaho community. They have given me a rewarding feedback after the Beginner's book. On the other side, my husband who without hesitation agreed to write the book with me. Without them I'm not sure I would have embarked on a new book project.

I'd also like to thank the technical reviewers for the time and dedication that they have put in reviewing the book. In particular, thanks to my colleagues at Webdetails; it's a pleasure and a privilege to work with them every day.

About the Reviewers

Jan Aertsen has worked in IT and decision support for the past 10 years. Since the beginning of his career he has specialized in data warehouse design and business intelligence projects. He has worked on numerous global data warehouse projects within the fashion industry, retail, banking and insurance, telco and utilities, logistics, automotive, and public sector.

Jan holds the degree of Commercial Engineer in international business affairs from the Catholic University of Leuven (Belgium) and extended his further knowledge in the field of business intelligence through a Masters in Artificial Intelligence.

In 1999 Jan started up the business intelligence activities at IOcore together with some of his colleagues, rapidly making this the most important revenue area of the Belgian affiliate. They quickly gained access to a range of customers as KPN Belgium, Orange (now Base), Mobistar, and other Belgian Telcos.

After this experience Jan joined Cap Gemini Ernst & Young in Italy and rapidly became one of their top BI project managers. After having managed some large BI projects (up to 1 million € projects) Jan decided to leave the company and pursue his own ambitions.

In 2002, he founded kJube as an independent platform to develop his ambitions in the world of business intelligence. Since then this has resulted in collaborations with numerous companies as Volvo, Fendi-LVMH, ING, MSC, Securex, SDWorx, Blinck, and Beate Uhse.

Over the years Jan has worked his way through every possible aspect of business intelligence from KPI and strategy definition over budgeting, tool selection, and software investments acquisition to project management and all implementation aspects with most of the available tools. He knows the business side as well as the IT side of the business intelligence, and therefore is one of the rare persons that are able to give you a sound, all-round, vendor-independent advice on business intelligence.

He continues to share his experiences in the field through his blog (`blog.kjube.be`) and can be contacted at `jan.aertsen@kjube.be`.

Pedro Alves, is the founder of Webdetails. A Physicist by formation, serious video gamer, volleyball player, open source passionate, and dad of two lovely children.

Since his early professional years he has been responsible for Business Software development and his career led him to work as a Consultant in several Portuguese companies.

In 2008 he decided it was time to get his accumulated experience and share his knowledge about the Pentaho Business Intelligence platform on his own. He founded Webdetails and joined the Mozilla metrics team. Now he leads an international team of BI Consultants and keeps nurturing Webdetails as a world reference Pentaho BI solutions provider and community contributor. He is the Ctools (CDF, CDA, CDE, CBF, CST, CCC) architect and, on a daily basis, keeps developing and improving new components and features to extend and maximize Pentaho's capabilities.

Slawomir Chodnicki specializes in data warehousing and ETL, with a background in web development using various programming languages and frameworks. He has established his blog at `http://type-exit.org` to help fellow BI developers embrace the possibilities of PDI and other open source BI tools.

I would like to thank all regular members of the ##pentaho IRC channel for their endless patience and support regarding PDI related questions. Very special thanks go to María Carina and Adrián Sergio for creating the Kettle Cookbook and inviting me to be part of the project.

Paula Clemente was born in Sintra, Portugal, in 1983. Divided between the idea of spending her life caring about people and animals or spending quality time with computers, she started studying Computer Science at IST Engineering College—"the Portuguese MIT"—at a time where Internet Social Networking was a synonym of IRC. She graduated in 2008 after completing her Master thesis on Business Processes Management. Since then she is proudly working as a BI Consultant for Webdetails, a Portuguese company specialized in delivering Pentaho BI solutions that earned the Pentaho "Best Community Contributor 2011" award.

Samatar Hassan is an application developer focusing on data integration and business intelligence. He was involved in the Kettle project since the year it was open sourced. He tries to help the community by contributing in different ways; taking the translation effort for French language, participating in the forums, resolving bugs, and adding new features to the software.

He contributed to the "Pentaho Kettle Solutions" book edited by Wiley and written by Matt Casters, the founder of Kettle.

I would first like to thank Adrián Sergio and María Carina Roldán for taking the time to write this book. It is a great idea to show how to take advantage of Kettle through step-by-step recipes. Kettle users have their own ETL bible now.

Finally, I'd like to thank all community members. They are the real power of open source software.

Nelson Sousa is a business intelligence consultant at Webdetails. He's part of the Metrics team at Mozilla where he helps develop and maintain Mozilla's Pentaho server and solution. He specializes in Pentaho dashboards using CDF, CDE, and CDA and also in PDI, processing vast amounts of information that are integrated daily in the various dashboards and reports that are part of the Metrics team day-to-day life.

www.PacktPub.com

Support files, eBooks, discount offers and more

You might want to visit www.PacktPub.com for support files and downloads related to your book.

Did you know that Packt offers eBook versions of every book published, with PDF and ePub files available? You can upgrade to the eBook version at www.PacktPub.com and as a print book customer, you are entitled to a discount on the eBook copy. Get in touch with us at service@packtpub.com for more details.

At www.PacktPub.com, you can also read a collection of free technical articles, sign up for a range of free newsletters and receive exclusive discounts and offers on Packt books and eBooks.

http://PacktLib.PacktPub.com

Do you need instant solutions to your IT questions? PacktLib is Packt's online digital book library. Here, you can access, read and search across Packt's entire library of books.

Why Subscribe?

- ▶ Fully searchable across every book published by Packt
- ▶ Copy and paste, print and bookmark content
- ▶ On demand and accessible via web browser

Free Access for Packt account holders

If you have an account with Packt at www.PacktPub.com, you can use this to access PacktLib today and view nine entirely free books. Simply use your login credentials for immediate access.

We dedicate this book to our family and specially our adorable kids.

- María Carina and **Adrián -**

Table of Contents

Preface

Pentaho Data Integration (PDI, also called Kettle), one of the data integration tools leaders, is broadly used for all kind of data manipulation, such as migrating data between applications or databases, exporting data from databases to flat files, data cleansing, and much more. Do you need quick solutions to the problems you face while using Kettle?

Pentaho Data Integration 4 Cookbook explains Kettle features in detail through clear and practical recipes that you can quickly apply to your solutions. The recipes cover a broad range of topics including processing files, working with databases, understanding XML structures, integrating with Pentaho BI Suite, and more.

Pentaho Data Integration 4 Cookbook shows you how to take advantage of all the aspects of Kettle through a set of practical recipes organized to find quick solutions to your needs. The initial chapters explain the details about working with databases, files, and XML structures. Then you will see different ways for searching data, executing and reusing jobs and transformations, and manipulating streams. Further, you will learn all the available options for integrating Kettle with other Pentaho tools.

Pentaho Data Integration 4 Cookbook has plenty of recipes with easy step-by-step instructions to accomplish specific tasks. There are examples and code that are ready for adaptation to individual needs.

Learn to solve data manipulation problems using the Pentaho Data Integration tool Kettle.

What this book covers

Chapter 1, Working with Databases helps you to deal with databases in Kettle. The recipes cover creating and sharing connections, loading tables under different scenarios, and creating dynamic SQL statements among others topics.

Chapter 2, Reading and Writing Files shows you not only the basics for reading and writing files, but also all the how-tos for dealing with files. The chapter includes parsing unstructured files, reading master/detail files, generating multi-sheet Excel files, and more.

Chapter 3, Manipulating XML Structures teaches you how to read, write, and validate XML data. It covers both simple and complex XML structures.

Chapter 4, File Management helps you to pick and configure the different options for copying, moving, and transferring lists of files or directories.

Chapter 5, Looking for Data explains the different methods for searching information in databases, text files, web services, and more.

Chapter 6, Understanding Data Flows focuses on the different ways for combining, splitting, or manipulating streams or flows of data in simple and complex situations.

Chapter 7, Executing and Reusing Jobs and Transformations explains in a simple fashion topics that are critical for building complex PDI projects. For example, building reusable jobs and transformations, iterating the execution of a transformation over a list of data and transferring data between transformations.

Chapter 8, Integrating Kettle and the Pentaho Suite. PDI aka Kettle is part of the Pentaho Business Intelligent Suite. As such, it can be used interacting with other components of the suite, for example as the datasource for reporting, or as part of a bigger process. This chapter shows you how to run Kettle jobs and transformations in that context.

Chapter 9, Getting the Most Out of Kettle covers a wide variety of topics, such as customizing a log file, sending e-mails with attachments, or creating a custom functionality.

Appendix, Data Structures describes some structures used in several recipes throughout the book.

What you need for this book

PDI is a multiplatform tool, meaning that you will be able to install the tool no matter what your operating system is. The only prerequisite to work with PDI is to have JVM 1.5 or a higher version installed. It is also useful to have Excel or Calc, a nice text editor, and access to a database engine of your preference.

Having an Internet connection while reading is extremely useful as well. Several links are provided throughout the book that complement what is explained. Besides, there is the PDI forum where you may search or post doubts if you are stuck with something.

Who this book is for

If you are a software developer or anyone involved or interested in developing ETL solutions, or in general, doing any kind of data manipulation, this book is for you. It does not cover PDI basics, SQL basics, or database concepts. You are expected to have a basic understanding of the PDI tool, SQL language, and databases.

Conventions

In this book, you will find a number of styles of text that distinguish between different kinds of information. Here are some examples of these styles, and an explanation of their meaning.

Code words in text are shown as follows: "Copy the .jar file containing the driver to the libext/JDBC directory inside the Kettle installation directory".

A block of code is set as follows:

```
NUMBER, LASTNAME, FIRSTNAME, EXT, OFFICE, REPORTS, TITLE
1188, Firrelli, Julianne,x2174,2,1143, Sales Manager
1619, King, Tom,x103,6,1088,Sales Rep
```

When we wish to draw your attention to a particular part of a code block, the relevant lines or items are set in bold:

```
<request>
    <type>City</type>
    <query>Buenos aires, Argentina</query>
    <preferredScale>C</preferredScale>
</request>
```

New terms and **important words** are shown in bold. Words that you see on the screen, in menus or dialog boxes for example, appear in the text like this: "Add a **Delete file** entry from the **File management** category"

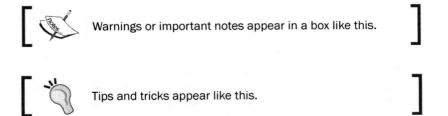

Warnings or important notes appear in a box like this.

Tips and tricks appear like this.

Reader feedback

Feedback from our readers is always welcome. Let us know what you think about this book—what you liked or may have disliked. Reader feedback is important for us to develop titles that you really get the most out of.

To send us general feedback, simply send an e-mail to feedback@packtpub.com, and mention the book title via the subject of your message.

If there is a book that you need and would like to see us publish, please send us a note in the **SUGGEST A TITLE** form on www.packtpub.com or e-mail suggest@packtpub.com.

If there is a topic that you have expertise in and you are interested in either writing or contributing to a book, see our author guide on www.packtpub.com/authors.

Customer support

Now that you are the proud owner of a Packt book, we have a number of things to help you to get the most from your purchase.

Downloading the example code

You can download the example code files for all Packt books you have purchased from your account at http://www.PacktPub.com. If you purchased this book elsewhere, you can visit http://www.PacktPub.com/support and register to have the files e-mailed directly to you.

Errata

Although we have taken every care to ensure the accuracy of our content, mistakes do happen. If you find a mistake in one of our books—maybe a mistake in the text or the code—we would be grateful if you would report this to us. By doing so, you can save other readers from frustration and help us improve subsequent versions of this book. If you find any errata, please report them by visiting http://www.packtpub.com/support, selecting your book, clicking on the **errata submission form** link, and entering the details of your errata. Once your errata are verified, your submission will be accepted and the errata will be uploaded on our website, or added to any list of existing errata, under the Errata section of that title. Any existing errata can be viewed by selecting your title from http://www.packtpub.com/support.

Piracy

Piracy of copyright material on the Internet is an ongoing problem across all media. At Packt, we take the protection of our copyright and licenses very seriously. If you come across any illegal copies of our works, in any form, on the Internet, please provide us with the location address or website name immediately so that we can pursue a remedy.

Please contact us at copyright@packtpub.com with a link to the suspected pirated material.

We appreciate your help in protecting our authors, and our ability to bring you valuable content.

Questions

You can contact us at questions@packtpub.com if you are having a problem with any aspect of the book, and we will do our best to address it.

1
Working with Databases

In this chapter, we will cover:

- Connecting to a database
- Getting data from a database
- Getting data from a database by providing parameters
- Getting data from a database by running a query built at runtime
- Inserting or updating rows in a table
- Inserting new rows when a simple primary key has to be generated
- Inserting new rows when the primary key has to be generated based on stored values
- Deleting data from a table
- Creating or altering a table from PDI (design time)
- Creating or altering a table from PDI (runtime)
- Inserting, deleting, or updating a table depending on a field
- Changing the database connection at runtime
- Loading a parent-child table

Introduction

Databases are broadly used by organizations to store and administer transactional data such as customer service history, bank transactions, purchases and sales, and so on. They also constitute the storage method for **data warehouses**, the repositories used in Business Intelligence solutions.

In this chapter, you will learn to deal with databases in Kettle. The first recipe tells you how to connect to a database, which is a prerequisite for all the other recipes. The rest of the chapter teaches you how to perform different operations and can be read in any order according to your needs.

 The focus of this chapter is on relational databases (RDBMS). Thus the term database is used as a synonym for relational databases through the recipes.

Sample databases

Through the chapter you will use a couple of sample databases. Those databases can be created and loaded by running the scripts available at the book's website. The scripts are ready to run under MySQL.

 If you work with a different DBMS you may have to modify the scripts slightly.

For more information about the structure of the sample databases and the meaning of the tables and fields, please refer to *Appendix, Data Structures*. Feel free to adapt the recipes to different databases. You could try some well known databases; for example Foodmart (available as part of the **Mondrian** distribution at `http://sourceforge.net/projects/mondrian/`) or the MySQL sample databases (available at `http://dev.mysql.com/doc/index-other.html`).

Pentaho BI platform databases

As part of the sample databases used in this chapter you will use the Pentaho BI platform Demo databases. The **Pentaho BI Platform Demo** is a pre-configured installation that lets you explore the capabilities of the Pentaho platform. It relies on the following databases:

Database name	Description
hibernate	Administrative information including user authentication and authorization data.
quartz	Repository for Quartz, the scheduler used by Pentaho.
sampledata	Data for Steel Wheels, a fictional company that sells all kind of scale replicas of vehicles.

By default, all those databases are stored in Hypersonic (HSQLDB). The script for creating the databases in HSQLDB can be found at `http://sourceforge.net/projects/pentaho/files`. Under **Business Intelligence Server | 1.7.1-stable** look for **pentaho_sample_data-1.7.1.zip**.

It can also be found at `svn://ci.pentaho.com/view/Platform/job/bi-platform-sample-data/`.

These databases can be stored in other DBMS as well. Scripts for creating and loading these databases in other popular DBMS as for example MySQL or Oracle can be found in Prashant Raju's blog, at `http://www.prashantraju.com/projects/pentaho/`.

Beside the scripts, you will find instructions for creating and loading the databases.

 Prashant Raju, an expert Pentaho developer, provides several excellent tutorials related to the Pentaho platform. If you are interested in knowing more about Pentaho, it's worth taking a look at his blog.

Connecting to a database

If you intend to work with a database, either reading, writing, looking up data, and so on, the first thing you will have to do is to create a connection to that database. This recipe will teach you how to do this.

Getting ready

In order to create the connection, you will need to know the connection settings. At least you will need:

- Host Name: Domain name or IP address of the database server.
- Port Number
- User Name
- Password

It's recommended that you also have access to the database at the moment of creating the connection.

How to do it...

1. Open Spoon and create a new transformation.
2. Select the **View** option that appears in the upper-left corner of the screen, right-click the **Database connections** option, and select **New**. The **Database Connection** dialog window appears.
3. Under **Connection Type**, select the database engine that matches your DBMS.

4. Fill the **Settings** options and give the connection a name by typing it in the **Connection Name:** textbox. Your window should look like this:

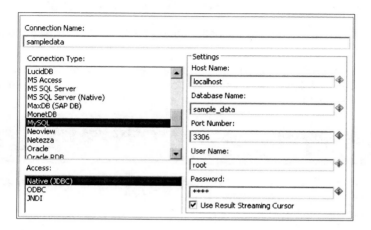

5. Press the **Test** button. A message should appear informing you that the connection to your database is **OK**.

 If you get an error message instead, you should recheck the data entered, as well as the availability of the database server. The server might be down, or it might not be reachable from your machine.

How it works...

A database connection is the definition that allows you to access a database from Kettle. With the data you provide, Kettle can instantiate real database connections and perform the different operations related with databases. Once you define a database connection, you will be able to access that database and execute arbitrary SQL statements: create schema objects like tables, execute SELECT statements, modify rows, and so on.

In this recipe you created the connection from the **Database connections** tree. You may also create a connection by pressing the **New...** button in the configuration window of any database-related step in a transformation or job entry in a job. Alternatively, there is also a wizard accessible from the **Tools** menu or by pressing *F3*.

Whichever the method you choose, a setting window like the one you saw in the recipe shows up allowing you to define the connection. This task includes:

▶   Selecting a database engine (**Connection type:**)

▶   Selecting the access method (**Access:**)

Native (JDBC) is recommended but you can also use a predefined ODBC data source, a JNDI data source, or an Oracle OCI connection.

▸ Providing the Host Name or IP

▸ Entering the User Name and Password for accessing the database.

A database connection can only be created with a transformation or a job opened. Therefore, in the recipe you were asked to create a transformation. The same could have been achieved by creating a job instead.

There's more...

The recipe showed the simplest way to create a database connection. However, there is more to know about creating database connections.

Avoiding creating the same database connection over and over again

If you intend to use the same database in more than one transformation and/or job, it's recommended that you share the connection. You do this by right-clicking the database connection under the **Database connections** tree, and clicking on **Share**. This way the database connection will be available to be used in all transformations and jobs. Shared database connections are recognized because they are bold. As an example take a look at the following sample screenshot:

The databases **books** and **sampledata** are shared; the others are not.

The information about shared connections is saved in a file named `shared.xml` located in the Kettle home directory.

No matter the Kettle storage method (repository or files) you can share connections. If you are working with the file method, namely `ktr` and `kjb` files, the information about shared connections are not only saved in the `shared.xml` file, but also saved as part of the transformation or job files even if they don't use the connections.

 You can avoid saving all the connection data as part of your transformations and jobs by selecting the option **Only save used connections to XML?** in the **Kettle options** window.

Avoiding modifying jobs and transformations every time a connection changes

Instead of typing fixed values in the database connection definition, it's worth using variables. For example, instead of typing `localhost` as the hostname, you can define a variable named `HOST_NAME` and as host name type its variable notation as `${HOST_NAME}` or `%%HOST_NAME%%`. If you decide to move the database from the local machine to a server, you just have to change the value of the variable and don't need to modify the transformations or jobs that use the connection.

This is especially useful when it's time to move your jobs and transformations between different environments: development, test, and so on.

Specifying advanced connection properties

The recipe showed you how to provide the general properties needed to create a connection. You may need to specify additional options—for example a preferred schema name, or supply some parameters to be used when the connection is initialized. In order to do that, look for those options in the extra tab windows under the **General** tab of the **Database Connection** window.

Connecting to a database not supported by Kettle

Kettle offers built-in support for a vast set of database engines. The list includes both commercial databases (such as Oracle) and open source (such as PostgreSQL), traditional row-oriented databases (such as MS SQL Server) and modern column-oriented databases (such as Infobright), disk-storage based databases (such as Informix) and in-memory databases (such as HSQLDB). However, it can happen that you want to connect to a database that is not in that list. In that case, you might still create a connection to that database. First of all, you have to get a JDBC driver for that DBMS. Copy the `jar` file containing the driver to the `libext/JDBC` directory inside the Kettle installation directory. Then, create the connection. In this case, as connection type choose **Generic database**. In the **Settings** frame specify the connection string (which should be explained along with JDBC), the driver class name, and the username and password. In order to find the values for these settings, you will have to refer to the driver documentation.

Checking the database connection at run-time

If you are not sure that the database connection will be accessible when a job or transformation runs from outside Spoon, you might precede all database-related operations with a **Check Db connection** job entry. The entry will return true or false depending on the result of checking one or more connections.

Getting data from a database

If you're used to working with databases, one of your main objectives while working with PDI must be getting data from your databases for transforming, loading in other databases, generating reports, and so on. Whatever operation you intend to achieve, the first thing you have to do after connecting to the database, is to get that data and create a PDI dataset. In this recipe you will learn the simplest way to do that.

Getting ready

To follow these instructions you need to have access to any DBMS.

How to do it...

1. Create a transformation and drop into the canvas a **Table Input** step. You will find it in the **Input** category of steps.

2. From the **Connection** drop-down list select the connection to the database where your data resides, or create it if it doesn't exist.

3. In the **SQL** text area, type the SQL statement that returns the data you need. So far you should have something like this:

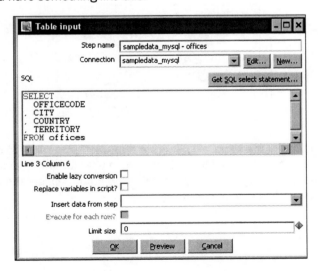

4. Click on **Preview**. This will bring a sample list of rows so you can confirm that the data is as expected.

5. Press **OK** to close the **Table Input** configuration window, and you'll be ready to use the data for further manipulation.

How it works...

The **Table Input** step you used in the recipe is the main PDI step to get data from a database. When you run or preview the transformation, Kettle executes the SQL and pushes the rows of data coming from the database into the output stream of the step. Each column of the SQL statement leads to a PDI field and each row generated by the execution of the statement becomes a row in the PDI dataset.

Once you get the data from the database, it will be available for any kind of manipulation inside the transformation.

There's more...

In order to save time, or in case you are not sure of the name of the tables or columns in the database, instead of typing the SQL statement press the **Get SQL select statement...** button. This will bring the **Database Explorer** window. This window allows you to explore the selected database. By expanding the database tree and selecting the table that interests you, you will be able to explore that table through the different options available under the **Actions** menu as shown below:

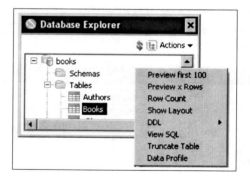

Double-clicking the name of the table will generate a SELECT statement to query that table. You will have the chance to include all the field names in the statement, or simply generate a SELECT * statement. After bringing the SQL to the **Table Input** configuration window, you will be able to modify it according to your needs.

By generating this statement you will loose any statement already in the SQL text area.

See also

▶ *Connecting to a database*. In order to get data from a database, you need to have a connection to it. This recipe explains how to do this.

▶ *Getting data from a database by providing parameters*. This recipe explains a more flexible way to run database queries.

▶ *Getting data from a database by running a query built at runtime*. This recipe explains an even more flexible method.

Getting data from a database by providing parameters

If you need to create a dataset with data coming from a database you can do it just by using a **Table Input** step. If the SELECT statement that retrieves the data doesn't need parameters, you simply write it in the **Table Input** setting window and proceed. However, most of the times you need flexible queries; queries that receive parameters. This recipe will show you how to pass parameters to a SELECT statement in PDI.

Assume that you need to list all products in Steel Wheels for a given product line and scale.

Getting ready

Make sure you have access to the sampledata database.

How to do it...

1. Create a transformation.
2. Before getting the data from the database, you have to create the stream that will provide the parameters for the statement.
3. Create a stream that builds a dataset with a single row and two columns: the product line parameter and the scale parameter. For this exercise, you can do it just by adding a **Data Grid** step or a **Generate Rows** step. Doing a preview on the last step of your stream you should see something like this:

Rows of step: parameters (1 row) (1 rows)		
#. ▲	productline_par	productscale_par
1	Classic Cars	1:10

4. Now drag to the canvas a **Table Input** step, and create a hop from the last step of the stream created above, towards this step.

5. Now you can configure the **Table Input** step. Double-click it, select the connection to the database, and type the following statement:

```
SELECT  productline
      ,  productscale
      ,  productcode
      ,  productname
FROM    products p
WHERE   productline  = ?
AND     productscale = ?
```

Downloading the example code

You can download the example code fles for all Packt books you have purchased from your account at http://www.PacktPub.com. If you purchased this book elsewhere, you can visit http://www.PacktPub.com/support and register to have the fles e-mailed directly to you.

6. In the **Insert data from step** list, select the name of the step that is linked to the **Table Input** step. Close the window.

7. Select the **Table Input** step and do a preview of the transformation. You will see a list of all products that match the product line and scale provided in the incoming stream:

Rows of step: steel wheels products (3 rows)

	productline	productscale	productcode	productname
1	Classic Cars	1:10	S10_1949	1952 Alpine Renault 1300
2	Classic Cars	1:10	S10_4757	1972 Alfa Romeo GTA
3	Classic Cars	1:10	S10_4962	1962 LanciaA Delta 16V

How it works...

When you need to execute a SELECT statement with parameters, the first thing you have to do is to build a stream that provides the parameter values needed by the statement. The stream can be made of just one step; for example a **Data grid** with fixed values, or a stream made up of several steps. The important thing is that the last step delivers the proper values to the **Table Input** step.

Then, you have to link the last step in the stream to the **Table Input** step where you will type the statement. What differentiates this statement from a regular statement is that you have to provide question marks. When you preview or run the transformation, the statement is prepared and the values coming to the **Table Input** step are bound to the placeholders; that is, the place where you typed the question marks.

Note that in the recipe the output of the stream was a single row with two fields, which is exactly the same number of question marks in the statement.

 The number of fields coming to a **Table Input** must be exactly the same as the number of question marks found in the query.

Also note that in the stream the product line was in the first place and the scale in the second place. If you look at the highlighted lines in the recipe, you will see that the statement expected the parameter values exactly in that order.

 The replacement of the markers respects the order of the incoming fields.

Finally, it's important to note that question marks can only be used to parameterize value expressions just as you did in the recipe.

Keywords or identifiers (for example; table names) cannot be parameterized with the question marks method.

If you need to parameterize something different from a value expression you should take another approach as explained in the next recipe.

There's more...

There are a couple of situations worth discussing.

Parameters coming in more than one row

In the recipe you received the list of parameter values in a single row with as many columns as expected parameter values. It's also possible to receive the parameter values in several rows. If instead of a row you had one parameter by row, as shown here:

Rows of step: parameters (1 by row) (2 rows)		
#. ^	parameter	
1	Classic Cars	
2	1:10	

The behavior of the transformation wouldn't have changed. The statement would have pulled the values for the two parameters from the incoming stream in the same order as the data appeared. It would have bound the first question mark with the value in the first row, and the second question mark with the value coming in the second row.

Note that this approach is less flexible than the previous one. For example, if you have to provide values for parameters with different data types you will not be able to put them in the same column and different rows.

Executing the SELECT statement several times, each for a different set of parameters

Suppose that you not only want to list the Classic Cars in 1:10 scale, but also the Motorcycles in 1:10 and 1:12 scale. You don't have to run the transformation three times in order to do this. You can have a dataset with three rows, one for each set of parameters, as shown below:

# ▲	productline_par	productscale_par
1	Classic Cars	1:10
2	Motorcycles	1:10
3	Motorcycles	1:12

Rows of step: parameters (several rows) (3 rows)

Then, in the **Table Input** setting window you have to check the **Execute for each row?** option. This way, the statement will be prepared and the values coming to the **Table Input** step will be bound to the placeholders once for each row in the dataset coming to the step. For this example, the result would look like this:

Rows of step: steel wheels products - execute for each row (7 rows)

▲	productline	productscale	productcode	productname
1	Classic Cars	1:10	S10_1949	1952 Alpine Renault 1300
2	Classic Cars	1:10	S10_4757	1972 Alfa Romeo GTA
3	Classic Cars	1:10	S10_4962	1962 LanciaA Delta 16V
4	Motorcycles	1:10	S10_1678	1969 Harley Davidson Ultimate Chopper
5	Motorcycles	1:10	S10_2016	1996 Moto Guzzi 1100i
6	Motorcycles	1:10	S10_4698	2003 Harley-Davidson Eagle Drag Bike
7	Motorcycles	1:12	S12_2823	2002 Suzuki XREO

See also

▶   *Getting data from a database by running a query built at runtime*. This recipe gives you an alternative way for using parameters in a SELECT statement.

Getting data from a database by running a query built at runtime

When you work with databases, most of the times you start by writing an SQL statement that gets the data you need. However, there are situations in which you don't know that statement exactly. Maybe the name of the columns to query are in a file, or the name of the columns by which you will sort will come as a parameter from outside the transformation, or the name of the main table to query changes depending on the data stored in it (for example sales2010). PDI allows you to have any part of the SQL statement as a variable so you don't need to know the literal SQL statement text at design time.

Assume the following situation: You have a database with data about books and their authors, and you want to generate a file with a list of titles. Whether to retrieve the data ordered by title or by genre is a choice that you want to postpone until the moment you execute the transformation.

Getting ready

You will need a book database with the structure explained in *Appendix, Data Structures*.

How to do it...

1. Create a transformation.
2. The column that will define the order of the rows will be a **named parameter**. So, define a named parameter named ORDER_COLUMN, and put title as its default value.

> Remember that Named Parameters are defined in the Transformation setting window and their role is the same as the role of any Kettle variable. If you prefer, you can skip this step and define a standard variable for this purpose.

3. Now drag a **Table Input** step to the canvas. Then create and select the connection to the book's database.
4. In the **SQL** frame type the following statement:
   ```
   SELECT * FROM books ORDER BY ${ORDER_COLUMN}
   ```
5. Check the option **Replace variables in script?** and close the window.
6. Use an **Output** step like for example a **Text file output** step, to send the results to a file, save the transformation, and run it.
7. Open the generated file and you will see the books ordered by title.
8. Now try again. Press *F9* to run the transformation one more time.
9. This time, change the value of the ORDER_COLUMN parameter typing genre as the new value.
10. Press the **Launch** button.
11. Open the generated file. This time you will see the titles ordered by genre.

How it works...

You can use Kettle variables in any part of the SELECT statement inside a **Table Input** step. When the transformation is initialized, PDI replaces the variables by their values provided that the **Replace variables in script?** option is checked.

In the recipe, the first time you ran the transformation, Kettle replaced the variable ORDER_COLUMN with the word title and the statement executed was:

```
SELECT * FROM books ORDER BY title
```

The second time, the variable was replaced by `genre` and the executed statement was:

```
SELECT * FROM books ORDER BY genre
```

 As mentioned in the recipe, any predefined Kettle variable can be used instead of a named parameter.

There's more...

You may use variables not only for the ORDER BY clause, but in any part of the statement: table names, columns, and so on. You could even hold the full statement in a variable. Note however that you need to be cautious when implementing this.

 A wrong assumption about the metadata generated by those predefined statements can make your transformation crash.

You can also use the same variable more than once in the same statement. This is an advantage of using variables as an alternative to question marks when you need to execute parameterized SELECT statements.

See also

> ▶ *Getting data from a database by providing parameters*. This recipe shows you an alternative way to parameterize a query.

Inserting or updating rows in a table

Two of the most common operations on databases besides retrieving data are inserting and updating rows in a table.

PDI has several steps that allow you to perform these operations. In this recipe you will learn to use the **Insert/Update** step. Before inserting or updating rows in a table by using this step, it is critical that you know which field or fields in the table uniquely identify a row in the table.

 If you don't have a way to uniquely identify the records, you should consider other steps, as explained in the *There's more...* section.

Assume this situation: You have a file with new employees of Steel Wheels. You have to insert those employees in the database. The file also contains old employees that have changed either the office where they work, or the extension number, or other basic information. You will take the opportunity to update that information as well.

Getting ready

Download the material for the recipe from the book's site. Take a look at the file you will use:

```
NUMBER, LASTNAME, FIRSTNAME, EXT, OFFICE, REPORTS, TITLE
1188, Firrelli, Julianne,x2174,2,1143, Sales Manager
1619, King, Tom,x103,6,1088,Sales Rep
1810, Lundberg, Anna,x910,2,1143,Sales Rep
1811, Schulz, Chris,x951,2,1143,Sales Rep
```

Explore the Steel Wheels database, in particular the `employees` table, so you know what you have before running the transformation. In particular execute these statements:

```
SELECT EMPLOYEENUMBER ENUM
     , concat(FIRSTNAME,' ',LASTNAME) NAME
     , EXTENSION EXT
     , OFFICECODE OFF
     , REPORTSTO REPTO
     , JOBTITLE
     FROM employees
     WHERE EMPLOYEENUMBER IN (1188, 1619, 1810, 1811);
+------+-----------------+-------+-----+-------+-----------+
| ENUM | NAME            | EXT   | OFF | REPTO | JOBTITLE  |
+------+-----------------+-------+-----+-------+-----------+
| 1188 | Julie Firrelli  | x2173 | 2   | 1143  | Sales Rep |
| 1619 | Tom King        | x103  | 6   | 1088  | Sales Rep |
+------+-----------------+-------+-----+-------+-----------+
2 rows in set (0.00 sec)
```

How to do it...

1. Create a transformation and use a **Text File input** step to read the file `employees.txt`. Provide the name and location of the file, specify comma as the separator, and fill in the **Fields** grid.

> Remember that you can quickly fill the grid by pressing the **Get Fields** button.

2. Now, you will do the inserts and updates with an **Insert/Update** step. So, expand the **Output** category of steps, look for the **Insert/Update** step, drag it to the canvas, and create a hop from the **Text File input** step toward this one.

3. Double-click the **Insert/Update** step and select the connection to the Steel Wheels database, or create it if it doesn't exist. As target table type `employees`.

4. Fill the grids as shown:

The key(s) to look up the value(s):

#.	Table field	Comparator	Stream field1	Stream field2
1	EMPLOYEENUMBER	=	EMPLOYEE_NUMBER	

Update fields:

#.	Table field	Stream field	Update
1	EMPLOYEENUMBER	EMPLOYEE_NUMBER	N
2	LASTNAME	LASTNAME	N
3	FIRSTNAME	FIRSTNAME	N
4	EXTENSION	EXT	Y
5	OFFICECODE	OFFICE	Y
6	REPORTSTO	REPORTS	Y
7	JOBTITLE	TITLE	Y

5. Save and run the transformation.

6. Explore the employees table. You will see that one employee was updated, two were inserted, and one remained untouched because the file had the same data as the database for that employee:

```
+------+----------------+-------+-----+-------+--------------+
| ENUM | NAME           | EXT   | OFF | REPTO | JOBTITLE     |
+------+----------------+-------+-----+-------+--------------+
| 1188 | Julie Firrelli| x2174 | 2   | 1143  |Sales Manager |
| 1619 | Tom King       | x103  | 6   | 1088  |Sales Rep     |
| 1810 | Anna Lundberg  | x910  | 2   | 1143  |Sales Rep     |
| 1811 | Chris Schulz   | x951  | 2   | 1143  |Sales Rep     |
+------+----------------+-------+-----+-------+--------------+
4 rows in set (0.00 sec)
```

How it works...

The **Insert/Update** step, as its name implies, serves for both inserting or updating rows. For each row in your stream, Kettle looks for a row in the table that matches the condition you put in the upper grid, the grid labeled **The key(s) to look up the value(s):**. Take for example the last row in your input file:

```
1811, Schulz, Chris,x951,2,1143,Sales Rep
```

When this row comes to the **Insert/Update** step, Kettle looks for a row where EMPLOYEENUMBER equals 1811. It doesn't find one. Consequently, it inserts a row following the directions you put in the lower grid. For this sample row, the equivalent INSERT statement would be:

```
INSERT INTO employees (EMPLOYEENUMBER, LASTNAME, FIRSTNAME,
            EXTENSION, OFFICECODE, REPORTSTO, JOBTITLE)
        VALUES (1811, 'Schulz', 'Chris',
            'x951', 2, 1143, 'Sales Rep')
```

Now look at the first row:

```
1188, Firrelli, Julianne,x2174,2,1143, Sales Manager
```

When Kettle looks for a row with EMPLOYEENUMBER equal to 1188, it finds it. Then, it updates that row according to what you put in the lower grid. It only updates the columns where you put Y under the **Update** column. For this sample row, the equivalent UPDATE statement would be:

```
UPDATE employees SET EXTENSION = 'x2174'
                  , OFFICECODE = 2
                  , REPORTSTO = 1143
                  , JOBTITLE = 'Sales Manager'
WHERE EMPLOYEENUMBER = 1188
```

Note that the name of this employee in the file (Julianne) is different from the name in the table (Julie), but, as you put N under the column **Update** for the field FIRSTNAME, this column was not updated.

 If you run the transformation with log level **Detailed**, you will be able to see in the log the real prepared statements that Kettle performs when inserting or updating rows in a table.

There's more...

Here there are two alternative solutions to this use case.

Alternative solution if you just want to insert records

If you just want to insert records, you shouldn't use the **Insert/Update** step but the **Table Output** step. This would be faster because you would be avoiding unnecessary lookup operations. The **Table Output** step is really simply to configure: Just select the database connection and the table where you want to insert the records. If the names of the fields coming to the **Table Output** step have the same name as the columns in the table, you are done. If not, you should check the **Specify database fields** option, and fill the **Database fields** tab exactly as you filled the lower grid in the **Insert/Update** step, except that here there is no **Update** column.

Alternative solution if you just want to update rows

If you just want to update rows, instead of using the **Insert/Update** step, you should use the **Update** step. You configure the **Update** step just as you configure the **Insert/Update** step, except that here there is no **Update** column.

Alternative way for inserting and updating

The following is an alternative way for inserting and updating rows in a table.

 This alternative only works if the columns in the Key field's grid of the **Insert/Update** step are a unique key in the database.

You may replace the **Insert/Update** step by a **Table Output** step and, as the error handling stream coming out of the **Table Output** step, put an **Update** step.

 In order to handle the error when creating the hop from the **Table Output** step towards the **Update** step, select the **Error handling of step** option.

Alternatively right-click the **Table Output** step, select **Define error handling...**, and configure the **Step error handling settings** window that shows up. Your transformation would look like this:

In the **Table Output** select the table **employees**, check the **Specify database fields** option, and fill the **Database fields** tab just as you filled the lower grid in the **Insert/Update** step, excepting that here there is no **Update** column.

In the **Update** step, select the same table and fill the upper grid—let's call it the Key fields grid—just as you filled the key fields grid in the **Insert/Update** step. Finally, fill the lower grid with those fields that you want to update, that is, those rows that had Y under the **Update** column.

In this case, Kettle tries to insert all records coming to the **Table Output** step. The rows for which the insert fails go to the **Update** step, and the rows are updated.

If the columns in the Key field's grid of the **Insert/Update** step are not a unique key in the database, this alternative approach doesn't work. The **Table Output** would insert all the rows. Those that already existed would be duplicated instead of updated.

This strategy for performing inserts and updates has been proven to be much faster than the use of the **Insert/Update** step whenever the ratio of updates to inserts is low. In general, for best practices reasons, this is not an advisable solution.

See also

▸ *Inserting new rows when a simple primary key has to be generated*. If the table where you have to insert data defines a primary key, you should generate it. This recipe explains how to do it when the primary key is a simple sequence.

▸ *Inserting new rows when the primary key has to be generated based on stored values*. Same as the previous bullet, but in this case the primary key is based on stored values.

Inserting new rows where a simple primary key has to be generated

It's very common to have tables in a database where the values for the primary key column can be generated by using a database sequence (in those DBMS that have that feature; for example, Oracle) or simply by adding 1 to the maximum value in the table. Loading data into these tables is very simple. This recipe teaches you how to do this through the following exercise.

There are new offices at Steel Wheels. You have the data of the offices in a file that looks like this:

```
CITY;PHONE;ADDRESS;COUNTRY;POSTALCODE
Sao Paulo;11 3289-3703;Avenida Paulista 1330;Brazil;01310-200
Sao Paulo;11 3104-1116;Rua Boa Vista, 51;Brazil;01014-001
Buenos Aires;11 4582-6700;Cabildo 2127;Argentina;C1428AAT
```

You have to insert that data into the Steel Wheels database.

Getting ready

For this recipe you will use the Pentaho sample database. If you don't have that database, you'll have to follow the instructions in the introduction of this chapter.

As you will insert records into the office table, it would be good if you explore that table before doing any insert operations. Here you have a sample query:

```
SELECT OFFICECODE, ADDRESSLINE1, CITY
FROM    OFFICES
ORDER BY OFFICECODE;
+------------+--------------------------+---------------+
| OFFICECODE | ADDRESSLINE1             | CITY          |
+------------+--------------------------+---------------+
| 1          | 100 Market Street        | San Francisco |
| 2          | 1550 Court Place         | Boston        |
| 3          | 523 East 53rd Street     | NYC           |
```

```
|  4          | 43 Rue Jouffroy D'abbans | Paris         |
|  5          | 4-1 Kioicho              | Tokyo         |
|  6          | 5-11 Wentworth Avenue    | Sydney        |
|  7          | 25 Old Broad Street      | London        |
+-------------+--------------------------+---------------+
7 rows in set (0.00 sec)
```

How to do it...

1. Create a transformation and create a connection to the `sampledata` database.

2. Use a **Text file input** step to read the `offices.txt` file with data about the new offices.

3. From the **Data Warehouse** category drag and drop a **Combination lookup/update** step, and create a hop from the previous step towards this one.

4. Double-click the step, select the connection to the `sampledata` database, and type `offices` as the **Target table**.

5. Fill the **Key fields** grid as shown:

#. ▲	Dimension field	Field in stream
1	ADDRESSLINE1	ADDRESS
2	CITY	CITY
3	COUNTRY	COUNTRY

6. In the **Technical key field** type `OFFICECODE`. For the **Creation of technical key** fields leave the default values. Close the window.

7. From the **Output** category of steps, add an **Update** step.

8. Double-click the step, select the connection to the `sampledata` database, and type `offices` as the **Target table**.

9. In the first grid add rows with the text `OFFICECODE` both under **Table field** and under **Stream field1**. As **Comparator** choose **=**. This way, you will update the rows where `OFFICECODE` is equal to the office code in your stream.

10. In the lower grid add a row and type `PHONE` both under **Table field** and **Stream field**. Add a second row and type `POSTALCODE` in both columns.

11. Close the window.

12. It's time to save the transformation and run it to see what happens.

13. As you might guess, three new offices have been added, with primary keys 8, 9, and 10. Look at the results:

```
SELECT OFFICECODE, ADDRESSLINE1, CITY
FROM    offices
ORDER BY cast(officecode as unsigned);
```

```
+------------+-----------------------------+----------------+
| OFFICECODE | ADDRESSLINE1                | CITY           |
+------------+-----------------------------+----------------+
| 1          | 100 Market Street           | San Francisco  |
| 2          | 1550 Court Place            | Boston         |
| 3          | 523 East 53rd Street        | NYC            |
| 4          | 43 Rue Jouffroy D'abbans    | Paris          |
| 5          | 4-1 Kioicho                 | Tokyo          |
| 6          | 5-11 Wentworth Avenue       | Sydney         |
| 7          | 25 Old Broad Street         | London         |
| 8          | Avenida Paulista 1330       | Sao Paulo      |
| 9          | Rua Boa Vista, 51           | Sao Paulo      |
| 10         | Cabildo 2127                | Buenos Aires   |
+------------+-----------------------------+----------------+
10 rows in set (0.00 sec)
```

How it works...

In many situations, before inserting data into a table you have to generate the primary key. If the primary key is a simple sequence or the maximum primary key plus one, you can generate it by using a **Combination lookup/update** step.

In the recipe, for each row in your file, with the **Combination lookup/update** step, you look for a record in the offices table with the same values for address, city, and country.

Because the offices are new, (there aren't offices in the table with the same combination of address, city, and country values) the lookup fails. As a consequence, the step generates a key value as the maximum OFFICECODE in the table, plus 1. Then, it inserts a row with the generated primary key and the fields you typed in the grid.

Finally, the step adds to the stream the generated primary key value.

As a last task, we used that key to update the other fields coming into the file: POSTALCODE and PHONE.

There's more...

The **Combination lookup/update** step is within the **Data Warehouse** category, because is mainly used for loading **junk dimension tables**. But as you could see, it can also be used in the particular situation where you have to generate a primary key.

In the recipe you generated the PK as the maximum plus one, but as you can see in the setting window, a database sequence can also be used instead.

When you use the **Combination lookup/update** step for inserting, make sure that the columns that are not part of the list of key fields are nullable or have default values.

Using the Combination lookup/update for looking up

In the recipe the **Combination lookup/update** step just inserted new rows. Now suppose that you have a row that existed in the table. In that case the lookup would have succeeded and the step wouldn't have inserted a new row. Instead, it would just have returned the found OFFICECODE. That field would have been added to the stream, ready to be used further in the transformation, for example for updating other fields as you did in the recipe, or for being used for inserting data in a related table.

Note that this is a potentially slow step, as it uses all the values for the comparison.

See also

▶   *Inserting new rows when the primary key has to be generated based on stored values*. This recipe explains the case where the primary key to be generated is not as simple as adding one to the last primary key in the table.

Inserting new rows where the primary key has to be generated based on stored values

There are tables where the primary key is not a database sequence, nor a consecutive integer, but a column which is built based on a rule or pattern that depends on the keys already inserted. For example imagine a table where the values for primary key are A00001, A00002, and A00003. In this case, you can guess the rule: putting an A followed by a sequence. The next in the sequence would be A00004. This seems too simple, but doing it in PDI is not trivial. This recipe will teach you how to load a table where a primary key has to be generated based on existing rows as in that example.

Suppose that you have to load author data into the book's database. You have the main data for the authors, and you have to generate the primary key as in the example above.

Getting ready

Run the script that creates and loads data into the book's database. You'll find it at http://packtpub.com/support.

Before proceeding, verify the current values for the primary keys in the table where you will insert data:

```
SELECT MAX(id_author) FROM authors;
+-----------------+
| MAX(id_author)  |
+-----------------+
| A00009          |
+-----------------+
1 row in set (0.00 sec)
```

How to do it...

1. Create a transformation and create a connection to the book's database.

2. Use a **Text file input** step to read the authors.txt file.

 For simplicity, the authors.txt file only has new authors, that is, authors who are not in the table.

3. To generate the next primary key, you need to know the current maximum. So use a **Table Input** step to get it. In this case the following statement will give you that number:

```
SELECT
cast(max(right(id_author,5)) as unsigned) max_id
FROM authors
```

 Alternatively you can simply get the id_author field and transform the field with Kettle steps until you get the current maximum. You will have a simple clear transformation, but it will take several Kettle steps to do it.

4. By using a **Join Rows (cartesian product)** step, join both streams. Your transformation should look like this:

5. Add an **Add sequence** step. Replace the default value `valuename` with `delta_value`. For the rest of the fields in the setting window leave the default values.

6. Add a **Calculator** step to build the keys. You do it by filling the setting window as shown:

Fields:

New field	Calculation	Field A	Field B	F..	Value ...	L...	P...	Remove	Conversion ...
new_id	A + B	max_id	delta_value		String			N	00000
prefix	Set field to constant value A	A			String			N	
new_author_id	A + B	prefix	new_id		String			N	

7. In order to insert the rows, add a **Table output** step, double-click it, and select the connection to the book's database.

8. As **Target table** type `authors`.

9. Check the option **Specify database fields**.

10. Select the **Database fields** tab and fill the grid as follows:

Fields to insert:

#. ▲	Table field	Stream field
1	id_author	new_author_id
2	lastname	lastname
3	firstname	firstname

11. Save and run the transformation.

12. Explore the authors table. You should see the new authors:

```
SELECT * FROM authors ORDER BY id_author;
+-----------+------------+-------------+-----------+----------+
| lastname  | firstname  | nationality | birthyear | id_author|
+-----------+------------+-------------+-----------+----------+
| Larsson   | Stieg      | Swedish     |      1954 | A00001   |
| King      | Stephen    | American    |      1947 | A00002   |
| Hiaasen   | Carl       | American    |      1953 | A00003   |
| Handler   | Chelsea    | American    |      1975 | A00004   |
| Ingraham  | Laura      | American    |      1964 | A00005   |
| Ramsey    | Dave       | American    |      1960 | A00006   |
| Kiyosaki  | Robert     | American    |      1947 | A00007   |
| Rowling   | Joanne     | English     |      1965 | A00008   |
| Riordan   | Rick       | American    |      1964 | A00009   |
| Gilbert   | Elizabeth  | unknown     |      1900 | A00010   |
| Franzen   | Jonathan   | unknown     |      1900 | A00011   |
| Collins   | Suzanne    | unknown     |      1900 | A00012   |
| Blair     | Tony       | unknown     |      1900 | A00013   |
```

```
       +----------+-----------+-------------+-----------+----------+
13 rows in set (0.00 sec)
```

How it works...

When you have to generate a primary key based on the existing primary keys, unless the new primary key is simple to generate by adding one to the maximum, there is no direct way to do it in Kettle. One possible solution is the one shown in the recipe: Getting the last primary key in the table, combining it with your main stream, and using those two sources for generating the new primary keys. This is how it worked in this example.

First, by using a **Table Input** step, you found out the last primary key in the table. In fact, you got only the numeric part needed to build the new key. In this exercise, the value was **9**. With the **Join Rows (cartesian product)** step, you added that value as a new column in your main stream.

Taking that number as a starting point, you needed to build the new primary keys as A00010, A00011, and so on. You did this by generating a sequence (1, 2, 3, and so on), adding this sequence to the max_id (that led to values 10, 11, 12, and so on), and finally formatting the key with the use of the calculator.

Note that in the calculator the first A+B performs an arithmetic calculation. It adds the max_id with the delta_value sequence. Then it converts the result to a **String** giving it the format with the mask 0000. This led to the values 00010, 00011, and so on.

The second A+B is a string concatenation. It concatenates the literal A with the previously calculated ID.

Note that this approach works as long as you have a single user scenario. If you run multiple instances of the transformation they can select the same maximum value, and try to insert rows with the same PK leading to a primary key constraint violation.

There's more...

The key in this exercise is to get the last or maximum primary key in the table, join it to your main stream, and use that data to build the new key. After the join, the mechanism for building the final key would depend on your particular case.

See also

   ▶   *Inserting new rows when a simple primary key has to be generated*. If the primary key to be generated is simply a sequence, it is recommended to examine this recipe.

Deleting data from a table

Sometimes you might have to delete data from a table. If the operation to do is simple, for example:

```
DELETE FROM LOG_TABLE WHERE VALID='N'
```

Or

```
DELETE FROM TMP_TABLE
```

You could simply execute it by using an **SQL** job entry or an **Execute SQL script** step. If you face the second of the above situations, you can even use a **Truncate table** job entry.

For more complex situations you should use the **Delete** step. Let's suppose the following situation: You have a database with outdoor products. Each product belongs to a category: tools, tents, sleeping bags, and so on. Now you want to delete all the products for a given list of categories, where the price is less than or equal to $50.

Getting ready

In order to follow the recipe, you should download the material for this chapter: a script for creating and loading the database, and an Excel file with the list of categories involved.

After creating the outdoor database and loading data by running the script provided, and before following the recipe you can explore the database. In particular execute the following statement:

```
SELECT     category, count(*) quantity
FROM       products p, categories c
WHERE      p.id_category=c.id_category
AND        price<=50
GROUP BY p.id_category;
+----------------+----------+
| category       | quantity |
+----------------+----------+
| kitchen        |       19 |
| lights         |       14 |
| sleeping bags  |        5 |
| tents          |        4 |
| tools          |        8 |
+----------------+----------+
5 rows in set (0.00 sec)
SELECT     category, count(*) quantity
FROM       products p, categories c
```

```
WHERE      p.id_category=c.id_category
AND        price>50
GROUP BY p.id_category;
+----------------+----------+
| category       | quantity |
+----------------+----------+
| kitchen        |        5 |
| lights         |        1 |
| sleeping bags  |        1 |
| tents          |        8 |
| tools          |        2 |
+----------------+----------+
5 rows in set (0.00 sec)
```

The highlighted lines above belong to the products that you intend to delete.

How to do it...

1. Create a transformation.

2. The value to which you will compare the price before deleting will be stored as a **named parameter**. So create it, name it MAX_PRICE, and set 50 as the default value.

3. Drag to the canvas an **Excel Input** step to read the Excel file with the list of categories.

4. Drag to the canvas a **Get Variables** step, to get the named variable as a field named max_price with type Number.

5. After that, add a **Database lookup** step. Configure it to get the id_category fields based on the category descriptions in the Excel file. So far, the transformation looks like this:

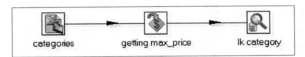

 For higher volumes it's better to get the variable just once in a separate stream and join the two streams with a **Join Rows (cartesian product)** step.

6. Select the **Database lookup** step and do a preview. You should see this:

Rows of step: lk category (2 rows)

# ▲	category	max_price	id_category
1	tents	50,00	4
2	tools	50,00	5

7. Finally, add a **Delete** step. You will find it under the **Output** category of steps.

8. Double-click the **Delete** step, select the outdoor connection, and fill in the key grid as follows:

The key(s) to look up the value(s):

# . ▲	Table field	Comparator	Stream field1	Stream field2
1	id_category	=	id_category	
2	price	<=	max_price	

9. Save and run the transformation.

10. Explore the database. If you run the same statements that you ran before starting the recipe, you'll note that all products belonging to the categories in the Excel file, with price less than or equal to $50 have been deleted. This is what you will see:

```
SELECT     category, count(*) quantity
FROM       products p, categories c
WHERE      p.id_category=c.id_category
AND        price<=50
GROUP BY p.id_category;
+----------------+----------+
| category       | quantity |
+----------------+----------+
| kitchen        |       19 |
| lights         |       14 |
| sleeping bags  |        5 |
+----------------+----------+
3 rows in set (0.00 sec)

SELECT     category, count(*) quantity
FROM       products p, categories c
WHERE      p.id_category=c.id_category
AND        price>50
GROUP BY p.id_category;
+----------------+----------+
| category       | quantity |
+----------------+----------+
| kitchen        |        5 |
| lights         |        1 |
| sleeping bags  |        1 |
| tents          |        8 |
| tools          |        2 |
+----------------+----------+
5 rows in set (0.00 sec)
```

How it works...

The **Delete** step allows you to delete rows in a table in a database based on certain conditions. In this case, you intended to delete rows from the table `products` where the price was less than or equal to 50, and the category was in a list of categories, so the **Delete** step is the right choice. This is how it works.

PDI builds a prepared statement for the `DELETE` operation. Then, for each row in your stream, PDI binds the values of the row to the variables in the prepared statement.

Let's see it by example. In the transformation you built a stream where each row had a single category and the value for the price.

If you run the transformation with log level **Detailed** and look at the log, you will see the statement that is executed:

```
DELETE FROM products
WHERE price < ?
AND id_category = ?
```

The `WHERE` clause is built based on the conditions you entered in the **Delete** configuration window. For every row, the values of the fields you typed in the grid—`max_price` and `id_category`—are bound to the question marks in the prepared statement.

Note that the conditions in the **Delete** step are based on fields in the same table. In this case, as you were provided with category descriptions and the products table does not have the descriptions but the ID for the categories, you had to use an extra step to get that ID: a **Database lookup**.

Suppose that the first row in the Excel file had the value `tents`. As the ID for the category `tents` is 4, the execution of the prepared statement with the values in this row has the same effect as the execution of the following SQL statement:

```
DELETE FROM products
WHERE price < 50
AND id_category = 4
```

See also

▶ *Looking for a value in a database table* (*Chapter 5, Looking for Data*). Refer to this recipe if you need to understand how the **Database lookup** step works.

Creating or altering a database table from PDI (design time)

It's not uncommon that someone asks you to load a table that doesn't exist yet. These are some use cases:

- You receive a flat file and have to load the full content in a temporary table
- You have to create and load a **dimension table** with data coming from another database

You could write a CREATE TABLE statement from scratch and then create the transformation that loads the table, or you could do all that in an easier way from Spoon.

In this case, suppose that you received a file with data about countries and the languages spoken in those countries. You need to load the full content into a temporary table. The table doesn't exist and you have to create it based on the content of the file.

Getting ready

In order to follow the instructions, you will need the countries.xml file available for downloading from the book's site.

How to do it...

1. Create a transformation and create a connection to the database where you will save the data.
2. In order to read the countries.xml file, use a **Get data from XML** step. As **Loop XPath** type /world/country/language.
3. Fill the **Fields** grid as follows:

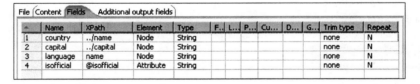

File	Content	Fields	Additional output fields											
▲	Name	XPath	Element	Type	F..	L..	P..	Cu...	D...	G..	Trim type	Repeat
1	country	../name	Node	String							none	N
2	capital	../capital	Node	String							none	N
3	language	name	Node	String							none	N
4	isofficial	@isofficial	Attribute	String							none	N

The @ symbol preceding the field isofficial is optional. By selecting **Attribute** as **Element** Kettle automatically understands that this is an attribute.

4. From the **Output** category, drag and drop a **Table Output** step.
5. Create a hop from the **Get data from XML** step to this new step.

6. Double-click the **Table Output** step and select the connection you just created.

7. In the **Target table** textbox type `countries_stage`.

8. Click on the **SQL** button. A window will appear with the following script:

```
CREATE TABLE countries_stage
(
  country TINYTEXT
, capital TINYTEXT
, language TINYTEXT
, isofficial TINYTEXT
)
;
```

 The syntax may be different for different DBMS.

Because you know that `isofficial` is just a simple flag with values `Y/N`, replace `isofficial TINYTEXT` with `isofficial CHAR(1)`.

After clicking on **Execute**, a window will show up telling that the statement has been executed, that is, the table has been created.

Save and run the transformation. All the information coming from the XML file is saved into the table just created.

How it works...

PDI allows you to create or alter tables in your databases depending on the tasks implemented in your transformations or jobs. To understand what this is about, let's explain the previous example.

A **Table Output** step causes Kettle to execute an `INSERT` statement against the database. The insert is made based on the data coming to the **Table Output** and the data you put in the **Table Output** configuration window, for example the name of the table or the mapping of the fields.

When you click on the **SQL** button in the **Table Output** setting window, this is what happens: Kettle builds the statements needed to execute that insert successfully. As in this example the table doesn't exist, and hence the statement generated by clicking on the button is a `CREATE TABLE`.

When the window with the generated statement appeared, you executed it. This causes the table to be created, so you could safely run the transformation and insert into the new table the data coming from the file to the step.

There's more...

The **SQL** button is present in several database-related steps. In all cases its purpose is the same: Determine the statements to be executed in order to run the transformation successfully. In the recipe the statement was a CREATE TABLE, but there are other situations. These are some examples:

- ▸ If you use an **Insert/Update** step and fill the **Update fields:** grid with a field that doesn't exist, Kettle generates an ALTER TABLE statement in order to add that field as a new column in the table.

- ▸ If you use an **Update** step and in the **The key(s) to look up the value(s):** grid type names of columns that are not indexed, Kettle generates a CREATE INDEX statement.

 Note that in this case the execution of the statement is not mandatory but recommended.

- ▸ If you use a **Dimension Lookup /Update** step in order to load a **Slowly changing dimension**, Kettle generates a CREATE TABLE statement including all the fields that are needed in order to keep that kind of dimension updated.

You can execute the SQL as it is generated, you can modify it before executing it (as you did in the recipe), or you can just ignore it. Sometimes the SQL generated includes dropping a column just because the column exists in the table but is not used in the transformation. In that case you shouldn't execute it.

 Read the generated statement carefully, before executing it.

Finally, you must know that if you run the statement from outside Spoon, in order to see the changes inside the tool you either have to clear the cache by right-clicking the database connection and selecting the **Clear DB Cache** option, or restart Spoon.

See also

- ▸ *Creating or altering a database table from PDI* (*runtime*). Instead of doing these operations from Spoon during design time, you can do them at runtime. This recipe explains the details.

Creating or altering a database table from PDI (runtime)

When you are developing with PDI, you know (or have the means to find out) if the tables you need exist or not, and if they have all the columns you will read or update. If they don't exist or don't meet your requirements, you can create or modify them, and then proceed. Assume the following scenarios:

- ► You need to load some data into a temporary table. The table exists but you need to add some new columns to it before proceeding.
- ► You have to load a dimension table. This task is part of a new requirement, so this table doesn't exist.

While you are creating the transformations and jobs, you have the chance to create or modify those tables. But if these transformations and jobs are to be run in batch mode in a different environment, nobody will be there to do these verifications or create or modify the tables. You need to adapt your work so these things are done automatically.

Suppose that you need to do some calculations and store the results in a temporary table that will be used later in another process. As this is a new requirement, it is likely that the table doesn't exist in the target database. You can create a job that takes care of this.

How to do it...

1. Create a job, and add a **Start job** entry.
2. From the **Conditions** category, drag and drop a **Table exists** entry, an **SQL** entry from **Scripting**, and a **Dummy** entry from **General**.
3. Link all the entries as shown:

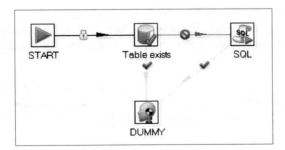

4. Double-click the **Table exists** entry, choose a database connection, and as **Table name** type my_tmp_table.

5. Double-click the **SQL** entry, choose the same database connection as above, and in the **SQL Script:** type:

```
CREATE TABLE my_tmp_table (
CALC_1 NUMERIC(10,2),
CALC_2 NUMERIC(10,2),
CALC_3 NUMERIC(10,2)
);
```

 The statement above is written with MySQL syntax. Please review and fix it if needed because you are using a different DBMS.

6. Save the job and run it.
7. The table `my_tmp_table` should have been created.
8. Run the job again.
9. Nothing should happen.

How it works...

The **Table exists** entry, as implied by its name, verifies if a table exists in your database. As with any job entry, this entry either succeeds or fails. If it fails, the job creates the table with an **SQL** entry. If it succeeds, the job does nothing.

There's more...

The **SQL entry** is very useful not only for creating tables as you did in the recipe, but also for executing very simple statements, as for example setting a flag before or after running a transformation. Its main use, however, is executing DDL statements.

On the other side, in order to decide if it was necessary to create the table or not, you used a **Table exists** entry. In addition to this entry and before verifying the existence of the table, you could have used the **Check Db connections**. This entry allows you to see if the database is available.

Now, let's suppose the table exists, but it is an old version that doesn't have all the columns you need. In this case you can use an extra useful entry: **Columns exist in a table**. If you can detect that a column is not present, you can alter the table by adding that column, also with an **SQL** job entry.

 Creating or altering tables is not a task that should be done as part of an ETL process. Kettle allows you to do it but you should be careful when using these features.

▶ *Creating or altering a database table from PDI (design time)*. Instead of doing these operations at runtime, you can do it from Spoon while you are designing the jobs and transformations. This recipe explains how to do this.

Inserting, deleting, or updating a table depending on a field

PDI allows you to do the basic operations that modify the data in your tables, that is: insert, update, and delete records. For each of those operations you have at least one step that allows you to do the task. It may happen that you have to do one or another operation depending on the value of a field. That is possible with a rather unknown step named **Synchronize after merge**.

Suppose you have a database with books. You received a file with a list of books. In that list there are books you already have, and there are books you don't have.

For the books you already have, you intend to update the prices.

Among the other books, you will insert in your database only those which have been published recently. You will recognize them because they have the text NEW in the comment field.

Getting ready

For this recipe you will need the database which can be created and filled by running the script books_2.sql. You also will need the file books_news.txt that accompanies the material for this chapter.

As the recipe will modify the data in the database, before proceeding, explore the database to see what is inside. In particular run these statements and pay attention to the results:

```
SELECT count(*)
FROM   books;
+----------+
| count(*) |
+----------+
|       34 |
+----------+
1 row in set (0.00 sec)
SELECT id_title, title, price
FROM   books
WHERE  author_id='A00001';
```

```
+-----------+-------------------------------------------+-------+
| id_title  | title                                     | price |
+-----------+-------------------------------------------+-------+
| 123-400   | The Girl with the Dragon Tattoo           |    37 |
| 123-401   | The Girl who Played with Fire             |  35.9 |
| 123-402   | The Girl who Kicked the Hornett's Nest    |    39 |
+-----------+-------------------------------------------+-------+
3 rows in set (0.00 sec)

SELECT *
FROM    books
WHERE   title="Mockingjay";

Empty set (0.00 sec)
```

How to do it...

1. Create a new transformation, and create a connection to the book's database.

2. Drop to the canvas a **Text file input** step and use the step to read the books_news. txt file. As separator, type |. Read all fields as **String** except the price that has to be read as a **Number** with 0.00 as the **Format**.

3. Do a preview to verify you have read the file properly. You should see this:

#	code	genre	title	author	comment	price
1	123-400	Fiction	The Girl with the Dragon Tattoo	Larsson, Stieg	In Stock	34.98
2	123-401	Fiction	The Girl Who Played with Fire	Larsson, Stieg	In Stock	35.99
3	123-402	Fiction	The Girl Who Kicked the Hornet's N...	Larsson, Stieg	In Stock	37.99
4	123-602	Fiction	Freedom: A Novel	Franzen, Jonathan	In Stock	28.00
5	223-655	Non-fiction	Eat, Pray, Love: One Woman's Se...	Gilbert, Elizabeth	NEW	36.00
6	223-701	Non-fiction	A Journey: My Political Life	Blair, Tony	NEW	35.00
7	323-609	Non-fiction	The Business of the 21st Century	Kiyosaki, Robert	NEW	24.45
8	523-110	Teens	Mockingjay	Collins, Suzanne	NEW	37.99
9	523-111	Teens	Catching Fire	Collins, Suzanne	In Stock	37.99
10	523-112	Teens	The Hunger Games	Collins, Suzanne	In Stock	37.99

Rows of step: book_news (10 rows)

4. Use a **Split Fields** step to split the name field into two: firstname and lastname.

5. Use a **Database lookup** step to look up in the authors table for an author that matches the firstname and lastname fields. As **Values to return from the lookup table:** add the id_author.

6. Check the option **Do not pass the row if the lookup fails** and close the window.

7. From the **Output** category of steps drag and drop to the canvas a **Synchronize after merge** step, and create a hop from the last step toward this one. Your transformation looks like this:

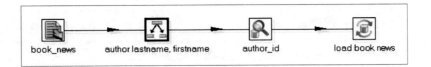

8. Double-click the step. As **Connection**, select the connection you just created. As **Target table**, type books.

9. Fill the grids as shown:

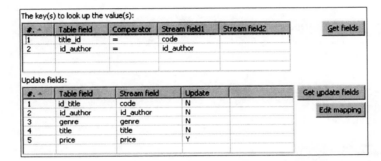

 Remember that you can avoid typing by clicking on the **Get Fields** and **Get update fields** buttons to the right.

10. Select the **Advanced** tab.

11. As **Operation fieldname**, select **comment**. As **Insert when value equal**, type NEW. As **Update when value equal**, type In Stock. Leave the other fields blank.

12. Close the window and save the transformation.

13. Run the transformation.

14. Explore the database again. In particular, run for the second time the same statements you ran before doing the recipe. Now you will get this:

```
SELECT count(*)
FROM    books;
+----------+
| count(*) |
+----------+
|       38 |
+----------+
1 row in set (0.00 sec)

SELECT id_title, title, price
FROM    books
WHERE   author_id='A00001';
```

```
+-----------+---------------------------------------------+-------+
| id_title  | title                                       | price |
+-----------+---------------------------------------------+-------+
| 123-400   | The Girl with the Dragon Tattoo             | 34.98 |
| 123-401   | The Girl who Played with Fire               | 35.99 |
| 123-402   | The Girl who Kicked the Hornett's Nest      | 37.99 |
+-----------+---------------------------------------------+-------+
3 rows in set (0.00 sec)
SELECT *
FROM    books
WHERE   title="Mockingjay";
+-----------+------------+-----------+-------+-------+
| id_title  | title      | id_author | price | genre |
+-----------+------------+-----------+-------+-------+
| 523-110   | Mockingjay | A00012    | 37.99 | Teens |
+-----------+------------+-----------+-------+-------+
1 row in set (0.00 sec)
```

How it works...

The **Synchronize after merge** step allows you to insert, update, or delete rows in a table based on the value of a field in the stream. In the recipe, you used the **Synchronize after merge** step both for inserting the new books (for example, Mockingjay) and for updating the prices for the books you already had (for example, The Girl with the Dragon Tattoo).

In order to tell PDI whether to execute an insert or an update, you used the field comment. Under the **Advanced** tab, you told PDI that it should insert the records where the comment was equal to NEW, and update those where the comment was In Stock.

Note that, because you didn't intend to delete rows, you left the **Delete when value equal** option blank. However, you could also have configured this option in the same way you configured the others. An example of that could be deleting the books that will stop being published. If you recognize those books after the expression out of market, you could type that expression in the **Delete when value equal** option and those books would be deleted.

The inserts and updates were made based on the fields you entered in the grids under the **General** tab, which work exactly as the grids in an **Insert/Update** or an **Update** step.

There's more...

Let's see a little more about the step you used in this recipe.

Insert, update, and delete all-in-one

The **Synchronize after merge** step is like an all-in-one step. It allows you to insert, update, and delete rows from a table all in a single step, based on a field present in the dataset. For each row Kettle uses the value of that column to decide which of the three basic operations to execute. This happens as follows.

Suppose that the **Operation fieldname** is called op and the values that should cause an insert, update, or delete are NEW, In Stock, and Discontinued respectively.

Operation	How it works
Insert	The insert is made for all rows where the field op is equal to NEW. The insert is made based on the key fields just like in an **Insert/Update** step.
Update	The update is made for all rows where the field op is equal to the value In Stock. The update is made based on the key fields just like in an **Insert/Update** or an **Update** step.
Delete	The delete is made for all rows where the field op is equal to the value Discontinued. The delete is made based on the key fields just like in a **Delete** step. For Delete operations the content of the lower grid is ignored.

Synchronizing after merge

You may wonder what the name **Synchronize after merge** has to do with this, if you neither merged nor synchronized anything. The fact is that the step was named after the **Merge Rows (diff)** step, as those steps can perfectly be used together. The **Merge Rows (diff)** step has the ability to find differences between two streams, and those differences are used later to update a table by using a **Synchronize after merge** step.

See also

▶ *Deleting data from a table*. For understanding how the delete operations work. Inserting or updating rows in a table and for understanding how the inserts and updates work.

▶ *Comparing two streams and generating differences (Chapter 6, Understanding Data Flows)*. For learning to use the **Synchronize after merge** step along with the **Merge Rows (dif)** step.

Changing the database connection at runtime

Sometimes you have several databases with exactly the same structure serving different purposes. These are some situations:

▶ A database for the information that is being updated daily and one or more databases for historical data.

> ► A different database for each branch of your business.

> ► A database for your sandbox, a second database for the staging area, and a third database fulfilling the production server purpose.

In any of those situations, it's likely that you need access to one or the other depending on certain conditions, or you may even have to access all of them one after the other. Not only that, the number of databases may not be fixed; it may change over time (for example, when a new branch is opened).

Suppose you face the second scenario: Your company has several branches, and the sales for each branch are stored in a different database. The database structure is the same for all branches; the only difference is that each of them holds different data. Now you want to generate a file with the total sales for the current year in every branch.

Getting ready

Download the material for this recipe. You will find a sample file with database connections to three branches. It looks like this:

```
branch,host,database
0001 (headquarters),localhost,sales2010
0002,183.43.2.33,sales
0003,233.22.1.97,sales
```

If you intend to run the transformation, modify the file so it points to real databases.

How to do it...

1. Create a transformation that reads the file with connection data and copy the rows to results.

2. Create a second transformation, and define the following **named parameters**: BRANCH, HOST_NAME, and DATABASE_NAME.

3. Create a database connection. Choose the proper **Connection Type:**, and fill the **Settings** data. Type a value for the **Port Number:**, the **User Name:**, and the **Password**. As **Host Name:** type ${HOST_NAME}, and as **Database Name:** type ${DATABASE_NAME}.

4. Use a **Table Input** step for getting the total sales from the database. Use the connection just defined.

5. Use a **Text file output** step for sending the sales summary to a text file. Don't forget to check the option **Append** under the **Content** tab of the setting window.

6. Create a job with two **Transformation** job entries, linked one after the other.

7. Use the first entry to call the first transformation you created, and the second entry to call the second transformation. The job looks like this:

8. Double-click the second transformation entry, select the **Advanced** tab, and check the **Copy previous results to parameters?** and the **Execute for every input row?** checkboxes.

9. Select the **Parameters** tab and fill it as shown:

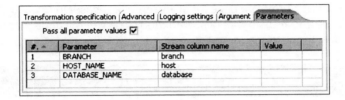

10. Save both transformations. Save the job, and run it.

11. Open the text file generated. It should have one line with sales information for each database in the file with the list of databases.

How it works...

If you have to connect to several databases, and you don't know in advance which or how many databases you will have to connect to, you can't rely on a connection with fixed values, or variables defined in a single place as for example in the `kettle.properties` file. In those situations, the best you could do is to define a connection with variables, and set the values for the variables at runtime.

In the recipe, you created a text file with a summary sales line for each database in a list.

The transformation that wrote the sales line used a connection with variables defined as **named parameters**. This means that whoever calls the transformation has to provide the proper values.

The main job loops on the list of database connections. For each row in that list, it calls the transformation copying the values from the file to the parameters in the transformation. In other words, each time the transformation runs, the **named parameters** are instantiated with the values coming from the file.

There's more...

In the recipe, you changed the host and the name of the database. You could have parameterized any of the values that made up a database connection, for example the user and password.

See also

▸ *Connecting to a database*. This recipe explains how to connect to a database by using variables.

▸ *Executing a transformation once for every row in a dataset* in *Chapter 7, Executing and Reusing Jobs and Transformations*. With this recipe you will understand better the way the loop over the database connection works.

Loading a parent-child table

A **parent-child table** is a table in which there is a self-referencing relationship. In other words, there is a hierarchical relationship among its rows. A typical example of this is a table with employees, in which one of the columns contains references to the employee that is above each employee in the hierarchy.

In this recipe you will load the parent-child table of employees of Steel Wheels. The hierarchy of roles in Steel Wheels is as follows:

▸ A sales representative reports to a sales manager

▸ A sales manager reports to a vice-president

▸ A vice-presidents reports to the president

▸ The president is the highest level in the hierarchy. There is a single employee with this role.

You will load all employees from a file. These are sample rows in that file:

```
EMPLOYEENUMBER|LASTNAME|FIRSTNAME|EXTENSION|EMAIL|OFFICECODE|JOBTITLE
|REP_TO

1002|Murphy|Diane|x5800|dmurphy@classicmodelcars.com |1|President|

1056|Patterson|Mary|x4611|mpatterso@classicmodelcars.com |1|VP
Sales|dmurphy@classicmodelcars.com

1076|Firrelli|Jeff|x9273|jfirrelli@classicmodelcars.com |1|VP
Marketing|dmurphy@classicmodelcars.com

1088|Patterson|William|x4871|wpatterson@classicmodelcars.com |6|Sales
Manager (JAPAN, APAC)|mpatterso@classicmodelcars.com

. . .
```

As you can see, among the fields you have the e-mail of the employee who is above in the hierarchy. For example, Gerar Bondur is a Sales Manager, and reports to the employee with e-mail mpatterso@classicmodelcars.com, that is, Mary Patterson.

Getting ready

In order to run this recipe, either truncate the employees table in Steel Wheels, or create the table employees in a different database.

How to do it...

1. Create a transformation that inserts the record for the president who is the first in the hierarchy, and doesn't report to anyone. The transformation should read the file, filter the record with JOBTITLE=President, and insert the data into the employees table.

2. Create another transformation to load the rest of the employees. Define a named parameter named LEVEL that will represent the role of the employees being loaded.

3. Use a **Text file input** step to read the file of employees.

4. Use a **Get Variables** step to add the variable LEVEL as a new field named level.

5. Add a **Filter rows** step to filter the employees to load based on their role. In order to do that, enter the following condition: JOBTITLE REGEXP level.

6. Add a **Database lookup** to find out the employee number of the employee who is one above in the hierarchy: In the upper grid add a row with the condition EMAIL = REP_TO. Use the lower grid to get the field EMPLOYEENUMBER and rename it to REPORTSTO.

7. Add a **Table Output** step, and use it to insert the records in the table employees. Your final transformation looks like this:

employees   Get level   match level?   lookup REPORTSTO   insert employees

8. Finally create a job to put all together. Drag to the work area a **START** entry, and four **Transformation** job entries. Link all of them in a row.

9. Use the first **Transformation** entry to execute the transformation that loads the president.

10. Double-click the second **Transformation** entry and configure it to run the transformation that loads the other employees. Under the **Parameters** tab, add a parameter named LEVEL with value VP.*.

11. Repeat step 10 for the third **Transformation** entry, but this time type
    `.*Manager.*` as the value for the LEVEL parameter.

12. Repeat step 10 for the fourth **Transformation** entry, but this time type `Sales`
    `Rep.*` as the value for the LEVEL parameter.

13. Save and run the job. The table should have all employees loaded, as you
    can see below:

```
SELECT
    EMPLOYEENUMBER N
, LASTNAME
, REPORTSTO
, JOBTITLE
FROM employees;
+------+-----------+-----------+---------------------------+
| N    | LASTNAME  | REPORTSTO | JOBTITLE                  |
+------+-----------+-----------+---------------------------+
| 1002 | Murphy    |      NULL | President                 |
| 1056 | Patterson |      1002 | VP Sales                  |
| 1076 | Firrelli  |      1002 | VP Marketing              |
| 1088 | Patterson |      1056 | Sales Manager (JAPAN, APAC)|
| 1102 | Bondur    |      1056 | Sale Manager (EMEA)       |
| 1143 | Bow       |      1056 | Sales Manager (NA)        |
| 1165 | Jennings  |      1143 | Sales Rep                 |
| 1166 | Thompson  |      1143 | Sales Rep                 |
| 1188 | Firrelli  |      1143 | Sales Rep                 |
| ...  | ...       |       ... | ...                       |
+------+-----------+-----------+---------------------------+
23 rows in set (0.00 sec)
```

How it works...

If you have to load a table with parent-child relationships, loading all at once is not always
feasible. Look at the `sampledata` database. There is no physical foreign key from the
REPORTSTO column to the EMPLOYEENUMBER column, but if the foreign key had existed,
loading all records at once would fail because of the foreign key constraint. Not only that; in
this case loading all at once would be impossible because in the file you missed the ID of the
parent employee needed for the REPORTSTO column.

So, in this recipe there was one possible solution for loading the table. We loaded all employees, one role at a time, beginning by the president and followed by the roles below in the hierarchy. The transformation that loaded the other roles simply read the file, kept only the employees with the role being loaded, looked for the ID of the parent employee in the hierarchy, and inserted the records. For the roles you could have used fixed values but you used regular expressions instead. In doing so, you avoided calling the transformation once for each different role. For example, for loading the vice-presidents you called the transformation once with the regular expression VP.* which matched both VP Sales and VP Marketing.

See also

► *Inserting or updating rows in a table*. If you are not confident with inserting data into a table see this recipe.

2
Reading and Writing Files

In this chapter, we will cover:

- Reading a simple file
- Reading several files at the same time
- Reading unstructured files
- Reading files having one field by row
- Reading files having some fields occupying two or more rows
- Writing a simple file
- Writing an unstructured file
- Providing the name of a file (for reading or writing) dynamically
- Using the name of a file (or part of it) as a field
- Reading an Excel file
- Getting the value of specific cells in an Excel file
- Writing an Excel file with several sheets
- Writing an Excel file with a dynamic number of sheets

Introduction

Files are the most primitive, but also the most used format to store and interchange data. PDI has the ability to read data from all kind of files and different formats. It also allows you to write back to files in different formats as well.

Reading and writing simple files is a very straightforward task. There are several steps under the input and output categories of steps that allow you to do it. You pick the step, configure it quickly, and you are done. However, when the files you have to read or create are not simple—and that happens most of the time—the task of reading or writing can become a tedious exercise if you don't know the tricks. In this chapter, you will learn not only the basics for reading and writing files, but also all the how-tos for dealing with them.

 This chapter covers plain files (txt, csv, fixed width) and Excel files. For recipes for reading and writing XML files, refer to *Chapter 3, Manipulating XML Structures.*

Reading a simple file

In this recipe, you will learn the use of the *Text file input* step. In the example, you have to read a simple file with a list of authors' information like the following:

```
"lastname","firstname","country","birthyear"
"Larsson","Stieg","Swedish",1954
"King","Stephen","American",1947
"Hiaasen","Carl ","American",1953
"Handler","Chelsea ","American",1975
"Ingraham","Laura ","American",1964
```

Getting ready

In order to continue with the exercise, you must have a file named authors.txt similar to the one shown in the introduction section of this recipe.

How to do it...

Carry out the following steps:

1. Create a new transformation.

2. Drop a **Text file input** step to the canvas.

3. Now, you have to type the name of the file (authors.txt) with its complete path. You do it in the **File or directory** textbox.

 Alternatively, you can select the file by clicking on the **Browse** button and looking for the file. The textbox will be populated with the complete path of the file.

4. Click on the **Add** button. The complete text will be moved from the **File or directory** textbox to the grid.

5. Select the **Content** tab and fill in the required fields, as shown in the following screenshot:

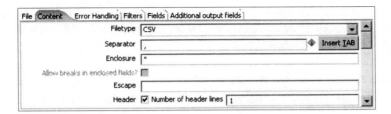

6. Select the **Fields** tab and click on the **Get Fields** button to get the definitions of the fields automatically. The grid will be populated, as shown in the following screenshot:

#.	Name	Type
1	lastname	String
2	firstname	String
3	country	String
4	birthyear	String

 Kettle doesn't always guess the data types, size, or format as expected. So, after getting the fields, you may change the data to what you consider more appropriate.

 When you read a file, it's not mandatory to keep the names of the columns as they are in the file. You are free to change the names of the fields as well.

7. Click on the **Preview** button and you will see some sample rows built with the data in your file.

How it works...

You use the **Text file input** in order to read text files, in this case, the `authors.txt` file.

Looking at the content of the file, you can see that the first line contains the header of the columns. In order to recognize that header, you have to check the **Header** checkbox under the **Content** tab, and type 1 in the **Number of header lines** textbox. You also have to indicate the field's separator. The separator can be made of one or more characters the most used being the semicolon, colon, or a tab. Finally, you can indicate the **Enclosure** string, in this case, ".

PDI takes all that information and uses it to parse the text file and fill the fields correctly.

There's more...

To work with these kinds of delimited text files, you could choose the **CSV file input** step. This step has a less powerful configuration, but it provides better performance.

If you explore the tabs of the **Text file input** setting window, you will see that there are more options to set, but the ones just explained are by far the most used. But there are a couple of additional features that may interest you:

Alternative notation for a separator

Instead of typing the separator for the fields, you can use the following notation:

```
$[H1, H2, ...]
```

Where the values `H1`, `H2`, `...` are the hexadecimal codes for the separators. For example, for specifying a tilde (~) as the separator, instead of typing it, you could type $[7E]. However, this notation makes more sense when your separators are non printable characters.

For the enclosure string the hexadecimal notation is also allowed.

About file format and encoding

If you are trying to read a file without success, and you have already checked the most common settings, that is, the name of the file, the header, the separator and the fields, you should take a look at and try to fix the other available settings. Among those, you have **Format** and **Encoding**.

Format allows you to specify the format of your file(s): **DOS** (default value) or **UNIX**. If your file has a Unix format, you should change this setting. If you don't know the format, but you cannot guarantee that the format will be DOS, you can choose the **mixed** option.

Encoding allows you to specify the character encoding to use. If you leave it blank, Kettle will use the default encoding on your system. Alternatively, if you know the encoding and it is different from the default, you should select the proper option from the drop-down list.

About data types and formats

When you read a file and tell Kettle which fields to get from that file, you have to provide at least a name and a data type for those fields. In order to tell Kettle how to read and interpret the data, you have more options. Most of them are self-explanatory, but the format, length, and precision deserve an explanation:

If you are reading a number, and the numbers in your file have separators, dollar signs, and so on, you should specify a *format* to tell Kettle how to interpret that number. The format is a combination of patterns and symbols as explained in the Sun Java API documentation at the following URL:

```
http://java.sun.com/javase/6/docs/api/java/text/DecimalFormat.html
```

If you don't specify a format for your numbers, you may still provide a *length* and *precision*. Length is the total number of significant figures, while precision is the number of floating point digits.

 If you don't specify format, length, or precision, Kettle will do its best to interpret the number, but this could lead to unexpected results.

In the case of dates, the same thing happens. When your text file has a date, you have to select or type a format mask, so Kettle can recognize the different components of the date in the field. For a complete reference on date formats, check the Sun Java API documentation, located at the following URL:

`http://java.sun.com/javase/6/docs/api/java/text/SimpleDateFormat.html`

Altering the names, order, or metadata of the fields coming from the file

If you want to reorder or delete some of the columns you read, you have to add another step to the transformation. Suppose you want to move the `country` name to the end of the list of columns, changing it to a more suitable field name, such as `nationality`.

In this case, add a **Select values** step. The *Select values* step allows you to select, rename, reorder, and delete fields, or change the metadata of a field.

Under the **Select & Alter** tab, select all the fields and manipulate those according to your needs as shown in the following example:

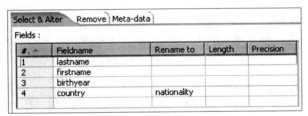

 If you just want to rename the columns, you don't need a *Select values* step. You can do it in the *Text file input* step by typing the names manually.

Reading files with fixed width fields

In the example, you read a **CSV (Comma Separated Values)** file type. This is the default value for the type of file, as you can see under the **Content** tab. You have another option here named **Fixed** for reading files with fixed-width columns. If you choose this option, a different helper GUI will appear when you click on the **Get fields** button. In the wizard, you can visually set the position for each of your fields.

There is also another step named *Fixed file input* in the **Input** category to apply in these cases. It provides better performance and has a simpler, but less flexible configuration.

Reading several files at the same time

Sometimes you have several files to read, all with the same structure, but different data. In this recipe, you will see how to read those files in a single step. The example uses a list of files containing names of museums in Italy.

Getting ready

You must have a group of text files in a directory, all with the same format. In this recipe, the names of these files start with `museums_italy_` for example, `museums_italy_1`, `museums_italy_2`, `museums_italy_roma`, `museums_italy_genova`, and so on.

Each file has a list of names of museums, one museum on each line.

How to do it...

Carry out the following steps:

1. Create a new transformation.
2. Drop a **Text file input** step onto the work area.
3. Under the **File or directory** tab, type the directory where the files are.
4. In the **Regular Expression** textbox, type: `museums_italy_.*\.txt`
5. Then click on the **Add** button. The grid will be populated, as shown in the following screenshot:

#. ▲	File/Directory	Wildcard (RegExp)
1	${Internal.Transformation.Filename.Directory}\museums\	museums_italy_.*\.txt

`${Internal.Transformation.Filename.Directory}` is a variable that will be replaced at run-time with the full path of the current transformation. Note that the variable will be undefined until you save the transformation. Therefore it's necessary that you save before running a preview of the step.

You don't have to type the complete name of the `${Internal.Transformation.Filename.Directory}` variable. It can be selected from a list automatically created when pressing *Ctrl+Space*.

6. Under the **Fields** tab, add one row: type `museum` for the **Name** column and **String** under the **Type** column.

7. Save the transformation in the same place, the `museum` directory is located. Previewing the step, you will obtain a dataset with the content of all files with names of museums.

How it works...

With Kettle, it is possible to read more than one file at a time using a single *Text File Input* step.

In order to get the content of several files, you can add names to the grid row by row. If the names of files share the path and some part of their names, you can also specify the names of the files by using regular expressions, as shown in the recipe. If you enter a regular expression, Kettle will take all the files whose names match it. In the recipe, the files that matched `museums_italy_.*\.txt` were considered as input files.

`museums_italy_.*\.txt` means "all the files starting with `museum_italy_` and having txt extension". You can test if the regular expression is correct by clicking on the **Show filename(s)...** button. That will show you a list of all files that matches the expression.

If you fill the grid with the names of several files (with or without using regular expressions), Kettle will create a dataset with the content of all of those files one after the other.

To learn more about regular expressions, you can visit the following URLs:

▸ `http://www.regular-expressions.info/quickstart.html`

▸ `http://java.sun.com/docs/books/tutorial/essential/regex/`

There's more...

In the recipe, you read several files. It might happen that you have to read just one file, but you don't know the exact name of the file. One example of that is a file whose name is a fixed text followed by the current year and month as in `samplefile_201012.txt`. The recipe is useful in cases like that as well. In this example, if you don't know the name of the file, you will still be able to read it by typing the following regular expression: `samplefile_20[0-9][0-9] (0[1-9]|1[0-2])\.txt`.

Reading unstructured files

The simplest files for reading are those where all rows follow the same pattern: Each row has a fixed number of columns, and all columns have the same kind of data in every row. However, it is common to have files where the information does not have that format. In many occasions, the files have little or no structure. Suppose you have a file with roller coaster descriptions, and the file looks like the following:

```
JOURNEY TO ATLANTIS
SeaWorld Orlando

Journey to Atlantis is a unique thrill ride since it is ...
Roller Coaster Stats
Drop: 60 feet
Trains: 8 passenger boats
Train Mfg: Mack

KRAKEN
SeaWorld Orlando

Named after a legendary sea monster, Kraken is a ...
Kraken begins with a plunge from a height of 15-stories ...
Roller Coaster Stats
Height: 151 feet
Drop: 144 feet
Top Speed: 65 mph
Length: 4,177 feet
Inversions: 7
Trains: 3 - 32 passenger
Ride Time: 2 minutes, 2 seconds

KUMBA
Busch Gardens Tampa
...
```

As you can see, the preceding file is far from being a structured file that you can read simply by configuring a *Text file input* step. Following this recipe, you will learn how to deal with this kind of file.

Getting ready

When you have to read an unstructured file, such as the preceding sample file, the first thing to do is to take a detailed look at it. Try to understand how the data is organized; despite being unstructured, it has a hidden format that you have to discover in order to be able to read it.

So, let's analyze the sample file, which is available for download from the book's site.

The file has data about several roller coasters. Let's take note of the characteristics of the file:

 As a useful exercise, you could do this yourself before reading the following list.

- ▶ Each roller coaster spans several lines.
- ▶ There are blank lines, which should be eliminated.

- What allows us to distinguish the first line for each roller coaster from the rest is that it is written in uppercase letters.

- The first line below the name of the roller coaster is the name of the amusement park where it is located.

- Most of the lines have a property of the roller coaster in the format of `code:description`, as for example `Drop: 60 feet`.

- Above the properties, there is a line with the text `Roller Coaster Stats`, which doesn't add any information. It should be discarded.

- There are lines with additional information about the roller coaster. There is nothing that distinguishes these lines. They simply do not fall into any of the other kinds of lines (lines with the name of the park, lines with properties of the roller coaster, and so on).

Once you understand the content of your file, you are ready to read it, and parse it.

How to do it...

Carry out the following steps:

1. Create a transformation and drag a **Text file input** step.

2. Use that step to read the file named `rollercoasters_II.txt`. Under the **Content** tab, uncheck the **Header** option and under the **Separator** tab, type `|`. Under the **Fields** tab, enter a single field named `text` of type **String**. As the character `|` is not present in any part of the file, you are sure that the whole line will be read as a single field.

3. From the **Scripting** category of steps, add a **Modified Java Script Value** step, double-click it, and under the **main** tab window type the following snippet of code:

```
var attraction;
trans_Status=CONTINUE_TRANSFORMATION;

if (getProcessCount('r') == 1) attraction = '';
if (text == upper(removeDigits(text))) {
   attraction = text;
   trans_Status=SKIP_TRANSFORMATION;
   }
else if (text == 'Roller Coaster Stats')
   trans_Status=SKIP_TRANSFORMATION;
```

4. Click on the **Get variables** button to populate the grid with the variable `attraction`.

5. From the **Transform** category, add an **Add value fields changing sequence** step.

6. Double-click the step. As **Result field** type `line_nr`. In the first row of the grid type `attraction`.

7. Do a preview on this last step. You will see the following:

Rows of step: numbering lines (200 rows)			
# ▲	**text**	**attraction**	**line_nr** ▲
1	Disney's Magic Kingdom	BIG THUNDER MOUNTAIN RAILROAD	1
2	Height: 45 feet	BIG THUNDER MOUNTAIN RAILROAD	2
3	Top Speed: 30 mph	BIG THUNDER MOUNTAIN RAILROAD	3
4	Length: 2,780 feet	BIG THUNDER MOUNTAIN RAILROAD	4
5	Trains: 6 - 30 passenger	BIG THUNDER MOUNTAIN RAILROAD	5
6	Train Mfg: Walt Disney Imagineering	BIG THUNDER MOUNTAIN RAILROAD	6
7	Busch Gardens Tampa	CHEETAH CHASE	1
8	Busch Gardens' family roller coaster, Cheetah...	CHEETAH CHASE	2
9	Height: 46 feet	CHEETAH CHASE	3
10	Top Speed: 28 mph	CHEETAH CHASE	4

So far, you've read the file, and identified all the rows belonging to each roller coaster. It's time to parse the different lines. In the first place, let's parse the lines that contain properties:

1. Add a **Filter rows** step and enter the condition `text REGEXP (.+):(.+)`.

2. From the **Scripting** category, add a **Regex Evaluation** step and send the true rows toward this step.

3. Configure the step as follows: As **Field to evaluate** select **text**. Check the **Create fields for capture groups** option. As **Regular expression**: type `(.+):(.+)`.

4. Fill the lower grid with two rows: as **New field** type `code` in the first row and `desc` in the second. In both rows, under **Type**, select **String**, and under **Trim** select **both**.

5. Finally add a **Select values** step to select the fields `attraction`, `code`, `desc`, and `line_nr`.

 In order to do a preview to see how the steps are transforming your data, you can add a *Dummy* step and send the false rows of the *Filter rows* step towards it. The only purpose of this is avoiding the transformation crash.

Now you will parse the other lines: the lines that contain the park name, and the additional comments:

1. Add another **Filter rows** step, and send the false rows of the other **Filter rows** step toward this one.

2. Add two **Add constants** steps, and a **Select values** step, and link all the steps as shown in the following diagram:

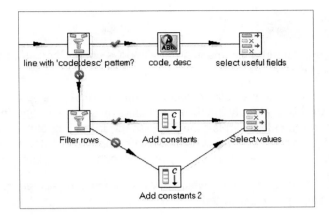

3. In the **Filter rows** enter the condition `line_nr=1`.

4. In the first **Add constants** step, add a String field named `code` with value `park`. Make sure the true rows of the **Filter rows** step go toward this step.

5. In the other **Add constants** step, add a String field named `code` with value `additional_information`. Make sure the false rows of the **Filter rows** step go toward this step.

6. Use the **Select values** step that joins the two **Add constants** steps to select the fields `attraction`, `code`, `text`, and `line_nr`. In the same step, rename `text` as `desc`.

 Make sure that the fields are in this exact order. The metadata of both **Select values** steps must coincide.

Now that you have parsed all the types of rows it's time to join the rows together.

1. Join both **Select values** with a **Sort rows** step. Sort the rows by `attraction` and `line_nr`.

2. Select the **Sort rows** step and do a preview. You should see the following:

Rows of step: Sort by attraction _code (200 rows)

	attraction	code	desc	line_nr
1	BIG THUNDER MOUN...	park	Disney's Magic Kingdom	1
2	BIG THUNDER MOUN...	Height	45 feet	2
3	BIG THUNDER MOUN...	Top Speed	30 mph	3
4	BIG THUNDER MOUN...	Length	2,780 feet	4
5	BIG THUNDER MOUN...	Trains	6 - 30 passenger	5
6	BIG THUNDER MOUN...	Train Mfg	Walt Disney Imagineering	6
7	CHEETAH CHASE	park	Busch Gardens Tampa	1
8	CHEETAH CHASE	additional_information	Busch Gardens' family ro...	2
9	CHEETAH CHASE	Height	46 feet	3
10	CHEETAH CHASE	Top Speed	28 mph	4

How it works...

When you have an unstructured file, the first thing to do is understand its content, in order to be able to parse the file properly.

If the entities described in the file (roller coasters in this example) are spanned over several lines, the very first task is to identify the rows that make up a single entity. The usual method is to do it with a *JavaScript* step. In this example, with the JavaScript code, you used the fact that the first line of each roller coaster was written with uppercase letter, to create and add a field named `attraction`. In the same code, you removed unwanted lines.

In this example, as you needed to know which row was the first in each group, you added an *Add value fields changing sequence* step.

After doing this, which as noted is only necessary for a particular kind of file, you have to parse the lines. If the lines do not follow the same pattern, you have to split your stream in as many streams as kind of rows you have. In this example, you split the main stream into three, as follows:

1. One for parsing the lines with properties, for example `Drop: 60 feet`.
2. One for setting the name of the amusement park where the roller coaster was.
3. One for keeping the additional information.

In each stream, you proceeded differently according to the format of the line.

The most useful step for parsing individual unstructured fields is the *Regexp Evaluation* step. It both validates if a field follows a given pattern (provided as a regular expression) and optionally, it captures groups. In this case, you used that step to capture a code and a description. In the preceding example (`Drop: 60 feet`), the *Regexp Evaluation* step allowed you to build two fields: `code` with value `Drop`, and `desc` with value `60 feet`.

Once you parsed the line with the *Regexp Evaluation* or the step of your choice, you can continue transforming or modifying the fields according to your needs and the characteristics of your particular file.

In the same way, depending on the purpose of your transformation, you can leave the streams separated or join them back together as you did in the recipe.

There's more...

There are some common kinds of files that can be parsed in the way you parsed the roller coasters file:

Master/detail files

Suppose that you have a file of invoices such as the following:

```
INV.0001-0045;02/28/2010;$323.99
CSD-031;2;$34.00
CSA-110;1;$100.99
LSK-092;1;$189.00
INV.0001-0046;02/28/2010;$53.99
DSD-031;2;$13.00
CXA-110;1;$40.99
INV.0001-0047;02/28/2010;$1149.33
...
```

The lines beginning with `INV.` are the invoice headers; the lines following the headers are the details of those invoices.

Files like these are not uncommon. If you have a file like this with records that represent headers followed by records that represent details about those headers, and the header and detail records have different structures, you could parse it as explained in the recipe.

Read the file, do whatever is necessary to find out if a row is a header or a detail, and split the stream in two. After that, parse header rows and detail rows accordingly.

Log files

Log files are among the most common kinds of unstructured files. Look at the following sample lines belonging to a Pentaho Server log:

```
...
2010-09-30 13:01:30,437 DEBUG [org.pentaho.platform.engine.
    services.solution.SolutionEngine] fd386728-ccab-11df-9...
2010-09-30 13:01:30,484 INFO  [org.pentaho.platform.reposit
    ory.solution.SolutionRepositoryBase] Solution Reposito...
2010-09-30 13:01:30,484 INFO  [org.pentaho.platform.reposit
    ory.solution.SolutionRepositoryBase] Solution Reposit...
2010-09-30 13:01:30,515 INFO  [org.pentaho.platform.reposit
    ory.solution.SolutionRepositoryBase] Could not find d...
2010-09-30 13:01:30,531 ERROR [org.pentaho.platform.engine.
    services.solution.SolutionEngine] fd386728-ccab-11df-...
2010-09-30 13:01:42,515 WARN  [org.hibernate.cache.EhCacheP
    rovider] Could not find configuration [file]; using d...
...
```

In this case, all lines begin with a timestamp, followed by the level of log (DEBUG, INFO, and so on), and then the details of the log.

Despite being unstructured, the lines in a log file—the one shown above—have some text that let you know what kind of data is in those lines. Using that knowledge, you can parse different lines as explained in the recipe.

In this particular example, you could read the file as containing two fields: one for the timestamp, the other with the rest of the line. Then you can parse the second field splitting it in two: the kind of log (DEBUG, INFO, and so on) and the detail. Optionally, if you wanted to treat each level of log differently, you could split the stream with a *Switch case* step or nested *Filter rows* steps and proceed.

Reading files having one field by row

When you use one of the Kettle steps meant for reading files, Kettle expects the data organized in rows, where the columns are the fields. Suppose that instead of having a file with that structure, your file has one attribute per row as in the following example:

```
Mastering Joomla! 1.5 Extension and Framework Development
Published: November 2007
Our price: £30.99

CakePHP 1.3 Application Development Cookbook: RAW
Expected: December 2010
Our price: £24.99

Firebug 1.5: Editing, Debugging, and Monitoring Web Pages
Published: April 2010
Our price: £21.99

jQuery Reference Guide
...
```

This file contains book information. In the file, each book is described in three rows: one for the title, one for the published or expected publishing date, and one row for the price.

There is no direct way to tell Kettle how to interpret these rows, but a simple transformation can do the trick.

Getting ready

Create a file containing the preceding text or download the sample file from the book's site.

How to do it...

Carry out the following steps:

1. Create a transformation and use a **Text file input** step to read the file `packt_books.txt`. Under the **Content** tab, uncheck the **Header** option and as **Separator**, type `|`. Under the **Fields** tab, enter a single String field named `text`.

2. From the **Transform** category, add a **Row flattener** step.

3. Double-click the step. As **The field to flatten** type or select `text`. Fill the grid with three rows with values `title`, `publishing_date`, and `price`.

4. Do a preview on the last step. You'll see the following:

	title	publishing_date	price
31	Mastering Joomla! 1.5 Extension and F...	Published: November 2007	Our price: £30.99
32	CakePHP 1.3 Application Development ...	Expected: December 2010	Our price: £24.99
33	Firebug 1.5: Editing, Debugging, and ...	Published: April 2010	Our price: £21.99
34	jQuery Reference Guide	Published: July 2007	Our price: £24.99
35	PHP Web 2.0 Mashup Projects	Published: September 2007	Our price: £24.99
36	3D Game Development with Microsoft ...	Published: September 2009	Our price: £30.99
37	Selenium 1.0 Testing Tools: Beginner's ...	Expected: December 2010	Our price: £24.99
38	Mahara 1.2 E-Portfolios: Beginner's Gu...	Published: February 2010	Our price: £24.99
39	Drupal 7 First Look: RAW	Expected: November 2010	Our price: £24.99
40	RESTful PHP Web Services	Published: October 2008	Our price: £24.99

Rows of step: Row flattener (49 rows)

You already have the fields as columns! Now, you can go a little further and do some cleansing, as follows:

1. From the **Scripting** category add a **Regexp Evaluation** step.

2. Configure the step as follows: As **Field to evaluate** type or select `publishing_date`. Check the option **Create fields for capture groups**. As **Regular expression:** type `(Published|Expected):(.+)`.

3. In the **Capture Group Fields** grid, add two rows. In the first row create a new **String** field named `status`. In the second, create a **Date** field named `pub_date` with **Format** MMM yyy. In both rows, under the **Trim** column, select **both**.

4. From the **Transform** category, add a **Replace in string** step. In the grid, add a row with the value `price` under the column **In stream field**, and `Our price:` under the column **Search**.

5. Finally, use a **Select values** step to change the metadata of the **price** field: Change it to `Number`. As **Format**, type `£#.00`

6. Do a preview and you'll see the following:

	title	publishing_date	price	r...	status	pub_date
31	Mastering Joomla! 1.5 Extension ...	Published: November 2007	£30.99	Y	Published	Nov 2007
32	CakePHP 1.3 Application Develop...	Expected: December 2010	£24.99	Y	Expected	Dec 2010
33	Firebug 1.5: Editing, Debugging, ...	Published: April 2010	£21.99	Y	Published	Apr 2010
34	jQuery Reference Guide	Published: July 2007	£24.99	Y	Published	Jul 2007
35	PHP Web 2.0 Mashup Projects	Published: September 2007	£24.99	Y	Published	Sep 2007
36	3D Game Development with Micro...	Published: September 2009	£30.99	Y	Published	Sep 2009
37	Selenium 1.0 Testing Tools: Begin...	Expected: December 2010	£24.99	Y	Expected	Dec 2010
38	Mahara 1.2 E-Portfolios: Beginner...	Published: February 2010	£24.99	Y	Published	Feb 2010
39	Drupal 7 First Look: RAW	Expected: November 2010	£24.99	Y	Expected	Nov 2010
40	RESTful PHP Web Services	Published: October 2008	£24.99	Y	Published	Oct 2008

Rows of step: change metadata (49 rows)

In the sample file, the months are written in English. Therefore, you put the mask MMM yyyy when capturing groups. If you get an error because of the Date format, there is a high possibility that you do not have English as the preferred language in your regional settings. Consequently, Kettle is not able to parse those dates.

How it works...

The *Row flattener* step is a simple step intended to flatten consecutive rows and is perfect for reading files such as the one in the recipe. In this case, you had a file with book information, each book occupying three consecutive rows. The *Row flattener* flattened the field text into three different new fields: title, publishing_date, and price.

This way, every three rows, it generated a single one.

Note that if one book has a different number of rows (for example, if it lacks the price row), then you get unexpected results.

 The *Row flattener* flattens the rows as indicated in its setting window, no matter the content of the field being flattened.

There's more...

If you are not sure about the content of the file, you'd best avoid this simple solution and go for a more sophisticated one, for example, a solution that uses a *Row denormalizer* step.

See also

The sectioned named, *Reading unstructured files* in this chapter. Look at this recipe if you have to read a file, such as the one in the recipe, but you are not sure of the number of rows occupied by each element.

Reading files with some fields occupying two or more rows

When you use one of the Kettle steps devoted for reading files, Kettle expects one entity per row. For example, if you are reading a file with a list of customers, then Kettle expects one customer per row. Suppose that you have a file organized by rows, where the fields are in different columns, but some of the fields span several rows, as in the following example containing data about roller coasters:

```
Roller Coaster          Speed        Location                    Year
Kingda Ka               128 mph      Six Flags Great Adventure
                                     Jackson, New Jersey         2005
Top Thrill Dragster 120 mph          Cedar Point
                                     Sandusky, Ohio              2003
Dodonpa                 106.8 mph    Fuji-Q Highland
                                     FujiYoshida-shi             2001
                                     Japan
Steel Dragon 2000       95 mph       Nagashima Spa Land
                                     Mie                         2000
                                     Japan
Millennium Force        93 mph       Cedar Point
                                     Sandusky, Ohio              2000
Intimidator 305         90 mph       Kings Dominion
...
```

The first row for each roller coaster has the name of the attraction, the speed, and the location in three different columns. The location however spans over two or three rows. Finally, the year is not in the first row as you would expect, but in the second one. How to read this file? Not with just a single *Text file input*, but by combining it with a couple of extra steps as you will learn in this recipe.

Getting ready

Create a file containing the preceding text or download the sample file from the book's site.

How to do it...

Carry out the following steps:

1. Create a transformation and use a **Text file input** step to read the file `rollercoasters.txt`. Under the **Content** tab, select **Fixed** as the **Filetype**.

2. Fill in the **Fields** tab. You can either click on **Get Fields** to use the wizard that let you configure the fixed-width columns, or you can type the fields' properties directly into the grid. Under **Trim type**, select **both** for all rows. Under **Repeat**, select **Y** for the first two fields: `Roller_Coaster` and `Speed`. Configure the `Year` field with **Format #**.

3. From the **Statistics** category, add a **Group by** step. In the grid **The fields that make up the group:** enter two rows with values `Roller_Coaster` and `Speed`. Fill the **Aggregates:** grid as shown in the following screenshot:

#. ▲	Name	Subject	Type	Value
1	Location	Location	Concatenate strings separated by	|
2	Year	Year	Concatenate strings separated by	

Note that the **Type** is **Concatenate string separated by** in both rows. The separators are | and space respectively. Do not confuse this type with **Concatenate string separated by** "," where the separator is a comma.

4. From the **Transform** category, add a **Split Fields** step. Double-click on it and configure it as follows: As **Field to split** type, select `Location`. For **Delimiter**, type |. Fill the **Fields** grid with three rows. Under **New field** type `park`, `location`, and `country`.

5. Close the window and do a preview on it. You will see the following:

Rows of step: Split location (21 rows)

	Roller_Coaster	Speed	park	location	country	Year
1	Kingda Ka	128 mph	Six Flags Great Adventure	Jackson, New Jersey		2005
2	Top Thrill Dragster	120 mph	Cedar Point	Sandusky, Ohio		2003
3	Dodonpa	106.8 mph	Fuji-Q Highland	FujiYoshida-shi	Japan	2001
4	Steel Dragon 2000	95 mph	Nagashima Spa Land	Mie	Japan	2000
5	Millennium Force	93 mph	Cedar Point	Sandusky, Ohio		2000
6	Intimidator 305	90 mph	Kings Dominion	Doswell, Virginia		2010
7	Goliath	85 mph	Six Flags Magic Mountain	Valencia, California		2000
8	Titan	85 mph	Six Flags Over Texas	Arlington, Texas		2001
9	Phantom's Revenge	85 mph	Kennywood	West Mifflin, Pennsylv…		2001

How it works...

If you have to read a file and some of the fields in your file span over several rows, you have to find a way to group all those fields together. The word group makes you think about the *Group by* step. First of all, in order to group rows, the rows should have some field or fields in common. In the sample file, you know that the rows following the one containing the name of the roller coaster belong to the same roller coaster, but Kettle does not. So, you selected **Y** under the **Repeat** field; this makes Kettle repeat the value of the `Roller_Coaster` and `Speed` fields in the rows, where the field is empty. If you do preview the data in the *Text file input step*, you see the following:

Rows of step: roller coasters (47 rows)

	Roller_Coaster	Speed	Location	Year
1	Kingda Ka	128 mph	Six Flags Great Adventure	
2	Kingda Ka	128 mph	Jackson, New Jersey	2005
3	Top Thrill Dragster	120 mph	Cedar Point	
4	Top Thrill Dragster	120 mph	Sandusky, Ohio	2003
5	Dodonpa	106.8 mph	Fuji-Q Highland	
6	Dodonpa	106.8 mph	FujiYoshida-shi	2001
7	Dodonpa	106.8 mph	Japan	
8	Steel Dragon 2000	95 mph	Nagashima Spa Land	
9	Steel Dragon 2000	95 mph	Mie	2000

This way, you are able to group all rows that share the same values for the `Roller_Coaster` and `Speed` fields. With the *Group by* step, you do that and concatenate the different values for the `Location` and `year` fields.

You know that the different rows for the `Location` field belong to the name of the park, where the attraction is located, the city or state, and the country. Therefore, the last thing you do is to split the location into three fields: `park`, `location`, and `country`.

See also

The section named *Reading files having one field by row* in this chapter. Read this if just one of the fields in your file spans several rows and the number of rows is known in advance.

Writing a simple file

In this recipe, you will learn the use of the *Text file output step* for writing text files.

Let's assume that you have a database with outdoor products and you want to export a catalog of products to a text file.

Getting ready

For this recipe, you will need a database with outdoor products with the structure explained in *Appendix, Data Structures*.

How to do it...

Carry out the following steps:

1. Create a new transformation.

2. Drop a **Table input** step into the canvas. Enter the following SQL statement:

   ```
   SELECT innerj.desc_product, categories.category, innerj.price FROM
   products innerj
   INNER JOIN categories
   ON innerj.id_category = categories.id_category
   ```

3. From the **Output** category, add a **Text file output** step.

4. In the **Filename** textbox under the **File** tab, type or browse to the name of the destination file.

5. In the **Extension** textbox, leave the default value txt.

6. Check the **Do not create file at start** checkbox. This checkbox prevents the creation of the file when there is no data to write to it.

 If you want to create the file anyway, uncheck the **Do not create file at start** checkbox and a file with at least 0 bytes will be created.

7. Under the **Content** tab, leave the default values.

[If you want to add lines to an existing file, select the **Append** checkbox.]

8. Under the **Fields** tab, fill in the grid as shown in the following screenshot:

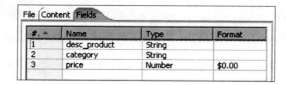

9. Running the transformation, a new text file will be created containing the list of products.

How it works...

The *Text file output* step allows you to generate files. In this recipe, you used it to generate a **Comma Separated Values (CSV)** file with data coming from a database.

Under the **File** tab, you entered the path and name of the file. Here you also have several options to include date or time in different formats as part of the name of the file. For this example, you didn't have to use those textboxes.

In the generated file you can see that the first column contains a line with the headers. Those headers are generated when the **Header** option from the **Content** tab is checked.

Under the **Fields** tab of this step, you must include the destination fields, including their types and formats. If you need it, you can include a field more than once.

[If you don't specify any field, the step will write all the fields from the previous step. This could be useful when you don't know the exact names of the fields or when these fields change dynamically.]

Under this same tab, the **Null** column specifies the string that will be written in case of a null value.

Finally, if you specify the **Length** of each column, a fixed width file will be created.

There's more...

Here are some considerations that make the process of writing files more flexible.

Changing headers

If you want to change the name of a header, you could insert a *Select values* step from the **Transform** category just before the *Text file output* step. Under the **Select & Alter** tab, select the fields you want to rename and give them a better description. For example, you could select the `desc_product` fieldname and rename the field as `Product`.

In order to send all the other fields toward the *Text file output* step, you also have to check the **Include unspecified fields, ordered by name** option.

Giving the output fields a format

When you write a file and tell Kettle which fields to write to that file, you have the option of specifying the format to apply to those fields. That is particularly useful when you have numeric or date fields.

In both cases, you may specify a format using a mask of patterns and symbols.

In the case of numeric fields, you can find more information about formats at the following URL:

```
http://java.sun.com/javase/6/docs/api/java/text/DecimalFormat.html
```

In the case of date fields, you will find a complete reference at the following URL:

```
http://java.sun.com/javase/6/docs/api/java/text/SimpleDateFormat.html
```

Writing an unstructured file

A standard file generated with Kettle is a file with several columns, which may vary according to how you configured the **Fields** tab of the *Output* step and one row for each row in your dataset, all with the same structure. If you want the file to have a header, the header is automatically created with the names of the fields. What if you want to generate a file somehow different from that?

Suppose that you have a file with a list of topics for a writing examination. When a student has to take the examination, you take that list of topics and generate a sheet like the following:

```
Student name: Mary Williams
-------------------------------------------------------------
Choose one of the following topics and write a paragraph about it
(write at least 300 words)
1. Should animals be used for medical research?
2. What do you think about the amount of violence on TV?
3. What does your country mean to you?
4. What would happen if there were no televisions?
5. What would you do if you found a magic wand?
```

Getting ready

Create a file with a list of topics or download the sample file from the book's site.

How to do it...

Carry out the following steps:

1. Create a transformation and read the file `writing_topics.txt`. Under the **Content** tab, uncheck the **Header** option, check the **Rownum in output?** option and as **Rownum fieldname**, type `topic_num`. Under the **Fields** tab, enter a single field named `text`.

2. From the **Scripting** category, drag a **User Defined Java Expression** (**UDJE** from now on). Use it to replace the `text` field with this: `topic_num +". " + text`.

3. With a **Select rows** step, select the `text` field and you have the list of topics. Now, you need to add the custom header.

4. With a **Get System Info** step, get the student name from the command line: Under **Name** type `text` and under **type** select **command line argument 1**.

5. Add a **UDJE** for replacing the `text` field with this: `"Student name: " + text`.

6. From the **Input** category, add a **Data Grid** step. Under the **Meta** tab, add a String field named `text`. Fill in the **Data** tab as shown in the following screenshot (including the empty fourth line):

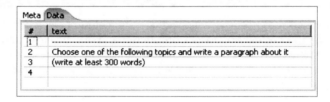

7. From the **Flow** category, add two **Append streams** steps and link them to the already created streams, as shown in the following diagram:

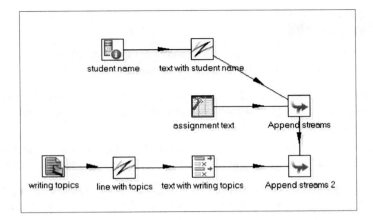

8. Double-click on the first **Append streams** step, as **Head hop**, select the name of the **UDJE** step, as **Tail hop**, select the name of the **Data Grid** step.

9. Double-click on the second **Append streams** step, as **Head hop**, select the name of the previous **Append streams** step, as **Tail hop** select the name of the **Select values** step.

10. After this last **Append streams** step, add a **Text file output** step, enter a path and name for the output file, and as fields, type the name of the only field that exists: the field named `text`.

11. Run the transformation. Don't forget to provide a student name as the first command line argument. See the generated file; it should look exactly as the one shown in the introduction.

How it works...

When you generate a file with any of the Kettle output steps, the rows have to be homogeneous, that is, all of them have to have the same format, the same number of columns, the same type of data, and so on. This recipe showed you one of the ways for creating a file with rows that differ in structure. In this case, you had a main stream with two columns: a number and a writing topic. However, you also had several lines that made up a header for those topics. What you did was to build separate streams; in each stream you concatenated the different fields that you wanted to send to the file, creating a single field named `text`. Then you joined the streams by using *Append streams* steps, and sent the final dataset to a file with a single column.

There's more...

The approach used in the recipe is useful for creating files with custom headers or footers. Now, suppose that you face any of the following scenarios:

- ► You have to generate a file with a custom header, but your main dataset has multiple columns and you want to take advantage of the formatting capabilities of the Kettle *Output* steps.

- ► You have more than one dataset, all with a different structure (different number or type of columns) and want to send all of them to the same file, one after each other.

In these situations, the problem can be addressed in a different way: create a different transformation for each stream (one for the header, one for each different dataset), and call them one after the other from a main job. Every transformation should append the rows to the same file (don't forget to check the **Append** option in the **Text file output** step). Creating this takes a little more time, but gives you much more flexibility.

Providing the name of a file (for reading or writing) dynamically

Sometimes, you don't have the complete name of the file that you intend to read or write in your transformation. That can be because the name of the file depends on a field or on external information. Suppose you receive a text file with information about new books to process. This file is sent to you on a daily basis and the date is part of its name (for example, `newBooks_20100927.txt`).

Getting ready

In order to follow this recipe, you must have a text file named `newBooks_20100927.txt` with sample book information such as the following:

```
"Title","Author","Price","Genre"
"The Da Vinci Code","Dan Brown","25.00","Fiction"
"Breaking Dawn","Stephenie Meyer","21.00","Children"
"Foundation","Isaac Asimov","38.50","Fiction"
"I, Robot","Isaac Asimov","39.99","Fiction"
```

How to do it...

Carry out the following steps:

1. Create a new transformation.

2. Drop a **Get System Info** step from the **Input** category into the canvas. Add a new field named today, and in the **Type** listbox, select System date (variable).

3. From the **Transform** category, add a **Selected values** step, in order to give the date the desired format. Click on the **Meta-data** tab and fill in the first row as follows:

   ❑ As **Fieldname**, type or select today

   ❑ As **Type** select **String**

   ❑ As **Format** type yyyyMMdd.

 In the recipe, the file is saved in the same directory as the transformation. In order to get this directory, you have to get it as a field in your dataset. That's the purpose of the next step.

4. Add the **Get Variables** step from the **Job** category. In the grid, add a new field named path. In the **Variable** column, press *Ctrl+Space* in order to show the list of possible variables, and select Internal.Transformation.Filename.Directory.

5. From the **Scripting** category, add a **User Defined Java Expression** (**UDJE**) step from now on.

6. In the step setting window, add a field named filename (type it in the **New field** column), and type path + "/newBooks_" + today +".txt" in the **Java Expression** column. Previewing this step, you will obtain the complete path for the file, for example, file:///C:/myDocuments/newBooks_20100927.txt.

 The recipe uses the UDJE for its simplicity and performance. However, you can obtain this calculated field in other ways, for example, using the **Calculator** step from the **Transform** category or the **Formula** step from the **Scripting** category.

7. Now that you have the filename, let's read the file. Add a **Text file input** step. Your transformation should look like the one shown in the following diagram (except possibly for the step names):

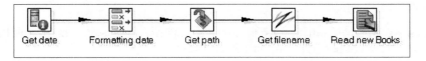

8. Double-click on the step. Under the **File** tab, go to the bottom section and check on the **Accept filenames from previous step** checkbox.

9. In the **Step to read filenames from** textbox, type or select the name of the **UDJE** step created earlier.

10. In the **Field in input to use as filename** textbox, type filename.

11. Select the **Content** tab. Type , in the **Separator**, and set the header to 1 line.

12. Under the **Fields** tab, add the following **Names** and **Types**: Title (String), Author (String), Price (Number), Genre (String).

> You can't use the **Get Fields** button in this case because the name of the file will be set dynamically. In order to obtain the headers automatically, you can fill the **File** tab with the name of a sample file. Then, clicking on the **Get Fields** button, the grid will be populated. Finally, you must remove the sample file from the **File** tab and set the **Accept filenames from previous step** section again.

13. Running the transformation, you will obtain a datasource with the text file information whose name was resolved dynamically.

How it works...

When you have to read a file and the filename is known only at the moment you run the transformation, you cannot set the filename explicitly in the grid located under the **File** tab of the *Input* step. However, there is a way to provide the name of the file.

First, you have to create a field with the name of the file including its complete path.

Once you have that field, the only thing to do is to configure the **Accept filenames from previous step** section of the *Input* step specifying the step from which that field comes and the name of the field.

In the recipe, you didn't know the complete name because part of the name was the system date, as for example, C:/myDocuments/newBooks_20100927.txt. In order to build a field with that name, you did the following:

▸ Getting the date of today (*Get System Info* step)

▸ Formatting this date as yyyyMMdd (*Selected values* step)

▸ Getting the path where the file were located (*Get Variables* step)

▸ Concatenating the path and the formatted date (*UDJE* step) generating the final field named filename

These steps are among the most used for these situations. However, the steps and the way of building the field will depend on your particular case.

In the recipe, you used a *Text File Input* step, but the same applies for other *Input* steps: *Excel Input*, *Property Input*, and so on.

It may happen that you want to read a file with a *CSV file input* step, but notice that it doesn't have the option of accepting the name of the file from a previous step. Don't worry! If you create a hop from any step toward this step, the textbox named **The filename field (data from previous steps)** will magically show up, allowing the name to be provided dynamically.

This method for providing the name of the file also applies when you write a file by using a *Text file output* step.

There's more...

What follows is a little background about the *Get System Info* step used in the recipe. After that, you will see how the *Accept file name from field?* feature can be used in the generation of files.

Get System Info

You can use the Get *System Info* step to retrieve information from the PDI environment. In the recipe, it was used to get the system date, but you can use it for bringing and adding to the dataset other environmental information, for example, the arguments from the command line, the transformation's name, and so on.

You can get further information about this step at the following URL:

```
http://wiki.pentaho.com/display/EAI/Get+System+Info
```

Generating several files simultaneously with the same structure, but different names

Let's assume that you want to write files with book information, but a different file for each genre. For example, a file named `fiction.txt` with all the fiction books, another file named `children.txt` with the children books, and so on. To do this, you must create the name of the file dynamically as shown in the recipe. In this case, supposing that your dataset has a field with the genre of the book, you could create a Java Expression that concatenates the path, the field that has the genre, and the string `.txt`. Then, in the **Text file output** step, you should check the checkbox named **Accept file name from field?** and in the **File name field** listbox, select the field just created.

Running this transformation will generate different text files with book's information; one file for each genre.

Using the name of a file (or part of it) as a field

There are some occasions where you need to include the name of a file as a column in your dataset for further processing. With Kettle, you can do it in a very simple way.

In this example, you have several text files about camping products. Each file belongs to a different category and you know the category from the filename. For example, `tents.txt` contains tent products. You want to obtain a single dataset with all the products from these files including a field indicating the category of every product.

Getting ready

In order to run this exercise, you need a directory (`campingProducts`) with text files named `kitchen.txt`, `lights.txt`, `sleeping_bags.txt`, `tents.txt`, and `tools.txt`. Each file contains descriptions of the products and their price separated with a |. For example:

```
Swedish Firesteel - Army Model|$19.97
Mountain House #10 Can Freeze-Dried Food|$53.50
Coleman 70-Quart Xtreme Cooler (Blue)|$59.99
Kelsyus Floating Cooler|$26.99
Lodge LCC3 Logic Pre-Seasoned Combo Cooker|$41.99
Guyot Designs SplashGuard-Universal|$7.96
```

How to do it...

Carry out the following steps:

1. Create a new transformation

2. Drop a **Text file input** step into the work area and use it to read the files: Under the **File** tab, type or browse to the `campingProducts` directory in the **File or directory** textbox, and use `.*\.txt` as **Regular Expression**. Click on the **Add** button.

3. Under the **Content** tab, type | as the **Separator** and complete the **Fields** tab as follows:

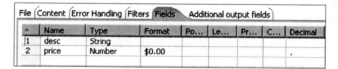

File	Content	Error Handling	Filters	**Fields**	Additional output fields			
.	**Name**	**Type**	**Format**	**Po...**	**Le...**	**Pr...**	**C...**	**Decimal**
1	desc	String						
2	price	Number	$0.00					.

4. Under the **Additional output fields** tab, type `filename` in the field **Short filename field**.

5. Previewing this step, you can see that there is a new field named `filename` with the name of the file (for example: `kitchen.txt`).

6. Now, you must split the filename text to get the category. Add a **Split Fields** from the **Transform** category, double-click on it and fill the setting windows, as shown in the following screenshot:

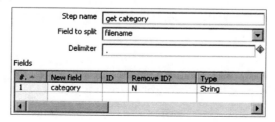

7. Previewing the last step of the transformation, you will see a dataset with the camping products, their price, and also a column named `category` with the proper product category.

How it works...

This recipe showed you the way to convert the names of the files into a new field named `category`. The source directory you entered in the *Text file* input step contains several files whose names are the categories of the products. Under the **Additional output fields** tab, you incorporated the **Short filename** as a field (for example `tents.txt`); you could also have included the extension, size, or full path among other fields.

The next step in the transformation, a **Split Fields** step uses a period (`.`) as the **Delimiter** value to use from the field only the first part, which is the category (`tents` in the example). It eliminates the second part, which is the extension of the filename (`txt`). If you don't want to discard the extension, you must add another field in the grid (for example, a field named `fileExtension`). Note that for this field, you set the type, but you can also specify a format, length, and so on.

Reading an Excel file

Kettle provides the *Excel input* step, in order to read data from Excel files. In this recipe, you will use this step to read an Excel file regarding museums in Italy. The file has a sheet with one column for the name of the museum and other for the city where it is located. The data starts in the C3 cell (as shown in the screenshot in the next section).

Getting ready

For this example, you need an Excel file named `museumsItaly.xls` with a `museums` sheet, as shown in the following screenshot:

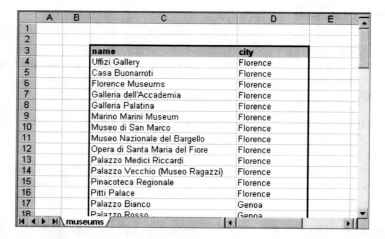

You can download a sample file from the book's site.

How to do it...

Carry out the following steps:

1. Create a new transformation.

2. Drop an **Excel input** step from the **Input** category.

3. Under the **Files** tab, browse to the `museumsItaly.xls` file and click on the **Add** button. This will cause the name of the file to be moved to the grid below.

4. Under the **Sheet** tab, fill in the first row as follows: type `museums` in the **Sheet name** column, 2 in the **Start row**, and 2 in the **Start column**.

> The rows and columns are numeric values (you cannot define the column with the identification letter you see in Excel). These values are zero-based (they start at the number 0).

5. Under the **Content** tab, leave the **Header** checked.

6. Under the **Fields** tab, click on the **Get fields from header row...** button to obtain the `name` and `city` fields.

7. Previewing the step, you will obtain a dataset with the museums data coming from the Excel sheet.

How it works...

The *Excel input* step allows you to read Excel files. Starting with Kettle 4.1.0, you can also use this step to read **OpenOffice** calc files.

This recipe showed you the way to read a simple Excel file, with a single sheet. However, the *Excel input* step allows you to read several Excel files at the same time. You do it just by adding more filename specifications to the grid located under the **File** tab. The step also allows you to read multiple sheets. You can click on the **Get Sheetname(s)** button to select from the list of sheets to read. If you don't specify any sheet in the grid, the step will read all of them.

 Take care when you leave the sheet name blank or when you select more than one sheet because if the sheets have different structures, you will get an error.

Except for the sheet information, configuring an *Excel input* step for reading an Excel file is quite the same as configuring a *Text file input* step. You should not have any troubles making it work.

See also

- The section named *Reading a simple file* in this chapter. As said, the configuration of an *Excel input* and a *Text file input* step are similar—you can learn more about how to configure the **Fields** tab in this recipe.

- The section named *Using the name of a file (or part of it) as a field* in this chapter. See this recipe for more information about the **Additional output fields** tab.

- The section named *Getting the value of specific cells in an Excel file* in this chapter. Refer to this recipe if you don't know exactly where your data is in a sheet.

Getting the value of specific cells in an Excel file

One of the good things about Excel files is that they give you freedom to write anywhere in the sheets, which sometimes is good if you want to prioritize the look and feel. However, that could cause you troubles when it's time to automatically process the data in those files. Suppose that you have an Excel file with values for a couple of variables you'd like to set, as shown in the following screenshot:

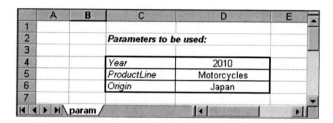

In this example, you want to set values for three variables: Year, ProductLine, and Origin. The problem is that you don't know where in the sheet that table is. It can be anywhere, near the upper left corner of the sheet. As you cannot ask Kettle to scan somewhere near the upper next corner, you will learn in this recipe how to get that data with a simple transformation.

Getting ready

Create an Excel file with the preceding table. Feel free to write the values anywhere within the first rows and columns, so long as the labels and values are in adjacent columns.

How to do it...

Carry out the following steps:

1. Create a transformation and drag an **Excel Input** step into the canvas.

2. Double-click on the step and type or browse to the path and name of the Excel file you just created.

3. Under the **Content** tab, uncheck the **Header** option, just in case one of the variables is in the very first row.

4. Select the **Field** tab, and add 10 rows. As **Name** type a, b, c, ..., j. As **Type**, select **String** for the 10 rows.

5. From the **Transform** category of steps, drag into the canvas a **Row Normalizer** and a **Row denormalizer** step.

6. From the **Statistics** category, drag an **Analytic Query**, and link all steps as shown in the following diagram:

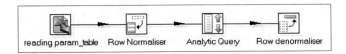

reading param_table   Row Normaliser   Analytic Query   Row denormaliser

7. Double-click on the **Row Normalizer**; click on **Get Fields** and the grid will be filled automatically with 10 rows. Fill the last column, **new field**, typing in all rows the value cell.

8. Double-click on the **Analytic Query** step. In the lower grid, add a row with the following values:

    ❑ Under **New field Name**, type value.

    ❑ Under **Subject** type or select cell.

    ❑ Under **Type**, select **LEAD "N" rows FORWARD and get Subject**.

    ❑ Under **N** type 1.

9. Double-click on the **Row denormalizer**. In the **Key** field, type or select cell. Fill the lower grid as follows:

▲	Target fieldname	Value fieldname	Key value	Type	Format
1	year	value	Year	String	#
2	productline	value	ProductLine	String	
3	origin	value	Origin	String	

10. Do a preview on the last step. You should see the following:

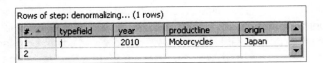

Rows of step: denormalizing... (1 rows)

#. ▲	typefield	year	productline	origin	
1	j	2010	Motorcycles	Japan	
2					

How it works...

The trick for getting data from an Excel sheet, if you don't know exactly where in the sheet the data is located, is to get rid of the leading rows and columns. Getting rid of rows is easy: just leave the **No empty rows** option on. The problem is getting rid of the columns.

In this recipe, you had an Excel file with some values: year, product line, and origin. You didn't know where exactly in the sheet the values were, but you had two clues: They were somewhere in the first cells and the values were next to the labels that identified them.

So, in order to find what you were looking for, you read the first 10 columns by using generic names a, b, c, and so on. By normalizing the cells, you put the cells row by row. This way, each value remained in the row just beneath its label. For example, if the cell with the value YEAR remained in the tenth row, the cell with value 2010 was in row 11.

You can confirm this by doing a preview on the *Row Normalizer* step.

For each row, the *Analytic Query* step went forward to get the value of the row below and brought it in as a new field in the current row. This way, the labels and the values were again next to each other, as shown in the following screenshot:

Rows of step: getting values ... (40 rows)			
# ▲	typefield	cell	value
11	a		
12	b		Year
13	c	Year	2010,0
14	d	2010,0	
15	e		
16	f		
17	g		
18	h		
19	i		
20	j		
21	a		
22	b		ProductLine
23	c	ProductLine	Motorcycles
24	d	Motorcycles	
25	e		
26	f		
27	g		
28	h		
29	i		
30	j		
31	a		
32	b		Origin
33	c	Origin	Japan
34	d	Japan	

Note that the result of combining these two steps was to remove the leading columns both to the right and to the left of our table. Now, you could just remove the useless rows by keeping only those with labels equal to Year, ProductLine, or Origin, or do what was done in the recipe: Denormalize the data to get just one row. This row is ready to be used for setting the variables Year, ProductLine, and Origin just by adding a **Set Variables** step at the end of the stream.

There's more...

As you don't know which columns will hold which kind of data, the advice is to read all as string. This way, you avoid unexpected errors. However, after getting the data, you can change the metadata accordingly by using a *Select values* step.

Also note that you only read the first 10 columns. If you cannot be sure that the values are going to be in this range of cells, feel free to increase that value.

The following are the two use cases related to the main example:

Labels and values horizontally arranged

What if, instead of having the labels and values as in the recipe, you have them horizontally arranged, as shown in the following screenshot:

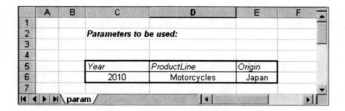

The recipe still works if you make a simple modification. Edit the *Analytic Query* step and change the 1 to 10. Just that. This is how it works: When you denormalize the rows, the labels and their values remain 10 rows apart from each other. So, instead of looking for the next row, the *Analytic Query* has to look 10 rows forward and get the values on those rows. You can see it in the following screenshot, which is the result of a preview on this step:

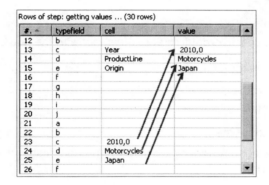

Looking for a given cell

If you just have to look for a specific cell, for example D5, the solution is quite different, but fortunately pretty straightforward. Firstly, you have to know the number of column and row where your data is. As Excel starts counting at zero, you conclude that the sample cell D5 is in the third column, fourth row. Then you take an *Excel input* step and enter the name of the Excel file to read. In the grid located under the **Sheets** tab, add a row. Under **Start row** and **Start column** type the number of row and column of interest, in this case, 4 and 3. Under the **Content** tab, uncheck the **Header** and the **No empty rows** options, checked by default, and in the **Limit** textbox, type 1. Under the **Fields** tab, add a single field to hold your value. You are done. Do a preview of the Excel and you will see the following:

Writing an Excel file with several sheets

Writing an Excel file with Kettle has a lot in common with writing a text file. Except for a couple of settings specific for Excel files, configuring an *Excel Output* step is quite similar to configuring a *Text file output* step. One of the differences is that when you write an Excel file, you add a sheet to the file. What if you want to write more than one sheet in the same file?

Suppose you have a datasource containing books and their authors and you want to create an Excel file with two sheets. In the first sheet, you want the authors and in the second, the books' titles. This recipe teaches you how to do this.

Getting ready

In order to run this recipe, you will need a database with books and authors with the structure described in *Appendix, Data Structures*.

How to do it...

Carry out the following steps, in order to create the sheet with the authors' details:

1. Create a new transformation.

2. Drop a **Table Input** step into the canvas, in order to read the author information:

   ```
   SELECT * FROM Authors order by lastname
   ```

3. Add an **Excel Output** step.

4. In the **Filename** textbox under the **File** tab, write the destination path and the name of the file (Books).

5. As the **Extension**, leave the default value xls.

6. Under the **Content** tab, make sure the **Header** checkbox is selected.

7. In the **Sheet name** textbox, type Authors.

8. Select the **Fields** tab and click on the **Get fields** button to fill the grid with the author data. The grid should look like the one shown in the following screenshot:

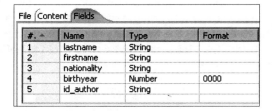

#. ▲	Name	Type	Format
1	lastname	String	
2	firstname	String	
3	nationality	String	
4	birthyear	Number	0000
5	id_author	String	

If you find that the default types or formats of the fields are not correct, you can fix them manually.

Carry out the following steps, in order to create the sheet with the book's details:

1. Create a new transformation.

2. Drop a **Table Input** step into the canvas, in order to read the book's titles information:

   ```
   SELECT * FROM Books order by title
   ```

3. Add an **Excel Output** step and set the same filename and extension configured in the previous transformation (`Books` and `xls`).

 Alternatively, you can use a new step named *Excel Writer*. You will find it in the Experimental category in Kettle 4.2 or later. This step allows writing Excel spreadsheets with more flexibility. One of its main features is the support for template files or sheets.

4. Under the **Content** tab, make sure the **Header** checkbox is selected.

5. In the **Sheet name** textbox type `Titles`.

6. Under the same tab, make sure to check the **Append** checkbox.

7. Select the **Fields** tab and press the **Get fields** button to fill the grid with book titles. The grid should look like the one shown in the following screenshot:

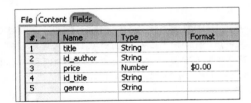

8. Create a job and drop a **Start** job entry into the canvas.

9. Then add two **Transformation** job entries and configure them for running the two transformations you created in the previous steps. The job should look like the following:

10. Run the job. It will generate an Excel file with two sheets, one for authors and the other for titles. It should look like the following screenshot:

	A	B	C	D	E
1	lastname	firstname	nationality	birthyear	id_author
2	Handler	Chelsea	American	1975	A00004
3	Hiaasen	Carl	American	1953	A00003
4	Ingraham	Laura	American	1964	A00005
5	King	Stephen	American	1947	A00002
6	Kiyosaki	Robert	American	1947	A00007
7	Larsson	Stieg	Swedish	1954	A00001
8	Ramsey	Dave	American	1960	A00006
9	Riordan	Rick	American	1964	A00009
10	Rowling	Joanne	English	1965	A00008

|◄ ◄ ► ►|\ **Authors** / Titles /

How it works...

The intuitive way to generate an Excel file with two sheets would be to create a single transformation with two *Excel Output* steps, one for each sheet. However, that approach does not work because Kettle cannot manage concurrent access to the same Excel file in a single transformation.

One way to avoid this issue is to create different transformations, one for each sheet, and then calling these transformations from a job. With this approach, the transformations are executed sequentially, which means that the sheets are generated one at a time, avoiding the concurrency problem.

There's more...

Another way to assure the sequential generation of the sheets would be using the *Block this step until steps finish* step from the *Flow* category. Using this step, the writing of the second sheet will wait for the first sheet to complete its writing process. For our recipe, the transformation should look like the following:

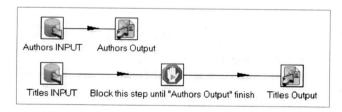

See also

The section named *Writing an Excel file with dynamic number of sheets* in this chapter. Read this recipe if you want to generate an Excel file with more than one sheet, but you do not know the name or number of sheets to generate beforehand.

Writing an Excel file with a dynamic number of sheets

When you generate an Excel file, you usually generate it with a single sheet. You can however generate a file with more sheets. With PDI, you can generate an Excel file with several sheets even if you don't know in advance how many sheets you will generate, or the name of those sheets.

In this recipe, you will create such an Excel file. Your file will have book title information separated in different sheets depending of the genre of the books.

Getting ready

You will need a database containing books and authors with the structure described in *Appendix, Data Structures*.

How to do it...

Carry out the following steps:

1. Create a new job.

2. From the **File Management** category, drop a **Delete file** job entry into the work area.

3. In the **File name** textbox, type the path and name of the Excel file you will create, in order to remove the file if it exists.

4. Then you have to add two *Transformation* entries: one for selecting the book's categories (`Transf_Categories`) and another to write the specific sheet for each category (`Trans_BookByCategory`). The job should look like the following:

5. Create the transformation named `Transf_Categories`.

6. In this transformation, drop a **Table input** step, in order to obtain the different book's categories. The SQL statement, should be similar to the following:

```
SELECT DISTINCT genre FROM Books ORDER BY genre
```

7. Add a **Copy rows to result** from the **Job** folder and create a hop from the **Excel output** step towards this one.

8. Create the second transformation called `Trans_BookByCategory`.

9. In the **Transformation settings** (*CTRL-T*), go to the **Parameters** tab, and add a new parameter named `GENRE` without default.

10. Drop a **Table input** step into the canvas. In the **SQL** frame, type the following statement, in order to select the books depending on the `GENRE` parameter:

```
SELECT * FROM Books WHERE genre='${GENRE}'
```

11. In this step, check the prompt **Replace variables in script?**

12. Add an **Excel output** step.

13. In the **Filename** textbox under the **File** tab, type the destination path and file. In the **Extension** textbox, leave the default value `xls`.

14. Under the **Content** tab, be sure to check **Append**.

15. Also here, in the **Sheet name** textbox, type `${GENRE}`.

16. Under the **Field** tab click on the **Get Fields** button.

17. Come back to the job; edit the job entry details for the transformation `Trans_BookByCategory`. Go to the **Advanced** tab and check **Copy previous result to parameters?** and **Execute for every input row?** checkboxes.

18. Under the **Parameters** tab, add a new value: type `GENRE` in the **Parameter** column, and `genre` for the **Stream column name**.

19. When you run the job, the Excel file created should have a different sheet for each category, for example:

	A	B	C	D	E
1	title	id_author	price	id_title	genre
2	Carrie	A00002	$41,00	123-346	Fiction
3	Salem's Lot	A00002	$33,00	123-347	Fiction
4	The Shining	A00002	$31,00	123-348	Fiction
5	The Dead Zone	A00002	$37,00	123-349	Fiction
6	Pet Sematary	A00002	$41,00	123-351	Fiction
7	The Tommyknockers	A00002	$39,00	123-352	Fiction
8	Bag of Bones	A00002	$40,90	123-353	Fiction
9	The Girl with the Dragon	A00001	$37,00	123-400	Fiction
10	The Girl who Played with	A00001	$35,90	123-401	Fiction
11	The Girl who Kicked the	A00001	$39,00	123-402	Fiction
12	Star Island	A00003	$36,00	123-505	Fiction
13	Basket Case	A00003	$31,00	123-506	Fiction

Business / Children \ **Fiction** / Non-fiction /

How it works...

When you have to execute the same task over and over again, the solution is to create a loop that executes a single transformation or job, as many times as needed. In this case, the goal was to create a new Excel sheet for each book category. So, the solution was:

- ▶ Creating a transformation (`Transf_Categories`) that builds the list of categories.
- ▶ Creating another transformation (`Trans_BookByCategory`) that appends a single sheet to the Excel file.
- ▶ Calling the second transformation once for each category in the list by copying the rows to result in the first transformation, and checking the **execute for every input row** checkbox in the Job entry belonging to the second transformation.

The main task was in the second transformation. In order to know which book categories to write each time, in that transformation you defined a parameter named GENRE. Then you used the GENRE parameter for filtering in the SQL statement and also for naming the Excel file sheet. The parameter is sent to the transformation because in the job, you set the **Copy previous result to parameters?** checkbox, and configured the **Parameters** tab properly.

 Note that in the **Excel Output** step, you checked the **Append** option, so that every time the transformation is executed, it creates a new sheet without loosing the sheets previously generated. Also note that you deleted the file at the beginning for cleaning purposes.

See also

- ▶ The section named *Writing an Excel file with several sheets* in this chapter. See this recipe for an example of generating an Excel file with a small fixed number of sheets.
- ▶ The section named *Executing a transformation once for every row in the dataset* in *Chapter 7, Executing and Reusing Jobs and Transformations*. See it in order to understand how loops work.

3
Manipulating XML Structures

In this chapter, we will cover:

- Reading simple XML files
- Specifying fields by using XPath notation
- Validating well-formed XML files
- Validating an XML file against DTD definitions
- Validating an XML file against an XSD schema
- Generating a simple XML document
- Generating complex XML structures
- Generating an HTML page using XML and XSL transformations

Introduction

XML is a markup language designed to describe data, the opposite of **HTML** which was designed only to display data. It is a self-descriptive language because its tags are not predefined. XML documents are not only used to store data, but also to exchange data between systems.

XML is recommended by **W3C**. You will find the details at the following URL:

```
http://www.w3.org/XML/
```

PDI has a rich set of steps and job entries for manipulating XML structures. The recipes in this chapter are meant to teach you how to read, write, and validate XML using those features.

Most of the recipes are based on a database with books and authors. To learn more about the structure of that database, see the *Appendix, Data Structures*, or the examples in *Chapter 1, Working with Databases*.

The recipes assume that you know the basics of XML, that is, you know what XML is, what an attribute is, and so on. If you don't, you should start by reading something about it before proceeding. The following tutorial is a good start:

`http://www.w3schools.com/xml/`

Reading simple XML files

PDI has a step named **Get XML Data** used to read XML structures. This recipe shows how to read an XML file containing the information about museums using this step.

Getting ready

In this exercise, you will use a file named `museum.xml` with the following structure:

```
<museums>
    <museum id_museum= '...'>
        <name>...</name>
        <city>...</city>
        <country>...</country>
    </museum>
</museums>
```

How to do it...

Carry out the following steps:

1. Create a new transformation.
2. Drop a **Get XML Data** step from the **Input** category into the canvas.
3. Under the **File** tab, you must select the XML document. Browse for the file `museums.xml` and click on the **Add** button.
4. Under the **Content** tab, type `/museums/museum` in the **Loop XPath** textbox. This will be the current node.

Alternatively, you can click on the **Get XPath nodes** and select it.

5. Under the **Fields** tab, you need to specify the fields by using XPath notation. Use the **Get Fields** button to get them automatically. You should get a result similar to the following:

# ▲	Name	XPath	Element	Type
1	name	name	Node	String
2	city	city	Node	String
3	country	country	Node	String
4	id_museum	@id_museum	Attribute	Integer

File / Content / Fields / Additional output fields

 In the case of XML attributes, if you include the @ character in the XPath as a prefix (for example, @id_museum), then it is not necessary to select **Attribute** under the **Element** column.

6. Doing a preview on this step, you will obtain the following results:

# ▲	name	city	country	id_museum
1	Fundacion Federico Klemm	Buenos Aires	Argentina	1
2	Fundacion Proa	Buenos Aires	Argentina	2
3	Museo de Arte Latinoamericano	Buenos Aires	Argentina	3
4	Museo Nacional de Bellas Artes	Buenos Aires	Argentina	4
5	Xul Solar Museum	Buenos Aires	Argentina	5
6	Museu de Arte Contemporanea de Niteroi	Niteroi	Brazil	6
7	Museu de Arte Contemporanea do Parana	Parana	Brazil	7
8	Museu de Arte Moderna	Rio de Janeiro	Brazil	8
9	Museu Nacional de Belas Artes	Rio de Janeiro	Brazil	9
10	Carlos Costa Pinto Museum	Salvador	Brazil	10
11	Itau Cultural	Sao Paulo	Brazil	11

How it works...

The **Get XML Data** step allows reading data in XML format by using XPath specification. In this recipe, you read a single file. However, as in any input step, you have the option to read a whole directory, multiple files, or even use a regular expression to specify which files to read. Alternatively, you can use this step to read XML structures from other sources, such as fields or URLs. For more details, see the section named *XML data in a field* later in this recipe.

In order to tell Kettle where to get the fields from, the first thing you have to do is to fill the **Loop XPath** textbox. You can do that by typing it or by clicking on the **Get XPath nodes** button and selecting it from the list of available nodes. For generating the dataset, Kettle will loop over the selected node.

 For each element that matches the selected node, Kettle will generate a new row.

The **XPath** and **Element** columns in the **Field** grid are the fields used to define the origin of the fields. The XPath should be relative to the current node. The **Element** column simply tells Kettle if the element is a node or an attribute. The rest of the columns in the grid should be filled just as you would in any input step: providing the type, format, and so on. If you are using this step for reading a file, then you have the option to fill this grid automatically, by clicking on the **Get fields** button.

There's more...

Most of the time, the XML file includes the encoding type. If none is specified, you have the option of selecting the encoding under the **Content** tab. For more on encoding, follow the link at `http://en.wikipedia.org/wiki/Character_encoding`.

If you have large XML files, then see the recommendations at `http://wiki.pentaho.com/display/EAI/Get+Data+from+XML+-+Handling+Large+Files`.

XML data in a field

In some situations, you don't have the XML as a file, but as a field in your dataset. An example of this is a transformation, where you call a web service that returns the result in XML format. In these situations, instead of specifying the name of the file, you must complete the section **XML source from field** under the **File** tab of the **Get data from XML** step. Checking the option **XML source is defined in a field?** will enable the drop-down list named **get XML source from a field**. From that list you have to select the field that contains the data in XML format.

The rest of the tabs should be filled exactly as when you read a file. The main difference is that the **Get fields** button will not be enabled. Consequently, you will have to fill the grid manually, or follow this tip:

> Copy the content of the field that contains the XML structure and save it in a file. Read that file by using the **Get data from XML** step, and use the **Get fields** button to fill the **Fields** grid automatically. Finally, change the settings under the **File** tab, in order to read the structure from the desired field.

XML file name in a field

It may happen that your XML structure is in a file, but you don't know its name in advance. If the name of the file is in a field, you still may read it by using the **Get data from XML** step. For reading the file, you must complete the section **XML source from field** under the **File** tab of the **Get data from XML** step. Check the two options: **XML source is defined in a field?**, **XML source is a filename?**. The **get XML source from a field** drop-down list will be filled with the names of the incoming fields. From that list, select the field that contains the name of the file. As in the previous case—XML data in a field—the **Get fields** button will be disabled. For advice on filling the **Fields** grid, read the preceding tip.

ECMAScript for XML

ECMAScript, more commonly known as **E4X**, is an extension to JavaScript whose main objective is to make it easier to work with XML.

This feature was included in *Pentaho Data Integration 3.1*. If you know E4X or if you are really confident with scripting, you can take advantage of it and use it to parse or to generate XML structures as a replacement for the XML-related steps.

You can learn more about E4X at the following URL:

```
http://en.wikipedia.org/wiki/E4X
```

You can find a tutorial at the following URL:

```
https://developer.mozilla.org/En/E4X/Processing_XML_with_E4X
```

See also

The recipe named *Specifying fields by using XPath notation*. See this recipe for understanding how to fill the fields grid.

Specifying fields by using XPath notation

If you intend to read or write XML structures, it's mandatory that you understand at least the basics of XPath, the language for finding information in an XML document, or defining parts of an XML document. In this recipe, you will be introduced to the XPath notation, so that you will find it easier to work with the rest of the recipes in the chapter.

Suppose you have an XML structure such as the following:

```
<w_cond>
  <data>
    <request>
      <type>City</type>
      <query>Buenos Aires, Argentina</query>
    </request>
    <current_condition>
      <observation_time>08:12 PM</observation_time>
      <temp scale="C">19</temp>
      <temp scale="F">66</temp>
      <weatherDesc>Sunny</weatherDesc>
      <windspeed unit="Miles">8</windspeed>
      <windspeed unit="Kmph">13</windspeed>
      <dirDegree>70</dirDegree>
      <dir16Point>ENE</dir16Point>
```

```
      . . .
    </current_condition>
    <weather>
      <date>2010-10-24</date>
      <tempMaxC>23</tempMaxC>
      . . .
    </weather>
    <weather>
      <date>2010-10-25</date>
      . . .
    </weather>
    . . .
  </data>
  <data>
    <request>
      <type>City</type>
      <query>Montevideo, Uruguay</query>
    </request>
    . . .
  </data>
  <data>
  . . .
  </data>
  . . .
</w_cond>
```

This structure contains the weather forecast for a group of cities. For each city, you have the current weather and the forecast for the next three days.

 The sample XML was obtained by using a free local weather API. To learn how to use that API, visit www.worldweatheronline.com. Note that the sample is a slightly modified version of the original result.

Now, you want to specify the XPath for the following data (highlighted in the sample structure):

- ▶ City
- ▶ Observation time
- ▶ Temperature (scale and degrees)
- ▶ Weather description

Getting ready

This recipe is theoretical and has the purpose of helping you when it's time to enter an XPath notation. You will not develop a transformation here. However, for a better understanding of what's being explained, you can do the following:

1. Download the sample XML file.
2. Read it by using the **Get data from XML** step.
3. Try introducing the different XPath notations in the **Fields** grid, as they are explained.
4. To check if you are entering the correct notations, do a preview and check it for yourself.

How to do it...

Carry out the following steps:

1. Pick the node that will be the base for specifying your fields. In the sample data, the node will be /w_cond/data.

    For each desired element, repeat steps 2 and 3:

2. Look at the XML structure to see if it is a node or an attribute. In the sample data, the temperature scale and the units for the windspeed are attributes. The rest of the fields are nodes.

3. Identify the absolute location of the element, that is, the complete path from the root element to the desired element. For example, for city the absolute location would be /w_cond/data/request/query. If the element is an attribute, prepend @ to the name.

4. Identify the location relative to the base node identified in step 1. For example, for the city the relative location would be request/query. If the element is an attribute, prepend @ to the name.

The following table shows the absolute and relative locations for the sample data:

data	absolute location	relative location
city	/w_cond/data/request/query	request/query
observation time	/w_cond/data/current_cond/ observation_time	current_cond/ observation_time
Temperature (degrees)	/w_cond/data/current_cond/temp	current_cond/temp
Temperature (scale)	/w_cond/data/current_cond/ temp/@scale	current_cond/temp/@scale
Weather description	/w_cond/data/current_cond/ weatherDesc	current_cond/weatherDesc

The preceding locations are the XPath notations for the selected data in the sample XML structure.

How it works...

XPath is a set of rules used for getting information from an XML document. XPath treats an XML structure as a tree of nodes. The tree can be compared to a directory tree in your system. The way you specify relative or absolute locations in that tree is much the same in both cases.

In Kettle you use XPath both for getting data from XML structures and for generating XML structures.

The reason for specifying both absolute and relative locations in the recipe is that in Kettle you need one or the other depending of what you are doing. For example when you read an XML structure you have to select a node, and define the fields as locations relative to that node. When you join two XML structures, the XPath statement that you need to specify is an absolute location.

There's more...

The XPath notations in the recipe are the simplest XPath notations you will find, but XPath allows you to write really complex expressions. The next sections provide you with more detail about specifying nodes with XPath notation. For more information on XPath, you can follow this link: `http://www.w3schools.com/XPath/` or see the **W3C** recommendation: `http://www.w3.org/TR/xpath`.

Getting data from a different path

When you read an XML structure, you don't specify absolute paths, but paths relative to a node selected as the current node. In the sample recipe, the current node was `/w_cond/data`. If the fields are inside that node, you get the relative location just by cutting the root part from the absolute location. For example, the absolute path for the weather description is `/w_cond/data/current_cond/weatherDesc`.

Then, for getting the location relative to the current node, just cut `/w_cond/data/` and you get `current_cond/weatherDesc`.

If the data you need is not in the tree below the selected node, you have to use the `..` notation, which is used to specify the parent of the current node. For example, suppose that the current node is `/w_cond/data/current_cond` and you want to know the name of the city to which this condition belongs. The `city` element is not inside the selected node. To reach it, you have to type `../request/city`.

Getting data selectively

If you are reading a structure where there might be more than one element with the same XPath notation, you have the option to select just the one that interests you. Look for example at the temperature elements in the sample structure:

```
<temp scale="C">19</temp>
<temp scale="F">66</temp>
```

These lines belong to the Celsius and the Fahrenheit scales respectively. Both lines share the same XPath notation. Suppose that you are interested in the Celsius line. To get that element, you have to use a **predicate**. A predicate is an expression used to find a specific node or a node that contains a specific value. In this case, you need a predicate to find a node that contains an attribute named `scale` with value `C`. The notation for getting that node is `temp[@ scale='C']`. In general, for getting a node that contains a specific value, the notation is `XPath[condition]`, that is, the XPath expression followed by the condition within brackets.

Now, let's make it a bit more complicated. Suppose that you don't even know which scale to return, because the scale is part of the XML structure, as shown in the following example:

```
<request>
    <type>City</type>
    <query>Buenos Aires, Argentina</query>
    <preferredScale>C</preferredScale>
</request>
```

Each city will have its own preferred scale and you should return the temperature in Celsius or Fahrenheit depending on the city's preferred scale.

What you need is a dynamic predicate. The way to implement this is through the use of a non standard extension named **Tokens**. Let's explain it based on our example:

1. The first thing you have to do is to add the field in which the token is based: `preferredScale`. So, add a field named `preferredScale` and for **XPath**, type:

    `../request/preferred_scale`.

2. Then, add a new field for the temperature in the desired scale. For **Name**, type `temperature` and as **XPath** type:

    `../temp[@scale =@_preferredScale-]/text()`

3. Finally, under the **Content** tab, check **Use tokens**. If you don't, this will not work!

Assuming that you defined the fields: `city`, `preferredScale`, `temperature_C`, and `temperature_F` for the temperature in Celsius and Fahrenheit degrees respectively, and `temperature`, if you do a preview you should see something like the following:

	city	preferredScale	temperature_C	temperature_F	temperature
1	Buenos aires, Argentina	C	19	66	19
2	Montevideo, Uruguay	C	16	61	16
3	Santiago, Chile	C	25	77	25
4	Brasilia, Brazil	C	23	73	23
5	Rio de janeiro, Brazil	C	25	77	25
6	New York, United States of America	F	19	67	67
7	Washington, United States of America	F	22	71	71
8	Barcelona, Spain	C	18	64	18

In general, the expression for a token is `@_<tokenized_field>-`, where `<tokenized_field>` is the field in which the token is based and has to be previously defined.

PDI will build a dynamic predicate by replacing each `<tokenized_field>` by its current value and then returning the proper node value.

Getting more than one node when the nodes share their XPath notation

Look at the `weather` nodes in the sample XML structure:

```
<weather>
  <date>2010-10-24</date>
  <tempMaxC>23</tempMaxC>
  . . .
</weather>
<weather>
  <date>2010-10-25</date>
  <tempMaxC>23</tempMaxC>
  . . .
</weather>
<weather>
  <date>2010-10-26</date>
  <tempMaxC>24</tempMaxC>
```

For each node `/w_cond/data` (the current node in the example), there are three different `weather` nodes.

Suppose that you want to read all of them. In this case, you have to use a predicate just as explained in the previous section. In this case the predicate is not used to find a node that contains a specific value, but to find the nodes by position: You need the first, second, and third `weather` nodes. The notation that you have to use is `XPath[position]`, that is, the XPath expression followed by the position of the desired element within brackets.

In the example, the notation for the first, second, and third `weather` nodes would be `weather[1]`, `weather[2]`, and `weather[3]` respectively. For getting nodes inside those, the notation is as usual. For example, for getting the date of the second node, you should write `weather[2]/date`.

Note that if you are reading an XML structure, each element that you get by using this notation may be used as a new column in the dataset. If, instead of that you want to generate a different row for each `weather` node, then you should take another approach: Instead of using this notation, simply change the current node (**Loop XPath** element) from `/w_cond/data` to `/w_cond/data/weather`.

Saving time when specifying XPath

In most of the Kettle steps where you have to provide an XPath, you must type it manually. That's why you need to understand this notation. However, when you read an XML structure by using the **Get Data from XML** step, you have the option to use the **Get Fields** button to get the nodes and attributes automatically. Note that Kettle will get only the trivial elements, that is:

- It will get only the fields that are below the node you typed as **Loop XPath**.
- It will bring all the elements. For getting elements selectively, as in the temperature example above, you'll have to modify the grid manually.
- If there is more than one element with the same XPath notation, as in the weather example above, it will bring only the first element.

To summarize, if you fill the grid with the **Get Fields** button, you will save time but on most occasions, you will still have to adjust the data in the grid manually.

Validating well-formed XML files

PDI offers different options for validating XML documents, including the validation of a well-formed document. The structure of an XML document is formed by tags that begin with the character < and end with the character >. In an XML document, you can find start-tags: `<exampletag>`, end-tags: `</exampletag>`, or empty-element tags: `<exampletag/>`, and these tags can be nested. An XML document is called **well-formed** when it follows the following set of rules:

- They must contain at least one element
- They must contain a unique root element – this means a single opening and closing tag for the whole document
- The tags are case sensitive
- All of the tags must be nested properly, without overlapping

In this recipe, you will learn to validate whether a document is well-formed, which is the simplest kind of XML validation. Assume that you want to extract data from several XML documents with museums information, but only want to process those files that are well-formed.

Getting ready

To use this recipe, you need a set of XML files in a directory named museums. This recipe reads a directory containing three files, where the first one has an intentional tag mistake. You can download sample files from the book's site.

How to do it...

Carry out the following steps:

1. Create a new job and add a **Start** entry.
2. Drop a **Check if XML is well formed** entry from the **XML** category into the canvas.
3. Under the **General** tab, you must type the path to the museum directory in the **File/Folder source** textbox, and type `.+\.xml` in the **wildcard** textbox, in order to use only the files with the .xml extension.
4. Click on the **Add** button to populate the **File/Folder** grid.
5. Under the **Advanced** tab, choose the following configuration:

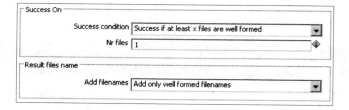

6. Then, create a new transformation in order to process the well-formed XML files obtained from the previous job entry. Add this transformation as the last step in the job.
7. In the transformation, drop a **GET files from result** step from the **Job** category.
8. Add the **GET data from XML** step.
9. Under the **File** tab, set the following:

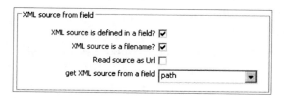

10. Under the **Content** tab, type `/museums/museum` in the **Loop XPath** textbox.

11. Finally, the grid under the **Fields** tab must be completed manually, as shown in the following screenshot:

# ▲	Name	XPath	Element	Type
1	name	name	Node	String
2	city	city	Node	String
3	country	country	Node	String
4	id_museum	@id_museum	Attribute	Integer

File | Content | Fields | Additional output fields

12. When you run the job, you will obtain a museums dataset with data coming only from the well-formed XML files. You can take a look at the **Logging** window to verify this. You will see something like the following:

```
2010/11/01 11:56:43 - Check if XML file is well formed - ERROR
(version 4.1.0, build 13820 from 2010-08-25 07.22.27 by tomcat) :
Error while checking file [file:///C:/museums1.xml].
Exception :
2010/11/01 11:56:43 - Check if XML file is well formed - ERROR
(version 4.1.0, build 13820 from 2010-08-25 07.22.27 by tomcat) :
org.xml.sax.SAXParseException:
Element type "museum" must be followed by either attribute
specifications, ">" or "/>".
```

13. Further, you can see in the **Logging** window that only two files out of three were read:

```
2010/11/01 11:56:43 - Get XMLs well-formed.0 - Finished processing
(I=0, O=0, R=2, W=2, U=0, E=0)
```

How it works...

You can use the _Check if XML is well-formed_ job entry to check if one or more XML files are well-formed.

In the recipe, the job validates the XML files from the source directory and creates a list with only the valid XML files.

As you saw in the logging window, only two files were added to the list and used later in the transformation. The first file (`C:/museums1.xml`) had an error; it was not well-formed and because of that it was not added to the list of files.

The _Get files from result_ step in the transformation get the list of well-formed XML documents created in the job. Then, a _Get data from XML_ step read the files for further processing. Note that in this case, you didn't set the names of the files explicitly, but used the field `path` coming from the previous step.

See also

▸ The recipe named *Specifying fields by using XPath notation* in this chapter. See this recipe to understand how to fill the **Fields** grid.

▸ The recipe named *Validating an XML file against DTD definitions* in this chapter. If you want more intelligence in the XML validation process, see this recipe. Also, *Validating an XML file against an XSD schema*. The same as above, but with a different method for validation.

Validating an XML file against DTD definitions

A **Document Type Definition** (**DTD**) defines the document structure of an XML document with a list of elements and attributes. Kettle provides the *DTD Validator* entry job to do a validation against a DTD definition file.

For example, suppose you have an XML file with museums information, as follows:

```
<museums>
   <museum>
       <name>Fundacion Federico Klemm</name>
       <city>Buenos Aires</city>
       <country>Argentina</country>
   </museum>
    <museum id_museum= '2'>
        <name>Fundacion Proa</name>
        <city>Buenos Aires</city>
        <country>Argentina</country>
   </museum>
   <museum id_museum= '9'>
        <name>Museu Nacional de Belas Artes</name>
         <country>Brazil</country>
   </museum>
   <museum id_museum= '19'>
      <name>Biblioteca Luis Angel Arango</name>
        <city>Bogota</city>
        <country>Colombia</country>
   </museum>
</museums>
```

You want to validate it against the following DTD definition file:

```
<!DOCTYPE museums [
<!ELEMENT museums (museum+)>
```

```
<!ELEMENT museum (name+, city, country)>
<!ELEMENT name (#PCDATA)>
<!ELEMENT city (#PCDATA)>
<!ELEMENT country (#PCDATA)>
<!ATTLIST museum id_museum CDATA #REQUIRED >
 ]>
```

With this definition, you are declaring the museum structure elements: name, city, and country, and defining the attribute id_museum as required.

Getting ready

For this recipe, you need a museum.xml document with DTD definition included. You can download it from the book's website.

 You can have the DTD definition as an independent file or inside the XML document. If the DTD is declared inside the XML file, it should be wrapped in a DOCTYPE definition with the following syntax:
<!DOCTYPE root-element [element-declarations]>

How to do it...

Carry out the following steps:

1. Create a new job and add a **Start** entry.

2. Drop a **DTD Validator** job entry from the **XML** category into the canvas.

3. Here, you must point to your XML file in the **XML File name** textbox.

4. Check the **DTD Intern** checkbox.

5. Run this job, so that the XML data gets validated against the DTD definitions, which are inside the XML file.

6. You can see the result of the validation including information about the errors under the **Logging** tab in the **Execution results** window. In this case, the results are as follows:

    □ For the first element, the job will detect this error: Attribute "id_museum" is required and must be specified for element type "museum".

    □ The second and fourth museum elements are correct.

    □ For the third element, you will receive the following message: The content of element type "museum" must match "(name+,city,country)".

How it works...

The *DTD Validator* job entry does the entire task of validating an XML file against a DTD definition. In the recipe, you checked the **DTD Intern** checkbox because the DTD definitions were inside the XML file. Otherwise, you must fill the DTD **File name** textbox with the name of the proper DTD file.

There's more...

DTD has a lot of limitations. For example, you cannot define types for the XML elements or attributes. If you need more flexibility, the recommendation is to use the *XSD validation* feature.

You can learn more about DTD definitions here: `http://www.w3schools.com/dtd/default.asp`.

See also

▶ The recipe named *Validating an XML file against an XSD schema* in this chapter. In this recipe, you can see an XSD validation example.

▶ The recipe named *Validating well-formed XML files* in this chapter. This recipe is for you if you only want to validate whether your XML is well-formed or not.

Validating an XML file against an XSD schema

In this recipe, you will learn how to use the *XSD Validator* step, in order to verify a particular XML structure using an **XSD (XML Schema Definition)**. For the example, you will use a database of books (with the structure shown in the *Appendix, Data Structures*) and an XSD schema file with the books structure. You want to validate each book element against the XSD schema file.

The XSD file is named `books.xsd` and it looks like following:

```
<xs:schema xmlns:xs="http://www.w3.org/2001/XMLSchema">
  <xs:simpleType name="idTitle">
    <xs:restriction base="xs:string">
      <xs:pattern value="\d{3}\-\d{3}"/>
    </xs:restriction>
  </xs:simpleType>
  <xs:simpleType name="positiveDecimal">
    <xs:restriction base="xs:decimal">
      <xs:minInclusive value="0.0" />
    </xs:restriction>
  </xs:simpleType>
```

```
    <xs:element name="book">
      <xs:complexType>
        <xs:sequence>
          <xs:element name="title" type="xs:string"/>
          <xs:element name="genre" type="xs:string"/>
          <xs:element name="price" type="positiveDecimal"/>
          <xs:element name="author" type="xs:string"/>
        </xs:sequence>
        <xs:attribute name="id_title" type="idTitle" />
      </xs:complexType>
    </xs:element>
  </xs:schema>
```

This schema file verifies the following features:

▶ Inside a sequence, there are three elements of string type: `title`, `genre`, and `author`.

▶ There is an element named `price` of a `simpleType` named `positiveDecimal`, declared earlier as a decimal type with `0.0` as its minimum value.

▶ There is a `simpleType` named `idTitle` for the `id_Title` attribute. This type is declared as a string with a pattern expression. In this case, you will use `\d{3}\-\d{3}` that means three decimal followed by a hyphen and then three more decimals, for example: `123-456`.

Getting ready

You need a database with books' and authors' information. You will also need the XSD schema as a separate file. You can download the file from the book's site.

How to do it...

Carry out the following steps:

1. Create a new transformation.

2. Drop a **Table Input** step and make a selection from the `Books` database with the following statement:

```
SELECT id_title
     , title
     , genre
     , price
     , concat(lastname,", ",firstname) author
FROM Books
LEFT JOIN Authors
ON Authors.id_author=Books.id_author
```

3. Use the **Add XML** step from the **Transform** category, in order to create a new column with the data for each book in XML format.

4. Under the **Content** tab, type xmlBook in **Output Value** and book as the **Root XML element**.

5. Under the **Fields** tab, use the **Get Fields** button to populate the grid automatically. Then, modify the **Format** and **Decimal** for the price column, as shown in the following screenshot:

Content	Fields										
	Fieldname	E...	Type	Format	P..	C...	Decimal	G...	N...	Attribute
1	title		String							N
2	genre		String							N
3	price		Number	0.00			.			N
4	author		String							N
5	id_title		String							Y

6. If you do a preview on this step, then you will see a new column with an XML structure for each book. The following is a sample XML structure created with this step:

```
<book id_title="423-006">
<title>Harry Potter and the Order of the Phoenix</title>
<genre>Childrens</genre>
<price>32.00</price>
<author>Rowling, Joanne</author>
</book>
```

 Note that the structure is shown in several lines for clarity. In the preview, you will see the structure in a single line.

7. Add an **XSD Validator** step from the **Validation** category.

8. In the **XML field** located under the **Settings** tab, select the column xmlBook that you created in the previous step.

9. Under the same tab, complete the **Output Fields** frame, as shown in the following screenshot:

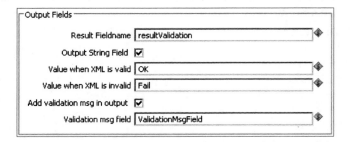

10. In the **XSD Source** listbox inside the **XML Schema Definition** frame, select the option **is a file, let me specify filename**.

11. Then, in **XSD Filename** textbox, type or select the `books.xsd` file.

12. When you run this transformation, you will obtain the dataset with books along with a field indicating the result of the validation and the validation message in case of failure. Assuming that you have some errors in the source data, your final dataset will look similar to the one shown in the following screenshot:

id_title	title	genre	price	result...	ValidationMsgField
123-351	Pet Sematary	Fiction	41	OK	
123-352	The Tommyknockers	Fiction	39	OK	
123-353	Bag of Bones	Fiction	40,9	OK	
123-400	The Girl with the D...	Fiction	-5	Fail	cvc-minInclusive-valid: Value '-5.00' is nc
123-401	The Girl who Playe...	Fiction	35,9	OK	
123-402	The Girl who Kicke...	Fiction	39	OK	
123505	Star Island	Fiction	36	Fail	cvc-pattern-valid: Value '123505' is not f
123-506	Basket Case	Fiction	31	OK	
223-200	Chelsea Chelsea B...	Non-fi...	25	OK	
223-201	My Horizontal Life	Non-fi...	24	OK	
223-202	Are You There, Vo...	Non-fi...	19,9	OK	

How it works...

An **XML Schema Definition** (**XSD**) file defines a set of rules for validating an XML document. An XSD file allows you to verify whether a document, written in XML format, is well-formed and also respects those rules.

In this example, you created a new column with each book in XML format, and then applied the *XSD Validator* step to verify this column against the `books.xsd` schema file.

In the result of your transformation, you could see that one book didn't follow the pattern expected for the `id_title` field, because it didn't contain a hyphen. In that case, you obtained the following message: `cvc-pattern-valid: Value '123505' is not facet-valid with respect to pattern '\d{3}\-\d{3}' for type 'idTitle'`.

Also, one book had an incorrect price (a negative one). In that case, you got the following error: `cvc-minInclusive-valid: Value '-5.00' is not facet-valid with respect to minInclusive '0.0' for type 'positiveDecimal'`.

There's more...

In the recipe, you used the *XSD Validation* step to validate an XML structure, which in turn was made from a field in a database. In general, you can use this step to validate any XML structure, both supplied as a field or saved in a file.

In cases where you want to validate a file, you can also take advantage of the same functionality from a job entry named **XSD Validation** inside the **XML** category. The configuration of that entry is simple - it's just setting the paths to the XML file and the XSD schema file.

You can learn more about XSD from the following URL:

```
http://www.w3.org/TR/xmlschema-0/
```

See also

- ▸ The recipe named *Validating well-formed XML files*. This recipe shows you the simplest method of XML validation.

- ▸ The recipe named *Validating an XML file against DTD definitions*. Yet another validation method.

Generating a simple XML document

In order to create a new XML document you can use the *XML Output* step. In this recipe, you will create a new XML file from a database containing books information.

Getting ready

You will need a books' database with the structure described in the *Appendix, Data Structures*.

How to do it...

Carry out the following steps:

1. Create a new transformation.

2. Drop a **Table Input** step, in order to obtain the books' information and type the following query:

```
SELECT id_title
     , title
     , genre
     , price
     , concat(lastname,",  ",firstname) author
FROM Books
LEFT JOIN Authors
ON Authors.id_author=Books.id_author
```

3. Add an **XML Output** step.

4. In the **Filename** textbox of the **File** tab, type the destination filename, including its complete path (without extension). In the **Extension** textbox, leave the default value, `xml`.

5. Fill the **Content** tab: As **Parent XML element**, type `Books` and as **Row XML element**, type `Book`.

6. Under the **Fields** tab, use the **Get Fields** button to get the fields. In the `price` field, set the **Format** to `$0.00`.

7. Run the transformation and look at the generated XML file. It should look like the following:

```
<Books>
    <Book>
        <id_title>123-346</id_title>
        <title>Carrie </title>
        <genre>Fiction</genre>
        <price>$41,00</price>
        <author>King, Stephen</author>
    </Book>
    <Book>
        <id_title>123-347</id_title>
        <title>Salem›s Lot </title>
        ...
    </Book>
    ...
</Books>
```

How it works...

The *XML output* step does the entire task. It creates the XML file with rows coming in the stream, using the **Parent XML element** and **Row XML element** values to complete the structure of the XML file. It encloses each row between tags with the name you provided for **Row XML element** (`<Book>` and `</Book>`) and the whole structure between tags with the name provided for **Parent XML element** (`<Books>` and `</Books>`).

The *XML output* step has some properties in common with other output steps. For example, the option to add the date and time as part of the name of the file or to split the output in several files using the **Split every ... rows** textbox from the **Content** tab.

There's more...

In the recipe, you wrote the XML information into a file, but you may want to have the information in XML format as a new column of your dataset. The following section explains how to do this.

Generating fields with XML structures

If, rather than generating the XML structure in a file, you want the structure as a new field, then you should use the **Add XML** step from the **Transform** category instead of using the **XML output** step.

The *Add XML* step encodes several fields into an XML fragment. In this step, you must set the **Root XML element** (for example Book) and the name for the new column. The **Fields** tab is quite similar to the same one in the **XML output** step, but here you can also specify if the element is a node or an attribute. In the example, you can set the field id_title as an attribute of the element Book: Set **Attribute** as Y and **Attribute parent name** as Book, and you will have the following XML structure:

```
<book id_title ="123-346">
    <title>Carrie </title>
    <genre>Fiction</genre>
    <price>41.00</price>
    <author>King, Stephen</author>
</book>
```

This step is particularly useful for generating complex structures, as you will see in the next recipe.

See also

The recipe named *Generating complex XML structures* in this chapter. This recipe explains how to generate more elaborate XML structures.

Generating complex XML structures

In previous recipes, you learned how to read and write simple XML structures. With Kettle, you can also generate more complex structures with different levels of information, which is more likely to be similar to the structures you find in real case scenarios.

Suppose you need to create a complex XML structure with a hierarchy of two levels: the authors in the first level and their books as their children. In this case, you can't use the *XML output* job entry, because it only works with simple structures. For theses cases, you must learn to use the *XML Join* step.

The objective for the recipe is to get the following XML structure:

```
<result>
  <authors>
      <author id_author =...>
          <lastname>...</lastname>
          <firstname>...</firstname>
          <nationality>...</nationality>
          <birthyear>...</birthyear>
          <books>
              <book id_title =...>
                  <title>...</title>
```

```
        <price>...</price>
        <genre>...</genre>
    </book>
  </books>
</author>
<author id_author =...>
...
</author>
...
</authors>
</result>
```

Getting ready

In this recipe, you will use a database of books with the structure shown in the *Appendix, Data Structures*.

How to do it...

You will do this recipe in the following three different steps:

1. First of all, you will create an empty XML root structure.
2. Then you will add the authors' information.
3. Finally, you will inject the books inside the authors tag.

The following steps explain how to create the XML root structure:

1. Create a new transformation.
2. Drop a **Generate Rows** step into the canvas, in order to create the authors tag.
3. In the **Fields** grid, type the **Name** authors and select **String** in the **Type** column.
4. For creating the root XML structure, add an **Add XML** step from the **Transform** category. Name this step Create XML root structure.
5. Under the **Content** tab of this step, type xmlResult in the **Output Value** textbox, and result in the **Root XML element** textbox.
6. Under the **Fields** tab, add the only field that you have: authors. Don't forget to set the type as **String**. If you do a preview on this step, you will see a new field named xmlResult with the following information:

   ```
   <result><authors/></result>
   ```

Now, the following steps explain how to create the authors piece of XML:

1. Drop a **Table Input** step into the canvas, and select the Authors table using the following SQL statement:

    ```
    SELECT *
    FROM authors
    ```

2. Use the **Add constants** step from the **Transform** folder and create the entry `books` (`String` type). This literal will be replaced later with the books' authors.

3. Add another **Add XML** step. Name this step as `Create Authors XML`.

4. Under the **Content** tab, type `author` for **Root XML element** and `xmlAuthors` for the **Output Value**.

5. Click on the **Get Fields** button to add to the grid all the fields (including the empty `books` field). For the `id_author` field, select **attribute** = `Y`. Doing a preview on this step, for each author you will see something like the following:

    ```
    <author id_author="A00001">
        <lastname>Larsson</lastname>
        <firstname>Stieg</firstname>
        <nationality>Swedish</nationality>
        <birthyear> 000000000001954</birthyear>
        <books/>
    </author>
    ```

 In the preview, you will see the XML structure in a single line. In the examples, the structures are shown over several lines and indented just for better understanding.

Now, you need to insert the authors' data inside the XML root structure created previously. The next steps explain how to merge both streams:

1. Add an **XML Join** step from the **Join** category and use it to link the streams, as shown in the following diagram:

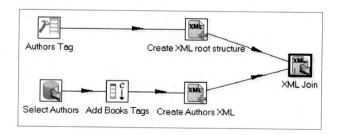

2. Name this step as `Merge Authors and root XML`.

3. Double-click on the step and fill the **Target stream properties**, **Source stream properties**, and **Join condition properties** frames, as shown in the following screenshot:

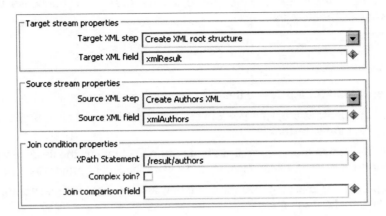

4. In the **Result XML field** inside the **Result Stream properties** frame, type `xmlauthors2`.

5. Do a preview of this step. You will see that there is a new field named `xmlauthors2` containing the XML structure for the root XML and the authors. Also note that there is an empty tag named `books` for each author's node:

```
<result>
   <authors>
      <author id_author ="A00001">
         <lastname>Larsson</lastname>
         <firstname>Stieg</firstname>
         <nationality>Swedish</nationality>
         <birthyear>1954</birthyear>
         <books/>
      </author>
      <author id_author ="A00002">
         <lastname>King</lastname>
         <firstname>Stephen</firstname>
         <nationality>American</nationality>
         ...
      </author>
   ...
   </authors>
</result>
```

Finally, it's time to create the XML structure for the books and merge them with the main structure:

1. Drop a **Table input** step into the canvas, in order to select all the books. Use the following SQL statement:

```
SELECT *
FROM Books
ORDER BY title
```

2. Add an **Add XML** step. Name this step as `Create Books XML`.

3. Under the **Content** tab, type `book` in the **XML root element** textbox and `xmlBooks` in the **Output Value** textbox.

4. Under the **Fields** tab, use the **Get Field** button to obtain all the fields. Select **attribute** = `Y` for the `id_title` field. Also, for the `price` field, set **Format** to `$0.00`.

5. Do a preview on this step. You will see a new XML field named `xmlBooks` with the book's data. For example:

```
<book id_title ="123-346">
    <title>Carrie </title>
    <price>$41,00</price>
    <genre>Fiction</genre>
</book>
```

6. Finally, you must do the last merge, this time between the output of the `Merge Authors and root XML` step and the output of the recently created `Create Books XML` step. Add one more **XML Join** step and link these two steps. The transformation must look like the following:

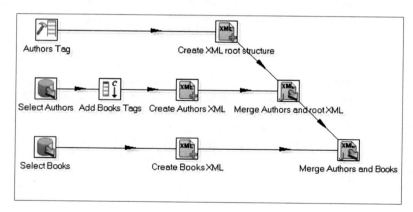

7. In this last step, set the following properties:

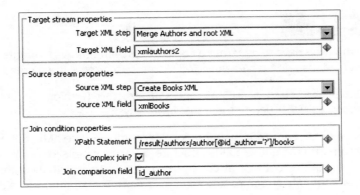

8. In the **Result XML field** inside the **Result Stream properties frame**, type `xmlfinalresult`. This field will contain the final result.

9. You can do a preview on this last step and you will obtain something like the following:

```
<result>
   <authors>
...
        <author id_author ="A00002">
            <lastname>King</lastname>
            <firstname>Stephen</firstname>
            <nationality>American</nationality>
            <birthyear>1947</birthyear>
            <books>
                <book id_title ="123-353">
                    <title>Bag of Bones</title>
                    <price>$40,90</price>
                    <genre>Fiction</genre>
                </book>
                <book id_title=" 123-346">
                    <title>Carrie</title>
                    ...
                </book>
                ...
            </books>
        </author>
        <author id_author=" A00007">
            <lastname>Kiyosaki</lastname>
            ...
        </author>
    </authors>
</result>
```

How it works...

The basic idea when you have to generate a complex XML structure is to create partial XML outputs in different steps and then use the *XML Join* step to create the merged structure.

The *XML Join* step allows you to incorporate one XML structure (with one or multiple rows) inside another leading XML structure that must have only one row.

In the first join step of the sample transformation, you combined the XML that contains the empty root structure with the authors XML structure. This is a simple join - the step replaces the tag `<authors/>` of the root XML structure (the target stream) with all of the authors coming from the author XML structure (the source stream). The XPath expression, `/result/authors` tells Kettle which node in the root structure is to be filled with the authors' structure.

The second *XML Join* step is a little more complex. It combines the result from the first *XML Join* step and the selection of books. In this case, you have a complex join because you need to join each group of books with their corresponding author. To do this, you must type the condition of the join with the following XPath expression:

```
/result/authors/author[@id_author='?']/books
```

The `?` character is used as a placeholder. During execution, this character will be replaced with the **Join Comparison Field** value (in this case, the `id_author` field value). So, all books in XML format with a particular `id_author` will replace the tag `<books/>` inside the tag `<author>` who have the same `id_author`. For example, the following book by Stieg Larsson (already converted to the XML format):

```
<book id_title="123-401">
<title>The Girl who Played with Fire</title>
<price>$35,90</price>
<genre>Fiction</genre>
</book>
```

is in a row where `id_author` is equal to "A00001". Therefore, this structure will be inserted in the main XML structure in the following path:

```
/result/authors/author[@id_author='A00001']/books
```

This is the path belonging to that author.

See also

- ▸ The recipe named *Generating a simple XML document* in this chapter. For understanding how the *Add XML* step works, see the section named *Generating fields with XML structures* inside this recipe.

- ▸ The recipe named *Specifying fields by using XPath notation* in this chapter. See this recipe if you need to understand the XPath specification.

Generating an HTML page using XML and XSL transformations

Sometimes, you don't have access to the source database from the web server, or you just want static pages in your site. Under this scenario, you can create a web page through **XSLT** and then publish it. In this recipe, you will take advantage of the *XSL Transformation* job entry features to do just that: taking an XML file and transforming it into HTML.

Suppose you want to publish a books catalog on a website. In this recipe, you will generate an HTML page taking as its source data that you have in a database.

Getting ready

You must have a database of books with the structure shown in the *Appendix, Data Structures*.

How to do it...

The first group of steps is meant for exporting the books' information from the database to an XML file, if you already have the information in this format, then you can skip to step 7.

1. Create a new transformation.

2. Drop a **Table Input** step into the canvas and select the books information. Use the following SQL statement:
```
SELECT *
FROM Books
LEFT JOIN Authors
ON Books.id_author = Authors.id_author
```

3. Add an **XML Output** step from **Output** category.

4. Fill in the **File** tab giving the file the name books and leaving the default xml as the proposed extension.

5. Under the **Content** tab, type Books in **Parent XML element** and Book in **Row XML element**.

6. Under the **Fields** tab, press the **Get Fields** button, in order to retrieve the entire fields information. Modify the price field giving it the **Format** $0.00.

   The result from these steps will be a file named books.xml with the books structure. It must look like the following:
```
<Books>
   <Book>
      <title>Carrie</title>
      <price>$41,00</price>
```

```
            <genre>Fiction</genre>
            <lastname>King</lastname>
            <firstname>Stephen</firstname>
        </Book>
        <Book>
            <title>Salem›s lot</title>
                ...
        </Book>
            ...
    </Books>
```

7. Now, you must create the XSL file (`booksFormat.xsl`), based on the `books.xml` structure. Create a new file with your preferred text editor and type the following:

```
<?xml version="1.0" encoding="UTF-8"?>
<xsl:stylesheet    version="1.0"
    xmlns:xsl="http://www.w3.org/1999/XSL/Transform"
    xmlns="http://www.w3.org/1999/xhtml">
    <xsl:output method="xml" indent="yes" encoding="UTF-8"/>
    <xsl:template match="/Books">
      <html>
        <head> <title>Books</title> </head>
        <body>
          <h1>Books</h1>
          <table border="1">
          <!-- grid header -->
          <tr bgcolor="lightblue"><td>Title</td><td>Author</td>
            <td>Price</td><td>Genre</td></tr>
            <xsl:apply-templates select="Book">
              <xsl:sort select="title" />
            </xsl:apply-templates>
          </table>
        </body>
      </html>
    </xsl:template>
    <xsl:template match="Book">
      <!-- grid value fields -->
      <tr>
        <td><xsl:value-of select="title"/></td>
        <td><xsl:value-of select="lastname"/>, <xsl:value-of
          select="firstname"/></td>
        <td><xsl:value-of select="price"/></td>
        <td><xsl:value-of select="genre"/></td>
      </tr>
    </xsl:template>
</xsl:stylesheet>
```

You can save a lot of time by downloading the sample XSL file from the book's website!

8. Create a new job and add a **Start** entry.

9. Add a **Transformation** entry to execute the preceding transformation.

10. Add an **XSL Transformation** job entry from the **XML** category. Set the **Files** frame to the following:

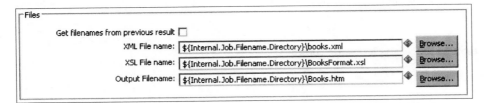

11. Run the job. A file named Book.htm will be created having the following layout:

Books

Title	Author	Price	Genre
Are You There, Vodka? It's me, Chelsea	Handler, Chelsea	$19,90	Non-fiction
Bag of Bones	King, Stephen	$40,90	Fiction
Basket Case	Hiaasen, Carl	$31,00	Fiction
Carrie	King, Stephen	$41,00	Fiction
Cashflow Quadrant	Kiyosaki, Robert	$25,00	Business
Chelsea Chelsea Bang Bang	Handler, Chelsea	$25,00	Non-fiction
Harry Potter and the Chamber of Secrets	Rowling, Joanne	$32,00	Children

How it works...

The **Extensible Stylesheet Language** (**XSL**) is used to transform and render XML documents. In this recipe, you generated an XML file with books information and then used an XSL file to transform that XML file into an HTML page.

Looking at the XSL file, you can see how it transforms the fields from the source into an HTML code. The file has different sections, which are as follows:

▶ One section for the header: a <table> tag with a row containing the fields' headers

▶ The tag <xsl:apply-templates select="Book"> indicating a loop over the template Book for each book

▶ The template Book, that creates a new row with the field's values

In order to apply the transformation defined in the XSL file effectively, you used the *XSL Transformation* job entry. The configuration of the entry is straightforward: you simply provide names of the XML file, the XSL file and the resulting file, and you're done.

There's more...

As an option, right after creating the page, you may publish it automatically on the website. For doing that, simply extend the job with a file transfer entry.

You will find more information about XSL at the following URL:

`http://en.wikipedia.org/wiki/XSLT`

You can also follow the following tutorial:

`http://www.w3schools.com/xsl/`

See also

The recipe named *Putting files on a remote server*, in *Chapter 4, File Management*. See this recipe for instructions on extending the job for transferring the generated page.

4
File Management

In this chapter, we will cover:

- ► Copying or moving one or more files
- ► Deleting one or more files
- ► Getting files from a remote server
- ► Putting files on a remote server
- ► Copying or moving a custom list of files
- ► Deleting a custom list of files
- ► Comparing files and folders
- ► Working with ZIP files

Introduction

On many occasions, the development of Kettle jobs and transformations involves manipulation of files, such as reading or writing a file along with other manipulations. Look at this sample scenario, where you have to:

- ► Get a file with orders from a remote server
- ► Validate and load the orders into a database
- ► Move the processed file to a designated folder
- ► If a file with that name already exists, rename the older version
- ► If the orders in the file are not valid, generate a log file with details of the errors and put that log file back on to the server for further review

In this situation besides reading and writing files, you also have to transfer, rename, and move them.

Copying, moving, deleting, and transferring files, list of files or directories are tasks not only needed for these situations, but in everyday life. It's common to have lot of files, which need to be organized in several ways, and for different purposes.

Kettle has a rich set of steps and job entries for doing this. However, you might get lost or frustrated trying to pick and then configure the option that suits your needs. The recipes in this chapter should help you with that task.

Copying or moving one or more files

The *Copy Files* job entry allows you to copy one or more files or folders. Let's see this step in action. Assume that you have a folder with a set of files, and you want to copy them to three folders depending on their extensions: you have one folder for text files, another for Excel files, and the last one for the rest of the files.

Getting ready

You will need a directory named `sampleFiles` containing a set of files with different extensions, including .txt and .xls. You will also need three destination directories, named `txtFiles`, `xlsFiles` and `OtherFiles`.

How to do it...

Carry out the following steps:

1. Create a new job and drop a **Start** job entry into the canvas.
2. Add a **Copy Files** job entry. In this entry, you will add the directions for copying the files into the three available destination folders. Double-click on the entry to open it.
3. In the **File/Folder source** textbox, type or browse for the `sampleFiles` folder. In the **File/Folder destination**, type or browse for the `txtFiles` folder. Also, type `.*\.txt` in the **Wildcard (regExp)** textbox. Click on the **Add** button.
4. In the **File/Folder source** textbox, type or browse for the `sampleFiles` folder. In the **File/Folder destination**, type or browse for the `xlsFiles` folder. Also, type `.*\.xls` in the **Wildcard (regExp)** textbox. Click on the **Add** button.
5. In the **File/Folder source** textbox, type or browse for the `sampleFiles` folder. In the **File/Folder destination**, type or browse for the `OtherFiles` folder. Also, type `.+(?<!(txt|xls))$` in the **Wildcard (regExp)** textbox. Click on the **Add** button.
6. Assuming that all folders are inside the directory where you have your job, the **Files/Folders** grid will look like the following screenshot:

	File/Folder source	File/Folder destination	Wildcard (RegExp)
1	${Internal.Job.Filename.Directory}\sampleFiles	${Internal.Job.Filename.Directory}\txtFiles	.*\.txt
2	${Internal.Job.Filename.Directory}\sampleFiles	${Internal.Job.Filename.Directory}\xlsFiles	.*\.xls
3	${Internal.Job.Filename.Directory}\sampleFiles	${Internal.Job.Filename.Directory}\OtherFiles	.+(?<!(txt|xls))$

Remember that `Internal.Job.Filename.Directory` is a predefined Kettle variable whose value is the full directory where the job is saved.

7. When you run the job, each file from the `sampleFiles` folder will be copied into the folder associated in the setting window, depending on its extension.

How it works...

You use the *Copy Files* job entry to perform the task of copying files. As you can see in the recipe, you can execute several copy instructions with a single job entry by entering different lines in the **Files/Folders** section from the **General** tab.

In the sample grid, you have three lines. For each line, the objective is to copy all the files from the source folder (first column) to the destination folder (second column) that match the regular expression (third column).

The first and second line copy the `.txt` and `.xls` files by using the regular expressions `.*\.txt` and `.*\.xls` respectively.

The third line copies the rest of the files. The regular expression that matches those files is a little more complex: The characters `?<!` represent a negation over the rest of the expression, so the expression `.+(?<!(txt|xls))$` means all files whose extension is neither `.txt` nor `.xls`.

There's more...

The recipe showed you the basics of copying files with Kettle. The following sections explain how to add more functionality, for example, validating the existence of files or folders before copying. You will also see the extra settings available for the *Copy Files* job entry.

Moving files

You can move the file (instead of copying) by checking the **Remove source files** checkbox in the **Settings** section under the **General** tab in the **Copy Files** job entry. If you check it, Kettle will delete the files after a successful copy. This is analogous to using a **Delete file** job entry right after the **Copy Files** entry.

Detecting the existence of the files before copying them

In the recipe, you simply wanted to organize some files in folders, and you didn't care if the files existed or not. However, the most common scenario is the one in which it's assumed that the files to copy or move already exist. You cannot perform that verification with the **Copy Files** entry, but there are other means.

Suppose that you want the files to be copied only if there is a mixture of file extensions. If there are only Excel files, or text files, they will not be copied and the situation will be recorded in a log.

In order to do that, you can create a transformation that succeeds if there is a mixture of files, or fails if you have only Excel files or only text files.

 The transformation should start with a *Get File Names* to get the list of files in the folder, and proceed differently according to the validations you want to do.

Then, in your job, you call the transformation before copying the files. The copy will be done only after the success of the transformation, as shown in the following diagram:

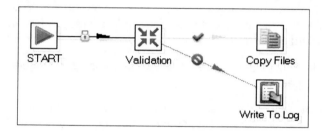

In the simplest case where you have to copy files specified by their exact name—that is, not expressed with regular expressions—you can verify their existence simply with a **File Exists** (for a single file) or a **Checks if files exist** (for multiple files) entry.

Creating folders

You can create the destination directory automatically by selecting the **Create destination folder** checkbox in the **Settings** section under the **General** tab in the **Copy Files** job entry. You could also create those directories by using a **Create a folder** job entry from the **File management** category. The difference is that, with the **Create a folder** entry, you can detect if the directory already exists; if you didn't expect that situation, you can act accordingly by, for example, aborting the job.

See also

The recipe named *Copying or moving a custom list of files* in this chapter. See this recipe if you have a set of files for copying, but the list cannot be specified with a regular expression.

Deleting one or more files

Kettle provides two job entries for deleting files: *Delete file* and *Delete files* entries. You can find both in the *File management* category of entries.

In this recipe, you will see an example of how to delete a file. You will delete a file that includes the current date as part of its name, for example `test_20101020.txt`.

Getting ready

You must create a sample file; for example, `test_20101020.txt`. Make sure to use your current date instead of `20101020`. Use the same format (`yyyyMMdd`).

How to do it...

1. Create a new transformation.

2. Drop a **Get System Info** step from the **Input** category into the work area.

3. Double-click on the step and add a field named `date`. In the **Type** column, select **system date(fixed)**.

4. Add a **Select values** step from the **Transform** category. Open it, and under the **Meta-data** tab, add the **Fieldname** `date`, set the type to **String** and type or select `yyyyMMdd` in the **Format** column.

5. From the Job category, add a **Set Variables** step. Double-click on it and fill in the grid, as shown in the following screenshot:

Field values:

	Field name	Variable name	Variable scope type	Default value
1	date	today	Valid in the parent job	

6. The transformation is ready. Save it. Now, create a new job and drop a **Start** entry.

7. Add a **Transformation** job entry and configure it to run the transformation created above: In the **Transformation Filename:** textbox type the complete path to the transformation file.

8. Add a **Delete file** entry from the **File management** category.

9. Double-click on this step. In the **File name** textbox, type the location of the file to be deleted and concatenate it with `test_` and the `today` variable, for example, `${Internal.Job.Filename.Directory}\test_${today}.txt`.

10. Run the job and the file will be deleted.

How it works...

The *Delete file* job entry simply deletes a file. In the recipe, you used it to delete a file whose name is not fixed, but depends on the current date.

The transformation has the purpose of building the last part of the name of the file: It gets the present date with a *Get System Info* step, converts the date to a `String` by using a *Select values* step, and sets a variable named `today` with this information. As the scope, you specified **Valid in the parent job**.

> In general, if you are unsure of the scope to set, you should choose **Valid in the root job**. That is usually the best choice. A variable with that scope will be valid in the root job and all sub-jobs and transformations.

In this case, `Valid in the parent job` will suffice because you will use the variable in the job that calls this transformation.

The main job runs the transformation and then uses the variable `${today}` to build the name of the file to delete. Assuming that your transformation is located in /home/my_work/, when you execute the job, the text `${Internal.Job.Filename.Directory}\ test_${today}.txt` will be replaced by /home/my_work/test_20101020.txt, and the *Delete file* step will remove that file if it exists.

There's more...

If you need to delete a set of files instead of just one, you can use the **Delete files** job entry from the **File Management** category. With this entry, you can delete several files or folders, including subfolders and can also use wildcards for the selection.

If you just want to delete folders instead of files, you can use the *Delete folders* job entry, whose configuration is quite straightforward.

Whichever is your use case, deleting one or more files, with or without folders, take a look at the following subsection. It gives you more tricks to use when deleting files.

Figuring out which files have been deleted

When you delete a single file by using the *Delete File* job entry, you can easily detect if the file was deleted or not, and act accordingly. Let's summarize how:

Result of the job	Method for detecting the result
File was deleted	The *Delete File* job entry succeeds
File wasn't deleted because of an error	The *Delete File* job entry fails
File wasn't deleted because it didn't exist	If you checked the **Fail if the file doesn't exist:**, the *Delete File* job entry fails

The problem arises when you try to delete several files with the *Delete Files* entry. How can you be sure whether your job is behaving correctly and deleting the expected files? How can you know the exact names of the files that were deleted?

There is no direct way of determining that list of files, but there are some interesting solutions.

When you run a job that deletes files, the names of the files being deleted are written into the log. If you are developing the job, just take a look at the **Logging** tab of the **Execution results** pane in Spoon. If you want to have the list of files for further processing, save the log into a file; then you can open that file and look for the lines containing the text `Deleting file`. To be more precise, you will find a bunch of lines with the details, as in the following example:

```
... - Delete some files - Processing folder [file:///C:/test]
... - Delete some files - Deleting file [file:///C:/test/
test_20101020.txt] ...
... - Delete some files - Deleting file [file:///C:/test/
test_20101021.txt] ...
...
... - Delete some files - Total deleted files = 5
```

Another way of getting the list of deleted files would be as follows: Create a transformation that lists the existing files with the same directory/file specifications as those in the *Delete Files* entry.

You should run the transformation with a *Transformation* entry just before the *Delete Files* entry. If the *Delete Files* entry succeeds, you know that the deleted files are those in the list you created. This method is easy, but you have to be careful. If more than one process or people are accessing the folder or files at the same time, there is a risk that the built list and the real names of the deleted files don't coincide.

See also

The recipe named *Deleting a custom list of files* in this chapter. This recipe is useful if you don't have the names of the files to delete beforehand or if the list cannot be specified with regular expressions.

Getting files from a remote server

When you need to copy files from or to remote machines, you can use the standard network protocol **File Transfer Protocol** (**FTP**) built on client-server architecture.

Kettle provides the *Get a file with FTP* job entry to get files from an FTP server. In the example, you will connect to a remote directory named `remoteDir` on an FTP server and copy some text files from that server to a local folder named `destinationDir`.

Getting ready

You need access to an FTP server.

How to do it...

Carry out the following steps:

1. Create a new job and drop a **Start** entry into the canvas.

2. Add a **Get a file with FTP** job entry from the **File transfer** category.

3. Under the **General** tab, type the server name or its IP address in the **FTP server name / IP address** textbox.

4. Type the port number in the **Server port** textbox. Usually, it is the port 21.

5. In the **Username** and **Password** textboxes, type the credentials to log into the FTP server.

> You can verify the connection information by clicking on the **Test connection** button.

6. In the **Remote directory** textbox under the **Files** tab, you must type the name of the remote directory on the FTP server from where the source files will be retrieved.

> You can check if folder exists by clicking on the **Check folder** button.

7. Type `.*\.txt` as the **Wildcard**.

8. In the **Target directory** textbox inside the **Local** frame, type the destination directory on the local machine. Under the **Files** tab, you have various fields as shown in the following screenshot:

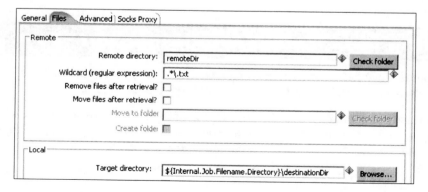

9. Run the job. The files with `.txt` extension will be copied from `remoteDir` on the FTP server to `destinationDir` on the local machine.

How it works...

The *Get a file with FTP* job entry performs the copy task; it uses the configuration set under the **General** tab to connect to the remote FTP server.

Under the **Files** tab, you defined the source directory (in the example, the remote folder `remoteDir`) and target directory (in the example, the local folder `destinationDir`).

 Try to avoid the use of directories with special characters, such as spaces. Some FTP servers don't allow these special characters.

You also provided a regular expression for the files to get. In this case, you typed `.*\.txt` which is a regular expression representing all `.txt` files.

There's more...

The following sections give you some additional information and useful tips when it's time to transfer files from a remote server.

Specifying files to transfer

In the recipe, you copied all files with a given extension; you did it by providing a regular expression that all those files matched. As another possibility, you may need to transfer a single file.

 Note that even if you have the exact name of the file, you still have to provide a regular expression.

For example, if the name of the file is `my_file.txt` you have to type `my_file\.txt`.

As a last possibility, instead of typing a wildcard, you may provide a Kettle variable name. Using a variable is particularly useful if you don't know the name of the file beforehand. Suppose that you have to get a file named `daily_update_yyyyMMdd.csv` where `yyyyMMdd` represents year, month, and day. In that case, you can create a transformation that builds a regular expression representing that file name (for example, `daily_update_20101215\.csv`) and sets a variable with that value. In the job, you should execute that transformation before the *Get a file with FTP* job entry.

Your job would look like the one shown in the following screenshot:

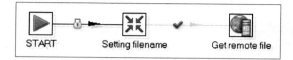

Finally, in the *Get a file with FTP* entry, you should type that variable (for example, `${DAILY_FILENAME}`) as the wildcard.

Some considerations about connecting to an FTP server

In order to be able to connect to an FTP server, you must complete the connection settings for the FTP server under the **General** tab of the **Get a file with FTP** job entry. If you are working with an anonymous FTP server, you can use `anonymous` as the username and free text as the password. This means that you can access the machine without having to have an account on that machine.

If you need to provide authentication credentials for access via a proxy, you must also complete the following textboxes: `Proxy host`, `Proxy port`, `Proxy username`, and `Proxy password`.

Access via SFTP

SFTP means **SSH File Transfer Protocol**. It's a network protocol used to secure the file transfer capability. With Kettle, you can get files from an SFTP server by using the *Get a file with SFTP* job entry. To configure this entry, you have to enter the name or IP of the SFTP server in the **SFTP server name / IP** textbox. The rest of the configuration of the **General** and **Files** tabs is pretty similar to the **Get a file with FTP** entry.

For more information on SFTP, you can visit the following URL:

`http://en.wikipedia.org/wiki/SSH_file_transfer_protocol`

Access via FTPS

An **FTPS** server extends the standard FTP protocol, adding cryptographic protocols, such as the **Transport Layer Security** (**TLS**) and the **Secure Sockets Layer** (**SSL**). You can use the *Get a file with FTPS* job entry to get files from an FTPS server. To configure this entry, you have to enter the name or IP address of the FTPS server in the **FTPS server name / IP address:** textbox. The rest of the configuration of the **General** and **Files** tabs is pretty similar to the **Get a file with FTP** entry.

More information about FTPS can be obtained from the following URL:

`http://en.wikipedia.org/wiki/Ftps`

Getting information about the files being transferred

A drawback when accessing an FTP server is that, from the job, you can only know if the entry succeeded or failed; you don't have control over how files behave, for example, how many files were transferred. To overcome this situation, it is recommended that you keep the log generated by the job, which is the only source of information about what happened. To see the details, you can simply take a look at the log, or parse it in a subsequent Kettle transformation.

See also

The recipe named *Putting files on a remote server* in this chapter. See this recipe if instead of getting files you have to transfer files to a remote server.

Putting files on a remote server

This recipe is similar to the previous one, *Getting files from a remote server*, but in this case, you want to copy the text files from a local machine to a remote machine using the FTP network protocol and the *Put a file with FTP* job entry.

Getting ready

You need write access to an FTP server.

How to do it...

Carry out the following steps:

1. Create a new job. Drop a **Start** entry into the canvas.

2. Add a **Put a file with FTP** job entry from **File transfer** category.

3. Under the **General** tab, type the server name (or its IP address) in the **FTP server name / IP address** textbox.

4. Type the port number in the **Port** textbox. Usually, it is the port 21.

5. In the **Username:** and **Password:** textboxes, type the credentials to log into the FTP server.

 You can verify if the connection settings are valid by clicking on the **Test connection** button.

6. Type the source folder in the **Local directory** textbox inside the **source (local) files** frame located under the **Files** tab. In this example: c:\sourceDir.

7. Type .*\.txt as the **Wildcard**.

8. In the **Remote directory** textbox, type the destination directory on the remote machine, for example: `remoteDir`.

> You can check for the existence of the folder by clicking on the **Test folder** button.

9. The **Files** tab will look like the one shown in the following screenshot:

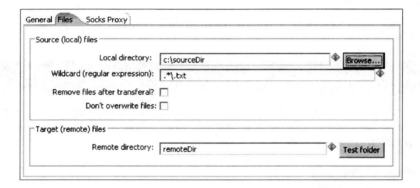

10. Run the job. The files with `.txt` extension will be copied from the `sourceDir` local folder to the `destinationDir` on the FTP Server.

How it works...

The *Put a file with FTP* job entry uses the configuration set under the **General** tab to connect to the remote FTP server. The entry copies the files from the local machine to the remote server by using the configuration typed under the **Files** tab. In the recipe, you set the source directory as `c:\sourceDir` and the destination directory as `remoteDir` and as the list of files to transfer you typed a regular expression representing all `.txt` files. You could have typed a regular expression representing the exact name of the file to transfer, as well as Kettle variables, both for the files and for the directories.

There's more...

In the recipe, you put some files on an FTP server. Kettle also provides job entries for putting files on SFTP and FTPS servers. They are the *Put a file with SFTP* and the *Upload files to FTPS* entries respectively. The configuration for these entries is quite similar to the one you used earlier.

See also

The recipe named *Getting files from a remote server* in this chapter. See this recipe for some tips about connecting to a remote server, specifying files for transferring or about using different protocols.

Copying or moving a custom list of files

Sometimes, you don't have the names of files to move or copy beforehand. In these cases, you can take advantage of the **Add filename to result** prompt existing in several Kettle steps and job entries.

Let's see an example. Suppose that you receive Excel files daily with book orders from different branches and, you need to process these files creating a new Excel file with all the incoming orders. Then, finally, you want to move the source files to a destination folder.

Getting ready

In order to do this exercise, you need a directory named booksOrders with several Excel files. Each file should have two columns: one for the id_title and another for the Quantity. Also, it is necessary to have a destination folder named processedOrders.

How to do it...

Carry out the following steps:

1. Create a new transformation. This transformation will take all Excel files from the source directory and write them into a single Excel file.
2. Drop an **Excel Input** step into the canvas.
3. Under the **Files** tab, fill in the grid in order to read all Excel files in the source directory. Under **File/Directory**, type ${Internal.Transformation.Filename.Directory}\booksOrders and under **Wildcard (RegExp)**, type .*\.xls.
4. Under the **Content** tab, make sure that the **Add filenames to result** prompt is checked.
5. Under the **Fields** tab, add to the grid a String field named id_title and a Number field named Quantity.
6. Add an **Excel Output** step after the **Excel Input** step.
7. Under the **File** tab, type the destination Excel file (for example allBookOrders) including the path, and leave .xls as the **Extension**. Also, check the **Include date in filename?** prompt. With these settings, your final file will have a name such as allBookOrders_101011.xls.

Note that yyMMdd is the default format for the appended date. If you want to append the date with a different format, then check the **Specify Date time format** option and select or type the desired format in the **Date time format** option.

8. Under the same tab, uncheck the **Add filename to result** prompt.

9. Under the **Fields** tab, click on the **Get Fields** button to fill in the grid.

10. Save the transformation.

Now, let's see how to move the source files between the folders.

1. Create a new job and add a **Start** entry.

2. Add a **Transformation** entry and configure it to run the transformation created above.

3. Add a **Copy or Move result filenames** entry from the **File management** category.

4. Open the step. In the **Destination folder** textbox, browse or type the target directory (for example ${Internal.Job.Filename.Directory}\processedOrders).

5. Run the job. It will execute the transformation and will move the source files from the booksOrders folder to the processedOrders folder.

How it works...

In the recipe, you used the Kettle **result filelist** feature to automatically build a list of files to copy.

In the transformation, you used an *Excel input* step to read all the files with the .xls extension from a source directory and an *Excel output* step to write this information to a new file.

The important setting here is the **Add filename to result** prompt in the **Excel input** step. When this option is checked (which is the default setting), the names of the files read in the step are saved to the result filelist, which is no more than a list of files in memory.

Back in the job, the **Copy or Move result filenames** entry reads the names saved in memory and moves the files in that list to the destination folder.

Note that in the *Excel output* step, you unchecked the **Add filename to result** prompt. If you had left this prompt checked, then the job would have moved the completeBookOrders_101011.xls file too.

See also

▶ The recipe named *Reading an Excel file* in *Chapter 2, Reading and Writing Files* for directions on how to read an Excel file.

▶ The recipe named *Writing an Excel file with several sheets* in *Chapter 2, Reading and Writing Files* for directions on how to write an Excel file.

Deleting a custom list of files

Suppose a scenario where you have to delete some files but you don't have the names of the files to delete beforehand. If you can specify that list with regular expressions, that wouldn't be a problem, but sometimes that is not possible. In these cases you should use a helper transformation that builds the list of files to delete. This recipe shows you how to do it.

For this recipe, assume you want to delete from a source directory all the temporary files that meet two conditions: the files have a .tmp extension and a size of 0 bytes.

Getting ready

In order to create and test this recipe, you need a directory with a set of sample files; some of them should have the .tmp extension and zero size. Some example files are shown in the following screenshot:

sample1.txt	1 KB
sample2.tmp	1 KB
sample3.tmp	0 KB
sample4.log	1 KB
sample5.tmp	0 KB
sample6.tmp	1 KB
sample7.tmp	0 KB
sample8.txt	0 KB
sample9.tmp	1 KB

In the preceding screenshot, the files that must be deleted are **sample3.tmp**, **sample5.tmp**, and **sample7.tmp**.

How to do it...

Carry out the following steps:

1. Create the transformation that will build the list of files to delete.
2. Drop a **Get File Names** step into the canvas.
3. Under the **File** tab, fill the **Selected files:** grid. Under **File/Directory**, type `${Internal.Transformation.Filename.Directory}\sample_directory` and under **Wildcard (RegExp)**, type `.*\.tmp`.
4. From the **Flow** category, add a **Filter rows** step.
5. Use this step to filter the files with size equal to zero. In order to do that, add the condition `size = 0`.

6. After the **Filter rows** step, add the **Select values** step. When asked for the kind of hop to create, select **Main output of step**. This will cause only those rows that meet the condition to pass the filter.

7. Use the **Select values** step to select the field's `path` and `short_filename`.

8. From the **Job** category of Steps, add a **Copy rows to result** step.

9. Save the transformation.

10. Create a new job and add a **Start** entry.

11. Add a **Transformation** entry and configure it to run the transformation previously created.

12. Add a **Delete files** entry from the **File management** category.

13. Double-click on it and check the **Copy previous Results to args?** prompt.

14. Save the job and run it. The files with a .tmp extension and size 0 bytes will be deleted.

How it works...

In this recipe, you deleted a list of files by using the *Delete files* job entry. In the selected files grid of that entry, you have to provide the complete name of the files to delete or the directory and a regular expression. Instead of typing that information directly, here you built the rows for the grid in a separate transformation.

The first step used in the transformation is the *Get File Names*. This step allows you to get information about a file or set of files or folders. In this example, the step gets the list of `.tmp` files from the `sample_directory` folder.

The following screenshot shows all of the information that you obtain with this step:

	Fieldname	Type	Length	Precision	Step origin	Sto...	Mask	De...	Group	Trim	C...
1	filename	String	500	-	dir tmp files	nor...		,	.	none	
2	short_filename	String	500	-	dir tmp files	nor...		,	.	none	
3	path	String	500	-	dir tmp files	nor...		,	.	none	
4	type	String	500	-	dir tmp files	nor...		,	.	none	
5	exists	Boolean	-	-	dir tmp files	nor...		,	.	none	
6	ishidden	Boolean	-	-	dir tmp files	nor...		,	.	none	
7	isreadable	Boolean	-	-	dir tmp files	nor...		,	.	none	
8	iswriteable	Boolean	-	-	dir tmp files	nor...		,	.	none	
9	lastmodifiedtime	Date	-	-	dir tmp files	nor...		,	.	none	
10	size	Integer	-	0	dir tmp files	nor...	#;-#	,	.	none	
11	extension	String	-	-	dir tmp files	nor...		,	.	none	
12	uri	String	-	-	dir tmp files	nor...		,	.	none	
13	rooturi	String	-	-	dir tmp files	nor...		,	.	none	

You can see these field names by pressing the space bar while having the focus on the **Get File Names** step.

After to that step, you used a **Filter rows** step to keep just the files with size 0 bytes.

If you do a preview on this step, you will see a dataset with the list of the desired files, that is, those that meet the two conditions: having the .tmp extension and size equal to 0 bytes.

After that, you selected just the fields holding the `path` and the `short_filename` and copied these rows to memory. You did that with the *Copy rows to result* step.

Now, let's go back to the job. The **Copy previous result to args?** prompt selected in the **Delete files** entry causes the job to read the rows coming from the transformation, and copy them to the grid. In other words, each row coming out of the transformation (a data pair: `path`, `short_filename`) becomes a row in the **Files/Folders:** grid.

With that information, the job is finally able to delete the specified files.

See also

▶ The recipe named *Deleting one or more files* in this chapter. See this recipe if the list of files to delete (or at least a regular expression specifying that list) is known in advance.

▶ The recipe named *Discarding rows in a stream based on a condition* in *Chapter 6, Understanding Flows of Data* to understand the use of the *Filter rows* step.

Comparing files and folders

Kettle allows you to compare files and folders through the following job entries: *File Compare* and *Compare folder*. In this recipe, you will use the first of those entries, which is used for comparing the content of two files. Assume that periodically you receive a file with new museums data to incorporate into your database. You will compare the new and the previous version of the file. If the files are equal, you do nothing, but if they are different, you will read the new file.

Getting ready

To create and test this recipe, you will need two files: the older version of the museum file (`LastMuseumsFileReceived.xml`), and the new file (`NewMuseumsFileReceived.xml`).

On the book's website, you will find sample files to play with. In particular, `NewMuseumsFileReceived(equal).xml` is equal to the `LastMuseumsFileReceived.xml` file, and `NewMuseumsFileReceived(different).xml`, as implied by its name, is different. With these files, you will be able to test the different situations in the recipe.

How to do it...

Carry out the following steps:

1. Create a new job, and drop a **Start** entry into the work area.

2. Add a **File Compare** job entry from the **File management** category. Here you must type or browse to the two files that must be compared, as shown in the following screenshot:

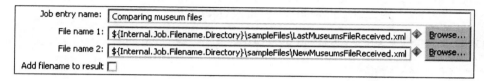

Job entry name:	Comparing museum files
File name 1:	${Internal.Job.Filename.Directory}\sampleFiles\LastMuseumsFileReceived.xml Browse...
File name 2:	${Internal.Job.Filename.Directory}\sampleFiles\NewMuseumsFileReceived.xml Browse...
Add filename to result ☐	

3. Add a **Transformation** job entry and a **DUMMY** job entry, both from the **General** category. Create a hop from the **File Compare** job entry to each of these entries.

4. Right-click on the hop between the **File Compare** job entry and the **Transformation** job entry to show the options, choose the Evaluation item and then select the Follow when result is false item.

5. Right-click on the hop between the **File Compare** job entry and the **DUMMY** job entry, choose the Evaluation item, and this time select the Follow when result is true item.

6. The job should look like the one shown in the following diagram:

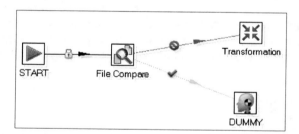

7. Then, create a new transformation in order to read the XML file. Drop a **Get data from XML** step from the **Input** category into the canvas and type the complete path for the XML file in the **File or directory** textbox under the **File** tab. In this case, it is ${Internal.Transformation.Filename.Directory}\sampleFiles\NewMuseumsFileReceived.xml. Use /museums/museum in the **Loop XPath** textbox under the **Content** tab, and use the **Get fields** button under the **Fields** tab to populate the list of fields automatically.

8. Save the transformation.

9. Configure the **Transformation** job entry for the main job to run the transformation you just created.

10. When you run the job, the two files are compared.

11. Assuming that your files are equal, in the **Logging** window you will see a line similar to the following:

```
2010/11/05 10:08:46 - fileCompare - Finished job entry [DUMMY]
(result=[true])
```

This line means that the flow went toward the **DUMMY** entry.

12. If your files are different, in the **Job metrics** window you will see that the **fileCompare** entry fails, and under the **Logging** tab, you will see something similar to the following:

```
. . .
... - Read XML file - Loading transformation from XML file
[file:///C:/readXMLFile.ktr]
... - readXMLFile - Dispatching started for transformation
[readXMLFile]
... - readXMLFile - This transformation can be replayed with
replay date: 2010/11/05 10:14:10
... - Read museum data.0 - Finished processing (I=4, O=0, R=0,
W=4, U=0, E=0)
... - fileCompare - Finished job entry [Read XML file]
(result=[true])
. . .
```

13. This means that the transformation was executed.

How it works...

The *File Compare* job entry performs the comparison task. It verifies whether the two files have the same content. If they are different, the job entry fails. Then, the job proceeds with the execution of the transformation that reads the new file. However, if the files are the same, the job entry succeeds and the flows continue to the *DUMMY* entry.

In other words, the new file is processed if and only if the *File Compare* fails, that is, if the two files are different.

There's more...

Besides comparing files with Kettle, you can also compare directories; let's see how it works.

Comparing folders

If you want to compare the contents of two folders, you can use the **Compare folder** job entry from the **File management** category.

In this job entry, you must browse to or type the complete paths of the two folders in the **File / Folder name 1** and **File / Folder name 2** textboxes respectively, and configure the comparison to be done. See the possible settings in the following screenshot:

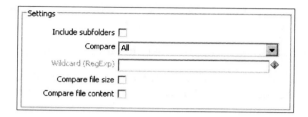

The **Compare** option, set to **All** by default, can be changed to compare just files, just folders or just the files indicated by a regular expression. The usual requirement would be to compare the list of files and then their sizes.

 Note that you can even compare the content of the files, but that will affect performance considerably.

Working with ZIP files

Compressed files are a convenient storage method. If you have many files or your files are very large, compressing them makes it easier to store them and transfer them through e-mails or between different media (PC, USB devices, and so on).

For example, consider managing the log information from a web server, which generates a new text file every day with data about the web traffic (pages, IPs, operations, status codes, and so on). After several months, you have a lot of files with a substantial amount of information.

Now, suppose that you want to create a local copy of those files. You don't have access to the server from your computer, so you have to copy the files onto some media and then onto your computer. As the size of these files can be huge, instead of directly copying the files, you will compress them first.

Once you have the ZIP file on your computer, you want to unzip it and create one separate .zip file per month. Assuming that the files are named `exYYMMDD.log` you will create .zip files named `YYMM.zip`. For example, a file named `ex101115.log` will be zipped along with all other logs from November 2010 as `1011.zip`.

Getting ready

You will need access to a directory containing log files.

How to do it...

You will create this recipe in two different steps. In the first step, you will compress the log files, and in the second step, you will uncompress them and organize them in monthly ZIP files.

So, let's compress the weblog files, by carrying out the following steps:

1. Create a new job and drop a **Start** job entry into the canvas.

2. Add a **Zip file** job entry from the **File management** category.

3. Under the **General** tab, select the source directory by clicking on the **Folder...** button. The example points to a web server log directory, such as `C:\WINDOWS\system32\Logfiles\W3SVC1\test_files`.

4. Type `.+\.log` in the **Include wildcard (RegExp):** textbox, in order to read all the files with the .log extension.

5. In the **Zip File name:** textbox, type the path and name for the destination ZIP file. For example: `C:\WINDOWS\system32\Logfiles\W3SVC1\test_files\weblogs.zip`.

6. You have several additional options for including date and time to the ZIP file name. You don't need to set those options for this recipe.

7. Under the **Advanced** tab, choose `Delete files` in the **After Zipping** drop-down list.

8. When running this job, a new file named `weblogs.zip` will be created containing the log information from the web server and the log files will be deleted.

Now assuming that you have copied the generated ZIP file to your computer, you want to unzip the weblogs and generate small ZIP files grouping them by month:

1. Create a new job and drop a **Start** job entry into the canvas.

2. Add an **Unzip file** job entry and open it.

3. In the **Zip File name** textbox, you must browse for the ZIP file you created previously (`weblogs.zip`).

4. Choose a **Target Directory**, for example: `${Internal.Job.Filename.Directory}\logs` and check the **Create folder** checkbox to create that folder, if it doesn't exist.

5. Type `.+\.log` in the **Include wildcard** textbox.

6. In the **After extraction** drop-down box select **Delete files**.

7. Under the **Advanced** tab, set the **Success on** condition to `At least we successfully unzipped x files`, and set the **Limit files** textbox to 1.

8. The next step for the job will be calling a transformation that creates the groups of logs for the smaller ZIP files. Add a **Transformation** job entry.

9. Double-click on the new entry. As **Transformation filename:** type `${Internal.Job.Filename.Directory}/read_log_list.ktr`. Click on the squared icon to the right of the name of the transformation, and a dialog window will appear asking if you want to create the transformation. Answer **Yes**.

10. In the transformation, add the following steps and link them one after the other:

    ❑ A **Get File Names (Input)**

    ❑ A **Strings cut (Transform)**

    ❑ A **User Defined Java Expression** or **UDJE** for short **(Scripting)**

    ❑ A **Select values (Transform)**

    ❑ A **Sort rows (Transform)**

    ❑ A **Copy rows to result (Job)** steps

    When asked about the kind of hop to create, always choose the **Main output of step** option. The transformation should look like the one shown in the following screenshot:

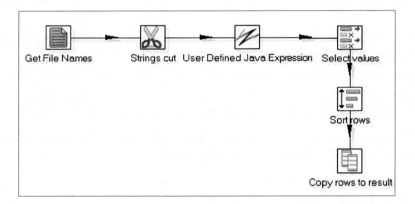

11. Double-click on the first step. With this step, you will get the complete list of log files.

> In order to test this transformation, copy some log files to the `logs` folder. This way, you will be able to preview each step.

12. Fill the grid by typing `${Internal.Transformation.Filename.Directory}\logs` under **File/directory** and `.+\.log` under **Wildcard (RegExp)**. Close the window.

13. Double-click the **Strings cut** step. This step will generate a `String` with the year and month part of the filenames. Then, fill the following fields:

    ❑ Under **In stream field**, type `short_filename`

    ❑ Under **Out stream field**, type `year_month`

    ❑   Under **Cut from** type 2

    ❑   Under **Cut to** type 6 and close the window.

14. Double-click on the **UDJE** step. With this step, you will create the fields for the .zip grid. Add three **String** fields named `wildcard`, `wildcardexc`, and `destination`. As **Java expression**, type `"ex"+year_month+"[0-9][0-9]\\.log"`, `""` and `path+"\\zip_files\\"+year_month+".zip"` respectively. Don't forget to set the **Value type** to **String**.

15. Double-click on the **Select values** step. Use it to select the field's `path`, `wildcard`, `wildcardexc`, and `destination`. Close the window.

16. Double-click on the **Sort rows** step. Use it to sort by `destination`. Check the **Only pass unique rows? (verifies keys only)** option. With this, you generate a single row by month.

17. Do a preview. You should see something like the following:

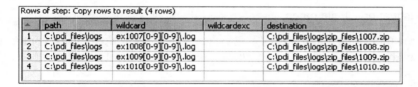

	path	wildcard	wildcardexc	destination
1	C:\pdi_files\logs	ex1007[0-9][0-9]\.log		C:\pdi_files\logs\zip_files\1007.zip
2	C:\pdi_files\logs	ex1008[0-9][0-9]\.log		C:\pdi_files\logs\zip_files\1008.zip
3	C:\pdi_files\logs	ex1009[0-9][0-9]\.log		C:\pdi_files\logs\zip_files\1009.zip
4	C:\pdi_files\logs	ex1010[0-9][0-9]\.log		C:\pdi_files\logs\zip_files\1010.zip

18. Save the transformation.

19. Go back to the job, and add a **Zip file** job entry.

20. Double-click on the entry, check the **Get arguments from previous** option and close the window.

21. Save the job, and run it.

22. Browse the log folder. You will see all log files that were compressed in the `weblogs.zip` file, and a subfolder named `zip`.

23. Browse the ZIP folder. You will see one ZIP file for each month for which you had log files.

How it works...

In this recipe, you saw the functionality of the *Zip File* and *Unzip File* job entries.

First, you zipped all log files in a folder. You specified the files to zip and the name and location of the ZIP file to generate. This is quite simple and doesn't require further explanation.

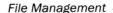

In the second part of the recipe, you performed two different tasks:

The first was to unzip a file. You specified the ZIP file, the regular expression that indicates which files to extract from the ZIP file, and the destination of the files. This is also a simple and intuitive operation.

The last part, the most elaborate task of the recipe, was compressing the log files grouped by month. In order to do this, you couldn't fill the grid in the *Zip file* job entry manually because you didn't know in advance the names of the log files. Therefore, instead of filling the grid you checked the **Get arguments from previous** option. The transformation was responsible for generating the values for the grid in the **Zip file** entry setting window. The columns generated by the transformation were:

> ▸ Folder of the files to zip
>
> ▸ Regular expression for the files to zip
>
> ▸ Regular expression for the files to exclude (in this case, you set a null value)
>
> ▸ Destination ZIP file name

These are the four fields that the *Zip file* entry needs in order to zip the files. For each row generated in the transformation, a new ZIP file was created based on these values.

There's more...

Look at some notes about zipping and unzipping files:

Avoiding zipping files

If you need to zip some files for attaching to an e-mail, then you don't have to use the *Zip file* entry. The *Mail* job entry does the task of zipping for you.

Avoiding unzipping files

In the recipe, you unzipped a file because you had to manipulate the files. If, instead of manipulating the files as you did, you need to read them you don't have to use the *Unzip file* entry. Kettle is capable of reading those files as they are. For a complete reference on this subject, you can take a look at the following entry in Slawomir Chodnicki's blog:

```
http://type-exit.org/adventures-with-open-source-bi/2010/11/directly-
accessing-remote-andor-compressed-files-in-kettle/
```

See also

The recipe named *Sending e-mails with attached files* of *Chapter 9, Getting the Most Out of Kettle*. This recipe will teach you how to attach ZIP files in an e-mail.

5
Looking for Data

In this chapter, we will cover:

- ► Looking for values in a database table
- ► Looking for values in a database (with complex conditions or multiples tables involved)
- ► Looking for values in a database with extreme flexibility
- ► Looking for values in a variety of sources
- ► Looking for values by proximity
- ► Looking for values consuming a web service
- ► Looking for values over an intranet or Internet

Introduction

With transformations, you manipulate data in many ways: doing mathematical or logical operations, applying string functions, grouping by one or more columns, sorting, and much more. Besides transforming the data you already have, you may need to search and bring data from other sources. Let's look at some examples:

- ► You have some product codes and you want to look for their descriptions in an Excel file
- ► You have a value and want to get all products whose price is below that value from a database
- ► You have some addresses and want to get the coordinates (latitude, longitude) for those locations from a web service

Searching for information in databases, text files, web services, and so on is a very common task and Kettle has several steps for doing it. In this chapter, you will learn about the different options.

Looking for values in a database table

In order to search for data in a database, Kettle offers several options. The simplest situation is the one in which you need to get one or more columns from a single database table. In this recipe, you will learn how to do this by using the *Database lookup* step.

We will work with the Steel Wheels sample data. If you don't know about it, refer to *Chapter 1, Working with Databases*. Suppose that you want to look for products that match a given search term and whose prices are below a given value. This recipe shows you how to do this.

Getting ready

In order to follow this recipe, you need the Steel Wheels database.

How to do it...

Carry out the following steps:

1. Create a new transformation.

2. Drop a **Data Grid** step (**Input** category). Open it. Under the **Meta** tab, add two `String` items: `prod` and `max_price`. Then, complete the **Data** tab, as shown in the following screenshot:

#. ▲	prod	max_price
1	Aston Martin	90
2	Ford Falcon	70
3	Corvette	70

3. Add a **User Defined Java Expression** step.

4. Use that step to add a **String** named `like_statement`. As **Java expression**, type `"%"+prod+"%"`.

5. Add a **Database lookup** step. You will find it in the **Lookup** category of steps.

6. Double-click on the step. As **Connection** select (or create if it doesn't exist) the connection to the `sampledata` database. As **Lookup table** type or browse for `PRODUCTS`.

7. Fill the upper and lower grid, as shown in the following screenshot:

The key(s) to look up the value(s):

#. ▲	Table field	Comparator	Field1	Field2
1	BUYPRICE	<	max_price	
2	PRODUCTNAME	LIKE	like_statement	

Values to return from the lookup table :

#. ▲	Field	New name	Default	Type
1	PRODUCTNAME		not available	String
2	PRODUCTSCALE			String
3	BUYPRICE			Integer

8. Close the **Database lookup** configuration window and do a preview on this step. You will see the following screen:

Rows of step: Database lookup (simple) (3 rows)

▲	prod	max_price	like_statement	PRODUCTNAME	PRODUCTSCALE	BUYPRICE
1	Aston Martin	90	%Aston Martin%	1965 Aston Martin DB5	1:18	66
2	Ford Falcon	70	%Ford Falcon%	not available		
3	Corvette	70	%Corvette%	1958 Chevy Corvette Limited Edition	1:24	16

How it works...

The *Database lookup* step allows you to look for values in a database table. To perform that search, you need to specify at least the following:

▶ The database connection and the database table you want to search

▶ The conditions for the search

▶ The fields to retrieve from the table

The upper grid is where you specify the conditions. Each row in the grid represents a comparison between a column in the table and a field in your stream, by using one of the provided comparators.

Take a look at the upper grid in the recipe. The conditions you entered were:

BUYPRICE < max_price and PRODUCTNAME LIKE like_statement

If we take, for example, the first row in the dataset, the condition can be restated as:

BUYPRICE<90 and PRODUCTNAME LIKE %Aston Martin%

That's exactly the search you wanted to perform for that row: look for the records where the column BUYPRICE was less than 90 and the column PRODUCTNAME contained Aston Martin.

As the result of the database lookup, you can retrieve any number of columns. Each database column you enter in the lower grid will become a new field in your dataset. You can rename them (this is particularly useful if you already have a field with the same name) and supply a default value if no record is found in the search.

In the recipe, you added three fields: PRODUCTNAME, PRODUCTSCALE, and BUYPRICE. By default, for PRODUCTNAME you typed not available. In the final preview, you can see that description in the second row. This means that there were no products with Ford Falcon as part of their description and price lower than 70.

There's more...

The recipe showed the minimal setting of the *Database lookup* step. The step has more options that can be useful as explained in the following subsections.

Taking some action when the lookup fails

When you perform a search with the *Database lookup* step, you expect that the search returns a row. If the data you are looking for doesn't exist in the table then the lookup fails. If this happens, the fields you added in the lower grid are added to the dataset anyway with null values or with the default values, if you provided them. That is the default behavior. However, you have two more options if you don't like that, which are as follows:

1. If the data should be present, then the failure of the lookup is considered an error. In that case, you can handle the error. You can, for example, send the rows that cause the failure to a different stream as in this example:

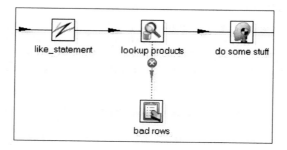

 Remember that you can capture errors by right-clicking on the **Database lookup** step, selecting the **Define error handling...** option and configuring the **Step error handling settings** window properly. At least, you have to check the **Enable the error handling?** option and select the **Write to log step** as the **Target step**.

If you do this, the rows for which the lookup fails go directly to the stream that captures the error, in this case, the **Write to log** step.

2. If the rows are useless without the fields that you are looking for, then you can discard them. You do that by checking the **Do not pass the row if the lookup fails** option. This way, only the rows for which the lookup succeeds will pass to the next step.

Taking some action when there are too many results

The *Database lookup* step is meant to retrieve just one row of the table for each row in your dataset. If the search finds more than one row, the following two things may happen:

1. If you check the **Fail on multiple results?** option, the rows for which the lookup retrieves more than one row will cause the step to fail. In that case, in the **Logging** tab window, you will see an error similar to the following:

   ```
   ... - Database lookup (fail on multiple res.).0 - ERROR... Because
   of an error, this step can't continue:
   ... - Database lookup (fail on multiple res.).0 - ERROR... :
   Only 1 row was expected as a result of a lookup, and at least 2
   were found!
   ```

   Then you decide if you leave the transformation or capture the error.

2. If you don't check the **Fail on multiple results?** option, the step will return the first row it encounters. You can decide which one to return by specifying the order. You do that by typing an order clause in the **Order by** textbox. In the `sampledata` database, there are three products that meet the conditions for the `Corvette` row. If, for **Order by**, you type `PRODUCTSCALE DESC`, `PRODUCTNAME`, then you will get `1958 Chevy Corvette Limited Edition`, which is the first product after ordering the three found products by the specified criterion.

If instead of taking some of those actions, you realize that you need all the resulting rows, you should take another approach: replace the *Database lookup* step with a *Database join* or a *Dynamic SQL row* step. For recipes explaining these steps, see the following *See also* section.

Looking for non-existent data

If instead of looking for a row you want to determine if the row doesn't exist, the procedure is much the same. You configure the *Database lookup* step to look for those rows. Then you capture the error, as depicted in the following diagram:

In this case, the stream that you use for capturing the error becomes your main stream. The rows that didn't fail will be discarded and the rows for which the lookup failed go directly to the main stream for further treatment.

See also

- ▶ The recipe named *Looking for values in a database* (*with complex conditions or multiples tables involved*) in this chapter. This recipe explains a more elaborate way of searching for data in a database.

- ▶ The recipe named *Looking for values in a database with extreme flexibility* in this chapter. As implied by its name, this recipe explains how to search for data in a database almost without restrictions.

Looking for values in a database (with complex conditions or multiple tables involved)

In the previous recipe, you saw how to search for columns in a database table based on simple conditions. With Kettle, you can also search by providing complex conditions or involving more than one table. In this recipe, you will learn how to perform that kind of search by using the *Database join* step.

In order to let you compare the different options for searching data in a database with ease, we will work with the same example that you saw in the preceding recipe: the Steel Wheels sample data. You want to look for products that match a given search term and whose prices are below a given value.

Getting ready

In order to follow this recipe, you need the Steel Wheels database.

How to do it...

Carry out the following steps:

1. Create a new transformation.
2. Create a stream that generates a dataset like the one shown in the following screenshot:

# ▲	prod	max_price
1	Aston Martin	90
2	Ford Falcon	70
3	Corvette	70

Rows of step: some conditions (3 rows)

> You can type the data into a file and
> read the file, or use a Data Grid.

3. Add a **Database join** step. You will find it in the **Lookup** category of steps.

4. Double-click on the step. As **Connection**, select (or create if it doesn't exist) the connection to the `sampledata` database.

5. In the SQL frame, type the following statement:

```
SELECT   PRODUCTNAME
       , PRODUCTSCALE
       , BUYPRICE
FROM     PRODUCTS
WHERE    PRODUCTNAME LIKE concat(<%>,?,>%>)
AND      BUYPRICE < ?
```

6. Check the **Outer join?** option.

7. Click on **Get Fields** to fill the grid with two parameters: `prod` and `max_price`.

8. Close the **Database join** configuration window and do a preview on this step. You will see the following screen:

	prod	max_price	PRODUCTNAME	PRODUCTSCALE	BUYPRICE
1	Aston Martin	90	1965 Aston Martin DB5	1:18	66
2	Ford Falcon	70			
3	Corvette	70	1958 Chevy Corvette Limited Edition	1:24	16
4	Corvette	70	2002 Chevy Corvette	1:24	62

Rows of step: Database join (4 rows)

How it works...

The *Database join* step is a powerful step for looking for data in a database based on given conditions. The conditions usually involve comparisons between columns in tables and fields in your stream; therefore it's called a join.

> Note that this is not really a database join. Instead of joining tables in a
> database, you are joining the result of a database query with a Kettle dataset.

The question marks you type in the SQL statement (those in the highlighted lines in the recipe) represent parameters. The purpose of these parameters is to be replaced with the fields you provide in the lower grid. For each row in your stream the **Database join** step replaces the parameters in the same order as they are in the grid, and executes the SQL statement.

If we take as an example the first row in the dataset, the SQL statement after the replacement of the parameters would look like this:

```
SELECT  PRODUCTNAME
     ,  PRODUCTSCALE
     ,  BUYPRICE
FROM    PRODUCTS
WHERE   PRODUCTNAME LIKE concat('%','Aston Martin','%')
AND     BUYPRICE < 90
```

And that's exactly the search you wanted to do for that row: look for the records where the column BUYPRICE was less than 90 and the column PRODUCTNAME contained Aston Martin.

As the result of the database join you can retrieve any number of columns. Each database column that you type in the SELECT clause will become a new field in your dataset. In the recipe, those fields were PRODUCTNAME, PRODUCTSCALE, and BUYPRICE. In particular, if you had typed SELECT *, you would have retrieved all columns in the tables involved in the statement.

In the recipe, you checked the **Outer join?** option. The effect of this is as follows: For the rows where the lookup fails, the new fields are retrieved with null values. That was the case for the second row. There were no products with Ford Falcon as part of its description and price lower than 70. Therefore, that row shows empty values for the PRODUCTNAME, PRODUCTSCALE, and BUYPRICE fields.

Note that in the recipe, you filled the grid with two fields. That is exactly the same number of question marks in the statement.

> The number of fields in the grid must be exactly the same as the number of question marks in the query.

Also, note that in the grid the prod field was in the first place and the max_price in the second place. If you look at the highlighted lines in the recipe, you will see that the statement expected the parameters in exactly that order.

> The replacement of the markers respects the order of the fields in the grid.

So far, the results are quite similar to those you got with a database lookup. There is a significant difference however. For the third row, the Corvette product, you can see two results. This means that the *Database join* found two matching rows in the database, and retrieved them both. This is not possible with a *Database lookup* step.

There's more...

The *Database join* step can be a little complicated to use or to understand compared to the *Database lookup* step. While the *Database lookup* step has a UI that makes the configuration of the step easy, in the *Database join* step, you have to write an SQL statement. That implies that you need a good knowledge of SQL. However, the *Database join* step has several advantages over the *Database lookup* one:

▶ It allows you to look up from a combination of tables.

▶ It allows you to retrieve fields from more than one table at a time.

▶ It allows you to retrieve aggregate results, fragments of a field (for example, a substring of a field), or a combination of fields (for example, two strings concatenated).

▶ It allows you to retrieve more than one row from the database for each incoming row in the Kettle dataset. This is by far the most important advantage! By default, all matching rows are retrieved. If you want to limit the number of rows to retrieve for each row in your stream, just change the **Number of rows to return** value.

See also

▶ The recipe named *Looking for values in a database table* in this chapter. This recipe shows the simplest way of looking for values in a database.

▶ The recipe named *Looking for values in a database with extreme flexibility* in this chapter. This recipe shows the most flexible way of searching for data in a database.

Looking for values in a database with extreme flexibility

The *Database join* step that you learned to use in the previous recipe is quite powerful and has several advantages over the simple *Database lookup* step. There is a still more powerful step for searching in a database: The *Dynamic SQL row* step. This recipe explains to you its capabilities and shows you how to use it.

In order to let you compare the different options for searching in a database with ease, we will work with an example similar to that you saw in the previous two recipes: we will work with the Steel Wheels sample data. You want to look for the following products:

▶ Products that contain `Aston Martin` in their description

▶ Products that contain `Ford Falcon` in their name and with scale `1:18`

▶ Products that contain `Corvette` in their name and with scale `1:24`

Getting ready

In order to follow this recipe, you need the Steel Wheels database.

How to do it...

Carry out the following steps:

1. Create a new transformation.

2. Create a stream that generates a dataset like the one shown in the following screenshot:

```
Rows of step: some conditions (3 rows)
```

# ▲	prod	column_name	cond
1	Aston Martin	PRODUCTDESCRIPTION	
2	Ford Falcon	PRODUCTNAME	PRODUCTSCALE="1:18"
3	Corvette	PRODUCTNAME	PRODUCTSCALE="1:24"

 You can type the data into a file and read the file, or use a Data Grid.

3. At the end of your stream, add a **User Defined Java Expression** step.

4. Use that step to add a **String** named `statement`. As **Java expression**, type
`"SELECT PRODUCTNAME, PRODUCTSCALE, BUYPRICE FROM PRODUCTS WHERE PRODUCTNAME LIKE '%"+prod+"%'"+(cond!=null?" AND "+cond:"")`.

5. Do a preview on this step. You will see a new column named `statement` with a complete SQL statement, for example:
```
SELECT PRODUCTNAME, PRODUCTSCALE, BUYPRICE FROM PRODUCTS WHERE
PRODUCTDESCRIPTION LIKE '%Aston Martin%'
```

6. Add a **Dynamic SQL row** step. You will find it in the **Lookup** category of steps.

7. Double-click on the step. As **Connection**, select (or create if it doesn't exist) the connection to the `sampledata` database.

8. As SQL field name, type or select `statement`.

9. Check the **Outer join?** option.

10. In the **Template SQL (to retrieve Meta data)** frame, type the following:
```
SELECT 'NAME', 'SCALE', 1 as BUYPRICE
```

11. Close the **Dynamic SQL row** configuration window and do a preview on this step. You will see the following screen (note that the `statement` field is hidden):

	prod	column_name	cond	NAME	SCALE	BUYPRICE
1	Aston Martin	PRODUCTDESCRI...		1965 Aston Martin DB5	1:18	66
2	Ford Falcon	PRODUCTNAME	PRODUCTSCALE='1:18'			
3	Corvette	PRODUCTNAME	PRODUCTSCALE='1:24'	1958 Chevy Corvette Limited...	1:24	16
4	Corvette	PRODUCTNAME	PRODUCTSCALE='1:24'	2002 Chevy Corvette	1:24	62

Rows of step: Dynamic SQL row (4 rows)

How it works...

The *Dynamic SQL row* step is a very powerful step for looking for data in a database.

If we take, for example, the first row in the dataset, the SQL statement (the one that you build with the Java expression) is similar to the following:

```
SELECT PRODUCTNAME, PRODUCTSCALE, BUYPRICE FROM PRODUCTS WHERE
PRODUCTDESCRIPTION LIKE '%Aston Martin%'
```

That's exactly the search you wanted to perform for that row: look for the records where the column `PRODUCTDESCRIPTION` contained `Aston Martin`.

Now look at the following SQL statement for the last row:

```
SELECT PRODUCTNAME, PRODUCTSCALE, BUYPRICE FROM PRODUCTS WHERE
PRODUCTNAME LIKE '%Corvette%' AND PRODUCTSCALE="1:24"
```

In this case, you are filtering both by the name and by the scale.

As you see, what you are doing is dynamically creating an SQL statement. Then, in the **Dynamic SQL row** configuration window, you just use the **SQL field name** to indicate which field contains the SQL statement to execute.

As the output of the **Dynamic SQL row** step, you can retrieve any number of columns. Each database column in the `SELECT` statement will become a new field in your dataset.

In order to tell Kettle the metadata of the new fields being added with this dynamic statement, you must fill in the **Template SQL (to retrieve Meta data)** frame. Here, you have to type any statement that returns the same structure as the new fields. Kettle will take from here both the names and the types for the new fields.

In the recipe, you typed `SELECT 'NAME', 'SCALE', 1 as BUYPRICE`. With this statement, you are telling Kettle that you are adding three fields: two strings named `NAME` and `SCALE` and an integer field named `BUYPRICE`.

 Both the statement and this template are written using MySQL syntax. It's mandatory that you restate them to match the syntax of the database engine you are using.

In the recipe, you checked the **Outer join?** option. The effect of this is the same as in the *Database join* step: for the rows where the lookup fails the new fields are retrieved with null values. That was the case for the second row. There were no products with `Ford Falcon` as part of its name and scale `1:18`. Therefore, that row shows empty values for the `PRODUCTNAME`, `PRODUCTSCALE`, and `BUYPRICE` fields.

For the third row, the `Corvette` product, you can see two results. This means that the *Dynamic SQL row* found two matching rows in the database and retrieved them both. This also resembles the behavior of the *Database join* step.

Finally, note that in the recipe, the statement was different for each row. It may happen however, that your statements do not change a lot. If this is the case, you can reduce the number of physical database queries by checking the **Query only on parameters change** option.

There's more...

The *Dynamic SQL row* step is the most flexible step for looking up data in a database. As you saw, there are a couple of similarities between this and the *Database join* step. What really makes a difference between them is that with the *Dynamic SQL row* step, any part of the statement can be built dynamically based on the fields in your stream. For example, the columns used for comparison in the recipe were the product description in the first row and the product name in the others. What you did in the recipe is not possible to achieve by using the *Database join*, at least in a simple fashion.

Note that you could also have had the statement already built, for example, in a property file or saved in a column in a database table. In that case, you also could have used the *Dynamic SQL row* step to execute the statement and that is definitely impossible to do with any other step.

See also

The recipe named *Looking for values in a database (with complex conditions or multiples tables involved)* in this chapter. Look at this recipe for understanding how to look in a database by using the *Database join* step.

Looking for values in a variety of sources

The first recipes in the chapter showed you how to look for additional information in a database. There are still many other sources of information. You may need to look in property files, in Excel files, in text files, and so on. Kettle allows you to look for data coming from all those sources with the *Stream lookup* step.

In this example, you have information about books coming from an Excel file and you need to complete this dataset by looking up the author's data and genre description, which are in external sources. In this case, the author's information is inside a text file and the genres are in a fixed predefined list.

Getting ready

For doing this recipe, you will need the following:

▸ A CSV file (`authors.txt`) with the author's data. The file should have the following columns: `lastname`, `firstname`, `nationality`, and `id_author`. The following are sample lines of this file:

```
"lastname","firstname","nationality","id_author"
"Larsson","Stieg","Swedish","A00001"
"King","Stephen","American","A00002"
"Hiaasen","Carl ","American","A00003"
"Handler","Chelsea ","American","A00004"
"Ingraham","Laura ","American","A00005"
```

▸ An Excel file with the book's information (`books.xls`). The sheet should have the following columns: `title`, `id_author`, `price`, `id_title`, and `id_genre` as shown in the following screenshot:

	A	B	C	D	E
1	title	id_author	price	id_title	id_genre
2	Carrie	A00002	41	123-346	F
3	Salem's Lot	A00002	33	123-347	F
4	The Shining	A00002	31	123-348	F
5	The Dead Zone	A00002	37	123-349	F
6	Pet Sematary	A00002	41	123-351	F
7	The Tommyknockers	A00002	39	123-352	F
8	Bag of Bones	A00002	40,9	123-353	F
9	The Girl with the Dragon Tatoo	A00001	35	123-400	F
10	The Girl who Played with Fire	A00001	35,9	123-401	F

Books

You can also download sample files from the book's website.

How to do it...

Carry out the following steps:

1. Create a new transformation.

2. Drop an **Excel input** step and a **Text file input** step into the canvas.

3. In the **Excel input** step, browse for the `books.xls` file under the **File** tab and click on the **Add** button. Populate the grid under the **Fields** tab by clicking on the **Get fields from header row** button.

4. In the **Text file** input step, browse for the `authors.txt` file and click on the **Add** button. Type , as the **Separator** under the **Content** tab and finally, populate the **Fields** tab grid by clicking on the **Get Fields** button.

5. Add a **Stream lookup** step from the **Lookup** category.

6. Create a hop from the **Excel input** step to the **Stream lookup** step and another from the **Text file input** also to the **Stream lookup** step.

7. Double-click on the **Stream lookup** step and in the **Lookup step** listbox select the name of the **Text file input** step previously created.

8. Complete the grids with the following information:

The key(s) to look up the value(s):

#. ▲	Field	LookupField	
1	id_author	id	

Specify the fields to retrieve :

#. ▲	Field	New name	Default	Type
1	firstname			String
2	lastname			String
3	nationality			String

> To save time, you can click on the **Get Fields** button to automatically load the fields in the upper grid, and the **Get lookup fields** button to populate the lower grid.

9. Previewing this step, you can verify that the dataset includes, for each book, the information for its author. Now, let's add the genre description.

10. Drop a **Data Grid** step from the **Input** category. Under its **Meta** tab, add two String items: id_genre and genre. Then, complete the **Data** tab as shown in the following screenshot:

Meta | Data

#	id_genre	genre
1	F	Fiction
2	NF	Non-fiction
3	B	Business
4	C	Children

11. Add a new **Stream lookup** step and create a hop from the **Data grid** step toward this new step.

12. Also, create a hop between both **Stream Lookups** steps. The transformation should look like the one shown in the following diagram:

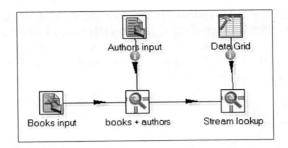

13. Double-click on the last **Stream lookup** step. In the **Lookup step** listbox, type or select the name of the **Data grid** step created earlier.

14. In the upper grid, add a row typing `id_genre` under the **Field** column and id under **LookupField**.

15. In the lower grid, add a genre **Field**, of String **Type**. Add Unknown as the **Default** value.

16. Doing a preview of this step, you will obtain a dataset of the books, their authors, and also the description of their genres. For example:

Rows of step: Adding genre (34 rows)

	title	id ...	price	i...	id_genre	firstname	lastname	nati...	genre
11	Star Island	A0...	36,0	1...	F	Carl	Hiaasen	Am...	Fiction
12	Basket Case	A0...	31,0	1...	F	Carl	Hiaasen	Am...	Fiction
13	Chelsea Chelsea Bang ...	A0...	25,0	2...	NF	Chelsea	Handler	Am...	Non-fiction
14	My Horizontal Life	A0...	24,0	2...	BG	Chelsea	Handler	Am...	Unknown
15	Are You There, Vodka?...	A0...	19,9	2...	NF	Chelsea	Handler	Am...	Non-fiction
16	The Obama Diaries	A0...	28,9	2...	NF	Laura	Ingraham	Am...	Non-fiction
17	Power to the People	A0...	33,0	2...	NF	Laura	Ingraham	Am...	Non-fiction
18	Rich Dad, Poor Dad	A0...	19,9	3...	B	Robert	Kiyosaki	Am...	Business

How it works...

The *Stream Lookup* step is the step that you should use to look for additional information in other sources. In this recipe, the main data comes from an Excel file with book titles and also, the identification for their author and genres. You used two *Stream Lookup* steps to look up for each title, the author's information, and the genre description respectively.

In the first *Stream Lookup* step the purpose is to look for the author's data; in this step, you configure the **Lookup step** listbox pointing to the **Text file input** step, which is where the author's data is coming from.

In the upper grid named **The key(s) to lookup the values(s)**, you have to specify the fields used to join both data sources. In this case, those fields are id_author and id.

The second grid titled **Specify the fields to retrieve** is to declare the fields to add to the main dataset. You have typed the fields: firstname, lastname, and nationality.

The last *Stream Lookup* step was created in order to retrieve the genre description that matches the genre identification in the main dataset. Here the key values are the fields `id_ genre` and `id` and the only data to retrieve is the field `genre`. Here you entered `Unknown` as the **Default** value. This means that if the **Stream Lookup** step doesn't find a matching genre for a row the genre description will be set to `Unknown`.

There's more...

The following sections provide you with some alternatives to the use of the *Stream Lookup* step.

Looking for alternatives when the Stream Lookup step doesn't meet your needs

The *Stream Lookup* step compares the fields with an equal operator. There are a couple of situations where this may not be what you need.

If you are not sure about the similarity of the values between the fields that you are comparing, a comparison by equal may fail. In that case, you could use the *Fuzzy match* step, which allows you to search for similar values.

If you need to compare using other operators, for example `<=`, then you should also look for an alternative step. One possible approach would be to use the *Join Rows (Cartesian product)* to retrieve all the data and filter the rows from that step with a *Filter rows* or a *Java Filter* step afterward.

 Keep in mind that this option might increase the number of records you are processing, slowing down your ETL process significantly.

Another option would be to transfer the source data to a database table and then lookup in the database. This approach takes a little more effort, but it has its advantages. You have more flexible ways for looking up data in a database compared with looking up in a stream. Besides, for big datasets, you can also gain performance as explained in the next subsection.

Speeding up your transformation

For big datasets, looking up in plain files with a *Stream Lookup* step will definitely slow down your transformation. As a workaround to speed things up, you should consider moving the data to a database table before looking up in it. The main advantage of this approach is that you can cache data, which makes the lookup task faster.

What if your ETL project doesn't involve database tasks? For these temporary lookup tables, you may want to use an in-memory database such as **HSQLDB** or **H2**.

For a practical example of this, take a look at the following blog post by Slawomir Chodnicki:

```
http://type-exit.org/adventures-with-open-source-bi/2011/01/using-an-
on-demand-in-memory-sql-database-in-pdi/
```

Using the Value Mapper step for looking up from a short list of values

The second *Stream Lookup* step in the recipe only returns a simple description and has a short list of possible values. In these cases, you can replace this step with a **Value Mapper** from the **Transform** category.

You should complete the step, as shown in the following screenshot:

Fieldname to use :	id_genre	
Target field name	genre	
Default upon non-matching	Unknown	

Field values:

#. ▲	Source value	Target value	
1	F	Fiction	
2	NF	Non-fiction	
3	B	Business	
4	C	Children	

In the **Source value** column, you define the possible values for the `id_genre` field, and in the **Target value** column, you define their descriptions. Also, in the **Default upon non-matching** textbox, you can enter a default value to be returned for the rows with invalid genre identification.

See also

- ▶ The recipe named *Looking up values by proximity* in this chapter for learning how to look for similar values.
- ▶ The recipe named *Generating all possible pairs formed from two datasets* from *Chapter 6, Understanding Flows of Data*. See this for understanding how to use the *Join Rows (Cartesian product)* step mentioned in the *There's more* section.

Looking for values by proximity

This chapter is about looking for values in different sources based on given conditions. Those conditions are comparison between fields in your stream and fields in the source that you are looking into. As you know or could see in the rest of the recipes, you usually compare by equality and sometimes you do it by using different operators such as LIKE, NOT EQUAL, <, and so on. What if you need to look for a value that is "more or less" equal to a field in your stream? None of the options you saw in the other recipes will give you the solution to this problem. In these situations, you need to perform a fuzzy search, that is, a search that looks for similar values. Kettle allows you to perform such a search by providing you the *Fuzzy match* step. In this recipe, you will learn how to use this step.

Suppose that you receive an external text file with book orders and you need to find the prices for these books. The problem is that you don't have the identification for that book, you only have the title and you are not sure if the spelling is correct.

Getting ready

You must have a books database with the structure shown in the *Appendix, Data Structures*.

The recipe uses a file named `booksOrder.txt` with the following book titles, which deliberately include some typos:

```
Carry
Slem's Lot
TheShining
The Ded sone
Pet Cemetary
The Tomyknockers
Bag of Bones
Star Island
Harry Potter
```

How to do it...

Carry out the following steps:

1. Create a new transformation.
2. Drop a **Text file input** step into the work area, in order to retrieve the book order.
3. In the **File or directory** textbox under the **File** tab, browse to the `booksOrder.txt` file and then click on the **Add** button.
4. Under the **Content** tab, uncheck the **Header** checkbox.
5. Under the **Fields** tab, add a new `String` field named `TitleApprox`.
6. Drop another step in order to read the books database. Use a **Table input** step and type the following SQL statement:

```
SELECT title
     , price
FROM Books
```

7. Add a **Fuzzy match** step from **Lookup** category. Add a hop from the **Table input** step toward this step. Add another hop from the **Text file input** step created before also toward the **Fuzzy match** step.
8. Double-click on the **Fuzzy match** step. Under the **General** tab, go to the **Lookup stream (source)** frame and as **Lookup step**, select the **Table input** step created before. In the **Lookup field**, select **title**.
9. In the **Main stream field**, select the **TitleApprox** field.

10. Now, you must select the fuzzy match algorithm to be used. In this case, you will use `Levenshtein`. Select it from the **Algorithm** drop-down list. Set the **minimal value** to 0 and the **Maximal value** to 3. Also, uncheck the **Case sensitive** checkbox.

11. Select the **Fields** tab and type `match` in the **Match field** and `measure_value` in **Value field**.

12. Under the same tab, add the `price` field to the grid.

13. After this, the transformation should look like the one shown in the following diagram:

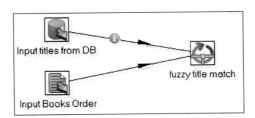

14. If you select the **Fuzzy match** step and preview the transformation, the result will be the following:

#. ▲	TitleApprox	match	measure_value	price
1	Carry	Carrie	3	41
2	Slem's Lot	Salem's Lot	2	33
3	TheShining	The Shining	2	31
4	The Ded sone	The Dead Zone	2	37
5	Pet Cemetary	Pet Sematary	2	41
6	The Tomyknockers	The Tommyknockers	1	39
7	Bag of Bones	Bag of Bones	0	40,9
8	Star Island	Star Island	0	36
9	Harry Potter			

How it works...

The *Fuzzy match* step is used to look in another stream for values that are similar to the value of a field in your stream. For each row in your dataset, a comparison is made between the main stream field (`TitleApprox` in this case) and each lookup field in the secondary stream (`title`). In other words, for each book in the list a comparison is made between the provided title and the real titles coming from the database.

The comparison consists of applying a given fuzzy match algorithm. A **fuzzy match algorithm** compares two strings and calculates a similarity index. The row with the lowest index is returned, as long as it is between the **Minimum value** and the **Maximum value**.

In this recipe, you used the `Levenshtein` match algorithm that calculates a metric distance. The similarity index for this algorithm represents the number of edits needed to transform one field into the other. These edits can be character insertion, deletion, or substitution of a single character.

As minimum and maximum values, you specified 0 (meaning that the exact title was found) and 3 (meaning that you will accept as valid a title with a maximum of three edits).

For example, when you preview the result of this step, you can see a title named `The Ded sone` which matches the real title `The Dead Zone` with a distance of 2. For the `Star Island` title the distance is 0 because the spelling was correct and a book with exactly the same title was found. Finally, for the `Harry Potter` row, there are no matching rows because you need too many editions to transform the provided title into one of the Harry Potter titles in the database.

There's more...

The *Fuzzy match* step allows you to choose among several matching algorithms, which are classified in the following two groups:

▸ Algorithms based on a metric distance: The comparison is based on how the compared terms are spelled.

▸ Phonetic algorithms: The comparison is based on how the compared terms sound, as read in English.

Let's see a brief comparative table for the implemented algorithms:

Algorithm	Classification	Explanation
Levenshtein	Metric distance	The distance is calculated as the minimum edit distance that transforms one string into the other. These edits can be character insertion or deletion or substitution of a single character.
Damerau-Levenshtein	Metric distance	Similar to Levenshtein, but adds the transposition operation.
Needleman-Wunsch	Metric distance	A variant of the Levenshtein algorithm. It adds a gap cost, which is a penalty for the insertions and deletions.
Jaro	Metric distance	Based on typical spelling deviations. The index goes from 0 to 1, with 0 as no similarity and 1 as the identical value.
Jaro-Winkler	Metric distance	A variant of the Jaro algorithm, appropriate for short strings such as names.
Pair letters Similarity	Metric distance	The strings are divided into pairs, and then the algorithm calculates an index based on the comparison of the lists of pairs of both strings.
SoundEx	Phonetic	It consists of indexing terms by sound. It only encodes consonants. Each term is given a Soundex code, each soundex code consists of a letter and three numbers. Similar sounding consonants share the same digit (for example, b, f, p, v are equal to 1).
Refined SoundEx	Phonetic	A variant of the SoundEx algorithm optimized for spell checking.

Algorithm	Classification	Explanation
Metaphone	Phonetic	The algorithm is similar to SoundEx algorithm, but produces variable length keys. Similar sounding words share the same keys.
Double Metaphone	Phonetic	An extension of the Metaphone algorithm where a primary and a secondary code are returned for a string.

The decision of which algorithm to choose depends on your problem and the kind of data you have or you expect to receive. You can even combine a fuzzy search with a regular search. For example, in the recipe, you didn't find a match for the `Harry Potter` row. Note that increasing the maximum value wouldn't have found the proper title. Try raising the maximum value to `10`, and you will see that the algorithm brings `Carrie` as the result, which clearly has nothing to do with the wizard. However, if you look for this value with a *Database join* step by comparing with the `LIKE` operator, you could retrieve not just one, but all the Harry Potter titles.

Further details on the individual similarity metrics can be found at the following URL:

`http://en.wikipedia.org/wiki/String_metrics`

You can also read more about them at the following URL:

`http://www.dcs.shef.ac.uk/~sam/simmetrics.html`

This documentation belongs to **SimMetrics**, an open source Java library of similarity metrics.

Looking for values consuming a web service

Web services are interfaces that are accessed through HTTP and executed on a remote hosting system. They use XML messages that follow the **SOAP** standard.

With Kettle, you can look for values in available web services by using the *Web service lookup* step. In this recipe, you will see an example that shows the use of this step.

Suppose that you have a dataset of museums and you want to know about their opening and closing hours. That information is available as an external web service.

The web service has a web method named `GetMuseumHour` that receives the `id_museum` as a parameter, and returns the museum schedule as a `String`. The request and response elements for the `GetMuseumHour` web method used in this recipe look like the following:

▶ Request:
```
<soap:Envelope xmlns:xsi="http://www.w3.org/2001/XMLSchema-
instance" xmlns:xsd="http://www.w3.org/2001/XMLSchema"
xmlns:soap="http://schemas.xmlsoap.org/soap/envelope/">
  <soap:Body>
    <GetMuseumHour xmlns="http://tempuri.org/">
```

```
        <idMuseum>int</idMuseum>
      </GetMuseumHour>
    </soap:Body>
  </soap:Envelope>
```

▶ Response:

```
<soap:Envelope xmlns:xsi="http://www.w3.org/2001/XMLSchema-
instance" xmlns:xsd="http://www.w3.org/2001/XMLSchema"
xmlns:soap="http://schemas.xmlsoap.org/soap/envelope/">
  <soap:Body>
    <GetMuseumHourResponse xmlns="http://tempuri.org/">
      <GetMuseumHourResult>string</GetMuseumHourResult>
    </GetMuseumHourResponse>
  </soap:Body>
</soap:Envelope>
```

Getting ready

You must have a database with the museum structure shown in the *Appendix, Data Structures* and access to a web service similar to the one detailed earlier. On the book's website, there is sample code for those services.

How to do it...

Carry out the following steps:

1. Create a new transformation.

2. Drop a **Table input** step into the work area in order to obtain the data with the list of museums. Type the following SQL statement:

```
SELECT id_museum
     , name
     , city
     , country
FROM museums
JOIN cities
ON museums.id_city=cities.id_city
```

3. Add a **Web service lookup** step from the **Lookup** category.

4. Double-click on the step. In the **Web Services** tab, type the URL address for the web service. It is important to point to the WSDL declaration path, for example: `http://localhost/museumHours/Service.asmx?wsdl`.

5. Click on the **Load** button in order to refresh the web methods for the **Operation** prompt.

6. In the **Operation** listbox, select the web method named `GetMuseumHour`. This

generates the necessary inputs and outputs tabs; you can also generate them by clicking on the **Add Input** and **Add Output** buttons.

 Additionally, you can also include authentication credentials for the web service and proxy information, if needed.

7. Select the **In** tab. Click on the **Get Fields** button and you will obtain the parameter name and type for the web service. Type `id_museum` in the **Name** column.

8. Under the output tab named **GetMuseumHourResult**, you must set the field where the result will be written. Clicking on the **Get Fields** button will obtain the return value name. Change the **Name** column to `Hours`.

9. You could execute the transformation now and examine the results. A better approach would be to check the availability of the web service before execution. So, create a new job and add a **Start** entry.

10. Add a **Check webservice availability** job entry from **Conditions** category.

11. Double-click on the step. Set the **URL** textbox to the WSDL address, in this case `http://localhost/museumsHours/Service.asmx?wsdl`.

12. After that entry, add a **Transformation** entry to run the transformation created earlier. Make sure that the transformation runs only if the previous entry succeeds. That is, right-click on the hop and check the **Follow when result is true** evaluation option.

13. Running the job will return a result like the one shown in the following screenshot:

id_museum	name	city	country	Hours
1	Fundacion Federico Klemm	Buenos Aires	Argentina	09:30 am - 5:30 pm
2	Fundacion Proa	Buenos Aires	Argentina	08:15 am - 5:45 pm
3	Museo de Arte Latinoamericano	Buenos Aires	Argentina	10:00 am - 6:30 pm
4	Museo Nacional de Bellas Artes	Buenos Aires	Argentina	09:00 am - 5:30 pm
5	Xul Solar Museum	Buenos Aires	Argentina	09:30 am - 5:30 pm
6	Museu de Arte Contemporane...	Niteroi	Brazil	09:30 am - 5:30 pm
7	Museu de Arte Contemporane...	Parana	Brazil	09:00 am - 6:00 pm
8	Museu de Arte Moderna	Rio de Janeiro	Brazil	09:00 am - 6:30 pm
9	Museu Nacional de Belas Artes	Rio de Janeiro	Brazil	09:00 am - 6:30 pm
10	Carlos Costa Pinto Museum	Salvador	Brazil	09:00 am - 6:30 pm
11	Itau Cultural	Sao Paulo	Brazil	09:00 am - 6:30 pm
12	Lasar Segall Museum	Sao Paulo	Brazil	09:00 am - 6:30 pm

How it works...

The objective in the example is to look for a value that is hosted on a web server. You do it by consuming a web service.

Note that the URL of the web service in the **Web service lookup** step points to a WSDL address. **WSDL (Web Services Description Language)** is an XML-based language used to describe web services.

When you click on the **Load** button in the **Web service lookup** step, the information retrieved from the WSDL contract is interpreted and used to fill the **Operation** combo with the web methods found in the web service. When you choose a method, it automatically sets the necessary values for the input and the output. You only need to write the local values that will be passed as parameters (**In** tab), and the value for the result (**GetMuseumHourResult** tab).

 If the tabs for the input and output are not created automatically, you can write the specifications manually, by clicking on the **Add Input** and **Add Output** buttons.

For each museum row, there will be a request to the web service passing the id_museum parameter declared in the **In** tab. The result containing the museum opening hours will be saved in the Hours field declared under the **GetMuseumHourResult** tab.

There's more...

There is also a step named **Check if webservice is available** from the **Lookup** category. You can use it to verify that the web service is available just before consuming it. In this step, you must have the URL address as a field in each row.

In some cases, the web server could be flooded due to the multiple simultaneous requests and it could return an error similar to: Too many users are connected.

In these cases, you can check the configuration of the web server. Alternatively, you can rerun the transformation consuming the web service by groups of rows, forcing a delay to avoid the web server saturation.

For more information about web services, you can follow this link:

http://en.wikipedia.org/wiki/Web_service

More information about WSDL can be obtained from the following URL:

http://www.w3.org/TR/wsdl

See also

The recipe named *Looking for values over an intranet or Internet* in this chapter. Check this recipe if the remote information is on a website instead of being provided as a web service.

Looking for values over an intranet or Internet

This example is similar to the previous one, with the difference being that you have to lookup the museum opening hours on a website instead of a web server. In this case, you will use the *HTTP Client* step.

Getting ready

You must have a database with the museum structure shown in the *Appendix, Data Structures* and a web page that provides the museum opening hours. The recipe uses an ASP page named `hours.asp`, but you can use the language of your preference. The page receives the museum's identification and returns a string with the schedule. You can download a sample web page from the book's website.

How to do it...

Carry out the following steps:

1. Create a new transformation.

2. Drop a **Table input** step into the canvas, in order to obtain the museum's information. Use the following SQL statement:

    ```
    SELECT id_museum
         , name
         , city
         , country
    FROM museums
    JOIN cities
    ON museums.id_city=cities.id_city
    ```

3. Add a **HTTP Client** step from the **Lookup** category.

4. Double-click on the step. In the **URL** field under the **General** tab, type the http web address of the webpage that provides the opening hours. For example: `http://localhost/museum/hours.asp`.

5. Set the **Result fieldname** textbox to `Hours`.

6. In the **HTTP status code fieldname**, type `status`.

 Under the **General** tab, you can include authentication credentials for the web service and proxy information, if it is needed.

7. Under the **Fields** tab, set the parameter that will be sent to the page as a GET parameter. Type `id_museum` in both in the **Name** and **Parameter** columns.

8. The result for the transformation will be the same as the one obtained in the previous recipe.

9. Take a look at that recipe for a preview of the final results.

How it works...

The *HTTP Client* step looks for the museums' opening hours over the intranet; the step does a request to the web page for each museum in the dataset. One example of this request passing the parameter would be the following:

```
http://localhost/museum/hours.asp?id_museum=25
```

Then, the response of the page containing the museum opening hours will set the `Hours` field.

The `status` field will hold the status code of the operation. For example, a status code equal to `200` means a successful request, whereas a status code `400` is a bad request. You can check the different status codes at the following URL:

```
http://en.wikipedia.org/wiki/List_of_HTTP_status_codes.
```

There's more...

Suppose that each museum has a different website (and different URL address) with a web page that provides its opening hours. In this case, you can store this specific URL as a new field in the museum dataset. Then in the **HTTP Client** step check the **Accept URL from field?** checkbox and select that field from the **URL field name** drop-down list.

 One alternative to this step is the *HTTP Post Lookup* step. Using this step, you connect to the website and pass the parameters through a POST method instead of a GET method.

See also

For an example using the *HTTP Client* step to get data from an Internet service take a look at the sample transformation in the Introduction of *Chapter 8, Integrating Kettle and the Pentaho Suite*.

6
Understanding Data Flows

In this chapter, we will cover:

- ► Splitting a stream into two or more streams based on a condition
- ► Merging rows from two streams with the same or different structure
- ► Comparing two streams and generating differences
- ► Generating all possible pairs formed from two datasets
- ► Joining two streams based on conditions
- ► Interspersing new rows in between existent rows
- ► Executing steps even when your stream is empty
- ► Processing rows differently based on the row number

Introduction

The main purpose of Kettle transformations is to manipulate data in the form of a dataset; this task is done by the steps of the transformation.

When a transformation is launched, all its steps are started. During the execution, the steps work simultaneously reading rows from the incoming hops, processing them, and delivering them to the outgoing hops. When there are no more rows left, the execution of the transformation ends.

The dataset that flows from step to step is not more than a set of rows all having the same structure or metadata. This means that all rows have the same number of columns, and the columns in all rows have the same type and name.

Suppose that you have a single stream of data and that you apply the same transformations to all rows, that is, you have all steps connected in a row one after the other. In other words, you have the simplest of the transformations from the point of view of its structure. In this case, you don't have to worry much about the structure of your data stream, nor the origin or destination of the rows. The interesting part comes when you face other situations, for example:

- You want a step to start processing rows only after another given step has processed all rows
- You have more than one stream and you have to combine them into a single stream
- You have to inject rows in the middle of your stream and those rows don't have the same structure as the rows in your dataset

With Kettle, you can actually do this, but you have to be careful because it's easy to end up doing wrong things and getting unexpected results or even worse: undesirable errors.

With regard to the first example, it doesn't represent a default behavior due to the parallel nature of the transformations as explained earlier. There are two steps however, that might help, which are as follows:

- **Blocking Step**: This step blocks processing until all incoming rows have been processed.
- **Block this step until steps finish**: This step blocks processing until the selected steps finish.

Both these steps are in the **Flow** category.

You will find examples of the use of the last of these steps in the following recipes:

- *Writing an Excel file with several sheets (Chapter 2, Reading and Writing Files)*
- *Generating a custom log file (Chapter 9, Getting the Most Out of Kettle)*

This chapter focuses on the other two examples and some similar use cases, by explaining the different ways for combining, splitting, or manipulating streams of data.

Splitting a stream into two or more streams based on a condition

In this recipe, you will learn to use the *Filter rows* step in order to split a single stream into different smaller streams. In the *There's more section*, you will also see alternative and more efficient ways for doing the same thing in different scenarios.

Let's assume that you have a set of outdoor products in a text file, and you want to differentiate the tents from other kind of products, and also create a subclassification of the tents depending on their prices.

Let's see a sample of this data:

```
id_product,desc_product,price,category
1,"Swedish Firesteel - Army Model",19,"kitchen"
2,"Mountain House #10 Can Freeze-Dried Food",53,"kitchen"
3,"Lodge Logic L90G3 Pre-Seasoned 10-1/2-Inch Round
Griddle",14,"kitchen"
. . .
```

Getting ready

To run this recipe, you will need a text file named `outdoorProducts.txt` with information about outdoor products. The file contains information about the category and price of each product.

How to do it...

Carry out the following steps:

1. Create a transformation.

2. Drag into the canvas a **Text file input** step and fill in the **File** tab to read the file named `outdoorProducts.txt`. If you are using the sample text file, type `,` as the **Separator**.

3. Under the **Fields** tab, use the **Get Fields** button to populate the grid. Adjust the entries so that the grid looks like the one shown in the following screenshot:

#. ▲	Name	Type	Format
1	id_product	Integer	#
2	desc_product	String	
3	price	Integer	0.00
4	category	String	

4. Now, let's add the steps to manage the flow of the rows. To do this, drag two **Filter rows** steps from the **Flow** category. Also, drag three **Dummy** steps that will represent the three resulting streams.

5. Create the hops, as shown in the following screenshot. When you create the hops, make sure that you choose the options according to the image: **Result is TRUE** for creating a hop with a green icon, and **Result is FALSE** for creating a hop with a red icon in it.

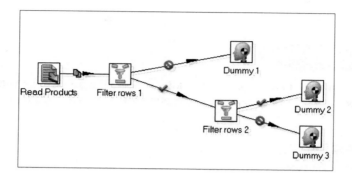

6. Double-click on the first **Filter rows** step and complete the condition, as shown in the following screenshot:

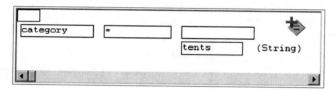

7. Double-click on the second **Filter rows** step and complete the condition with `price < 100`.

8. You have just split the original dataset into three groups. You can verify it by previewing each **Dummy** step. The first one has products whose category is not tents; the second one, the tents under 100 US$; and the last group, the expensive tents; those whose price is over 100 US$.

9. The preview of the last **Dummy** step will show the following:

	id_product	desc_product	price	category
1	47	Coleman Instant 14- by 10- Foot 8- Person ...	183.00	tents
2	49	Eureka Apex 2XT Adventure 7' 5" by 4' 11" ...	104.00	tents
3	52	Coleman WeatherMaster 8 Tent	206.00	tents
4	56	Eureka Solo Backcountry 1 Tent	122.00	tents
5	57	Kelty Grand Mesa 2-Person Tent (Ruby/Tan)	107.00	tents

How it works...

The main objective in the recipe is to split a dataset with products depending on their category and price. To do this, you used the *Filter rows* step.

In the **Filter rows** setting window, you tell Kettle where the data flows to depending on the result of evaluating a condition for each row. In order to do that, you have two list boxes: **Send 'true' data to step** and **Send 'false' data to step**. The destination steps can be set by using the hop properties as you did in the recipe. Alternatively, you can set them in the **Filter rows** setting dialog by selecting the name of the destination steps from the available drop-down lists.

You also have to enter the condition. The condition has the following different parts:

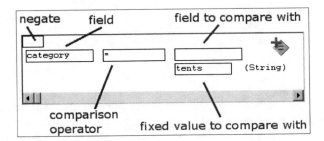

- ▸ The upper textbox on the left is meant to negate the condition.
- ▸ The left textbox is meant to select the field that will be used for comparison.
- ▸ Then, you have a list of possible comparators to choose from.
- ▸ On the right, you have two textboxes: The upper textbox for comparing against a field and the bottom textbox for comparing against a constant value.

Also, you can include more conditions by clicking on the **Add Condition** button on the right. If you right-click on a condition, a contextual menu appears to let you delete, edit, or move it.

In the first *Filter rows* step of the recipe, you typed a simple condition: You compared a field (category) with a fixed value (tents) by using the equal (=) operator. You did this to separate the tents products from the others.

The second filter had the purpose of differentiating the expensive and the cheap tents.

There's more...

You will find more filter features in the following subsections.

Avoiding the use of Dummy steps

In the recipe, we assumed that you wanted all three groups of products for further processing. Now, suppose that you only want the cheapest tents and you don't care about the rest. You could use just one *Filter rows* step with the condition `category = tents AND price < 100`, and send the 'false' data to a **Dummy** step, as in shown in the following diagram:

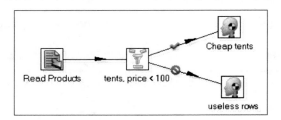

The rows that don't meet the condition will end at the **Dummy** step. Although this is a very commonly used solution for keeping just the rows that meet the conditions, there is a simpler way to implement it. When you create the hop from the **Filter rows** toward the next step, you are asked for the kind of hop. If you choose **Main output of step**, the two options **Send 'true' data to step** and **Send 'false' data to step** will remain empty. This will cause two things:

1. Only the rows that meet the condition will pass.
2. The rest will be discarded.

Comparing against the value of a Kettle variable

The recipe above shows you how to configure the condition in the *Filter rows* step to compare a field against another field or a constant value, but what if you want to compare against the value of a Kettle variable?

Let's assume, for example, you have a **named parameter** called `categ` with `kitchen` as **Default Value**. As you might know, named parameters are a particular kind of Kettle variable.

 You create the named parameters under the **Parameter** tab from the **Settings** option of the **Edit** menu.

To use this variable in a condition, you must add it to your dataset in advance. You do this as follows:

1. Add a **Get Variables** step from the **Job** category. Put it in the stream after the **Text file input** step and before the **Filter Rows** step; use it to create a new field named `categ` of **String** type with the value `${categ}` in the **Variable** column.

2. Now, the transformation looks like the one shown in the following screenshot:

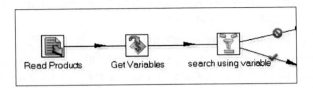

Read Products   Get Variables   search using variable

3. After this, you can set the condition of the first **Filter rows** step to `category = categ`, selecting `categ` from the listbox of fields to the right. This way, you will be filtering the `kitchen` products.

4. If you run the transformation and set the parameter to `tents`, you will obtain similar results to those that were obtained in the main recipe.

Avoiding the use of nested Filter Rows steps

Suppose that you want to compare a single field against a discrete and short list of possible values and do different things for each value in that list. In this case, you can use the *Switch / Case* step instead of nested *Filter rows* steps.

Let's assume that you have to send the rows to different steps depending on the category. The best way to do this is with the *Switch / Case* step. This way you avoid adding one *Filter row* step for each category.

In this step, you have to select the field to be used for comparing. You do it in the **Field name to switch** listbox. In the **Case values** grid, you set the **Value—Target step** pairs. The following screenshot shows how to fill in the grid for our particular problem:

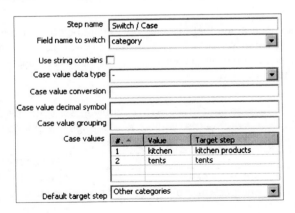

The following are some considerations about this step:

- You can have multiple values directed to the same target step
- You can leave the value column blank to specify a target step for empty values
- You have a listbox named **Default target step** to specify the target step for rows that do not match any of the case values
- You can only compare with an equal operator
- If you want to compare against a substring of the field, you could enable the **Use string contains** option and as **Case Value**, type the substring you are interested in. For example, if for **Case Value**, you type `tent_` then all categories containing `tent_` such as `tent_large`, `tent_small`, or `best_tents` will be redirected to the same target step.

Overcoming the difficulties of complex conditions

There will be situations where the condition is too complex to be expressed in a single *Filter rows* step. You can nest them and create temporary fields in order to solve the problem, but it would be more efficient if you used the **Java Filter** or **User Defined Java Expression** step as explained next.

You can find the **Java Filter** step in the **Flow** category. The difference compared to the *Filter Rows* step is that in this step, you write the condition using a Java expression.

The names of the listboxes—**Destination step for matching rows (optional)** and **Destination step for non-matching rows (optional)**—differ from the names in the **Filter rows** step, but their purpose is the same.

As an example, the following are the conditions you used in the recipe rewritten as Java expressions: `category.equals("tents")` and `price < 100`. These are extremely simple, but you can write any Java expression as long as it evaluates to a Boolean result.

 If you can't guarantee that the category will not be null, you'd better invert the first expression and put `"tents".equals(category)` instead. By doing this, whenever you have to check if a field is equal to a constant, you avoid an unexpected Java error.

Finally, suppose that you have to split the streams simply to set some fields and then join the streams again. For example, assume that you want to change the category as follows:

CONDITION	NEW CATEGORY
Category equal to `tents` and price below `100`	`cheap_tents`
Category equal to `tents` and price above or equal to `100`	`expensive_tents`
Category different from tents	Keep the old category

Doing this with nested **Filter rows** steps leads to a transformation like the following:

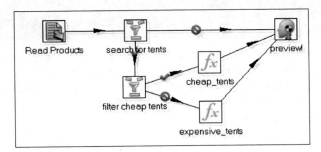

You can do the same thing in a simpler way:

1. Replace all the steps but the **Text file input** with a **User Defined Java Expression** step located in the **Scripting** category.

2. In the setting window of this step, add a row in order to replace the value of the category field: As **New field** and **Replace value** type `category`. As **Value type** select **String**. As **Java expression**, type the following:

```
(category.equals("tents"))?(price<100?"cheap_tents":"expensive_
tents"):category
```

The preceding expression uses the Java ternary operator `? :`. If you're not familiar with the syntax, think of it as shorthand for the `if-then-else` statement. For example, the inner expression `price<100?"cheap_tents":"expensive_tents"` means `if (price<100) then return "cheap_tents" else return "expensive_tents"`.

3. Do a preview on this step. You will see something similar to the following:

Rows of step: preview! (67 rows)

id_prod...	desc_product	price	category
50	50 Wenzel Alpine 8.5 X 8-Feet Dome Tent (Light Grey/Blue/Gold)	45.00	cheap_tents
51	51 Coleman Hooligan 2 Backpacking Tent	49.00	cheap_tents
52	52 Coleman WeatherMaster 8 Tent	206.00	expensive_tents
53	53 Coleman Sundome Tent (10-Feet x 10-Feet)	98.00	cheap_tents
54	54 Wenzel Pine Ridge 10-by-8 Foot Four-to-Five-Person 2-Room ...	47.00	cheap_tents
55	55 Wenzel Twin Peaks Sport Dome Tent, Red/Black	38.00	cheap_tents
56	56 Eureka Solo Backcountry 1 Tent	122.00	expensive_tents
57	57 Kelty Grand Mesa 2-Person Tent (Ruby/Tan)	107.00	expensive_tents
58	58 Victorinox Swiss Army Classic Pocket Knife	20.00	tools
59	59 Victorinox Swiss Army Tinker and Classic Knife Combo	17.00	tools
60	60 Victorinox Swiss Army Champion Plus Pocket Knife	34.00	tools
61	61 Leatherman 830039 New Wave Multitool with Leather/Nylon C...	93.00	tools

Merging rows of two streams with the same or different structures

It's a common requirement to combine two or more streams into a single stream that includes the union of all rows. In these cases, the streams come from different sources and don't always have the same structure. Consequently, combining the streams is not as easy as not just putting in a step that freely joins the streams. You have to take a couple of things into account. This recipe gives you the tips to make it easier.

Suppose that you received data about roller coasters from two different sources. The data in one of those sources looks like the following:

```
roller_coaster|speed|park|location|country|Year
Top Thrill Dragster|120 mph|Cedar Point|Sandusky, Ohio||2003
Dodonpa|106.8 mph|Fuji-Q Highland|FujiYoshida-shi|Japan|2001
Steel Dragon 2000|95 mph|Nagashima Spa Land|Mie|Japan|2000
Millennium Force|93 mph|Cedar Point|Sandusky, Ohio||2000
Intimidator 305|90 mph|Kings Dominion|Doswell, Virginia||2010
Titan|85 mph|Six Flags Over Texas|Arlington, Texas||2001
Furious Baco|84 mph|PortAventura|Spain||2007
. . .
```

The other source data looks like the following:

```
attraction|park_name|top_speed|trains_qt|ride_time
Expedition Everest|Disney's Animal Kingdom|50 mph|6 - 34 passenger|
Goofy'S Barnstormer|Disney's Magic Kingdom|25 mph|2 - 16 passenger|
Gwazi|Busch Gardens Tampa|50 mph|4 - 24 passenger|2 minutes, 30
seconds
Journey To Atlantis|SeaWorld Orlando||8 passenger boats|
Kraken|SeaWorld Orlando|65 mph|3 - 32 passenger|2 minutes, 2 seconds
. . .
```

You want to merge those rows into a single dataset with the following columns:

▶ `attraction`

▶ `park_name`

▶ `speed`

▶ `trains_qt`

▶ `ride_time`

Getting ready

Download from the book's site the files `roller_coasters_I.txt` and `roller_coasters_II.txt`. These files represent the two sources mentioned in the introduction.

How to do it...

Carry out the following steps:

1. Create a transformation and drag two **Text file input** steps into the canvas.

2. Use one of the steps to read the file `roller_coasters_I.txt`. Set the data types as follows: The speed as a `Number` with **Format** `#0.###` mph, and the rest of the fields as `String`. Do a preview to make sure that you are reading the file properly.

3. Drag the cursor over the step and press *Space* to see the output fields:

	Fieldname	Type	L...	P...	Step origin	Stor...	Mask	D...	G..	Trim	Comments
1	roller_coaster	String	-	-	roller_coasters_I	normal				none	
2	speed	Number	-	-	roller_coasters_I	normal	#0.### mph	.		none	
3	park	String	-	-	roller_coasters_I	normal				none	
4	location	String	-	-	roller_coasters_I	normal				none	
5	country	String	-	-	roller_coasters_I	normal				none	
6	year	String	-	-	roller_coasters_I	normal				none	

4. Use the other step to read the file `roller_coasters_II.txt`. Set the data type of `top_speed` to `Integer` and the rest of the fields to `String`. Do a preview to make sure that you are reading the file properly.

5. Drag the cursor over the step and press *Space* to see the output fields:

	Fieldname	Type	L...	P...	Step origin	Storage	Mask	D...	G...	Trim	Comments
1	attraction	String	-	-	roller_coasters_II	normal				none	
2	park_name	String	-	-	roller_coasters_II	normal				none	
3	top_speed	Integer	-	0	roller_coasters_II	normal				none	
4	trains_qt	String	-	-	roller_coasters_II	normal				none	
5	ride_time	String	-	-	roller_coasters_II	normal				none	

As you can see, the outputs of the streams are different. You have to insert the necessary steps to make them alike. That's the purpose of the next steps.

6. After the first **Text file input** step add an **Add constants** step. Use it to add two fields of type **String**. Name the fields `trains_qt` and `ride_time` and as **Value**, type `Not available`.

7. After it, add a **Select values** step. Fill in the **Select & Alter** tab as shown in the following screenshot:

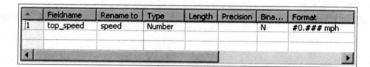

#. ▲	Fieldname	Rename to	Length	Precision
1	Roller_Coaster	attraction		
2	park	park_name		
3	Speed			
4	trains_qt			
5	ride_time			

8. After the second **Text file input** step, add another **Select values** step. Select the **Meta-data** tab and fill it in as shown in the following screenshot:

▲	Fieldname	Rename to	Type	Length	Precision	Bina...	Format
1	top_speed	speed	Number			N	#0.### mph

9. Repeat the procedure to see the output fields of the streams: Drag the cursor over the last step of each stream and press *Space*. Now, both streams should have the same layout.

You can keep both windows open at the same time: the one showing the output fields of the upper stream, and the one showing the output fields of the lower one. If you put one next to the other, you can immediately see if they are equal or not.

10. Finally, join the streams with a **Dummy** step as depicted in the following diagram:

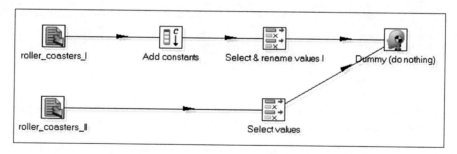

11. Do a preview on the *Dummy* step. You will see something similar to the result shown in the following screenshot:

Rows of step: preview! (25 rows)				
attraction	park_name	speed	trains_qt	ride_time
11	Son of Beast	Kings Island	78.3 mph		
12	Colossos	Heide Park	74.6 mph		
13	The Boss	Six Flags St. Louis	66.3 mph		
14	Mean Streak	Cedar Point	65 mph		
15	T Express	Everland	65 mph		
16	Expedition Everest	Disney's Animal Kingdom	50 mph	6 - 34 passenger	
17	Goofy'S Barnstormer	Disney's Magic Kingdom	25 mph	2 - 16 passenger	
18	Gwazi	Busch Gardens Tampa	50 mph	4 - 24 passenger	2 minutes, 30 seconds
19	Journey To Atlantis	SeaWorld Orlando		8 passenger boats	
20	Kraken	SeaWorld Orlando	65 mph	3 - 32 passenger	2 minutes, 2 seconds

How it works...

When you need to merge the rows of two streams into a single stream, you have to do all you can to make the metadata of the streams alike. That's what you did in this recipe. In the first stream, you added the fields you needed that were absent. You also selected and reordered the desired fields to resemble the second stream. After that you changed the metadata of the `top_speed` field in the second stream. You converted the field from `Integer` to `Number`, which was the type of the analogous field in the first stream.

When you did the preview, you could see the rows from both incoming steps.

There's more...

In the recipe, you merged two streams with data coming from different sources. However, that is not the only situation in which you may need to merge streams. It is common to split a stream into two or more streams to perform some particular manipulations, and then merge them back together, as depicted in the following diagram:

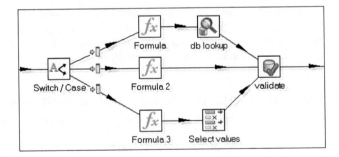

Whichever the case, when you have to merge two or more streams, there are two things that you should remember:

▶ Make sure that the metadata of all streams is exactly the same

▶ Decide and tell Kettle how you want to merge the streams

The following subsections explain these things in detail.

Making sure that the metadata of the streams is the same

In order to merge two or more streams their metadata has to coincide. This basically means that all streams have to have the same layout: same number of columns, same names, same types, and the columns must be in the same order.

If you try to merge streams that don't meet that requirement, you will receive a warning. A window will show up with the title **This hop cause the target step to receive rows with mixed layout!** and a text explaining the differences found. That means that you have to find the way to fix that situation. Here you have a quick-list that will help you make the metadata of several streams alike:

> ▸ Identify the fields that you want in the final dataset that are not present in all streams. In the streams that don't have those fields, add them. You can get the value from any source (a text file, the command line, and so on), or simply think of a default value and add the field with an **Add constant** step from the **Transformation** category. This is what you did with the fields: `trains_qt` and `ride_time`.

> ▸ Identify the fields that you want to keep that are present in all streams, but with different structure. Change the metadata of those fields in the streams where the metadata is not as desired. You can do this with a **Select values** step by using the **Metadata** tab. This is what you did for the field, `top_speed`.

> ▸ Verify the layouts of the streams. If they still differ, for each stream that does not have the proper layout, add a **Select values** step at the end. With this step, select the fields you want to keep (implicitly deleting the others), rename and reorder them, in order to match the desired layout. This was what you did with the first **Select values** step.

Now, you are free to merge the streams as explained in the next subsection.

> If you have to merge streams in a subtransformation, it's advisable to read the tip under the recipe, *Moving the reusable part of a transformation to a subtransformation* (Chapter 7, *Executing and Reusing Jobs and Transformations*)

Telling Kettle how to merge the rows of your streams

Once your streams are ready to be merged, you can then proceed in the following ways:

> ▸ Suppose that you want to put all the rows of one of the streams below all the rows of the other. If you don't care about the order of the streams, you can use any step to merge them. This was what you did in the recipe with the **Dummy** step.

> ▸ If you care about the order of the streams, you should use the **Append Streams** step from the **Flow** category, in order to merge the streams. By selecting a **Head hop** and a **Tail hop**, you can tell Kettle which stream goes first.

This only works for just two streams. If you need to merge several streams, then you need to add nested *Append Streams* steps.

▶ Now, suppose that you really want to merge the rows of the streams and leave them ordered by certain fields. You do it with a **Sorted Merge** step from the **Join** category. The step assumes that each stream in turn is sorted by the same fields.

▶ Note that Kettle warns you, but it doesn't prevent you from mixing row layouts when you merge streams. If you see a warning of this kind, refer to the tips in the previous subsection.

If you want Kettle to prevent you from running a transformation with mixed layout, check the option **Enable safe mode** located in the windows that shows up when you run the transformation. Note that the use of the **Enable safe mode** option will cause a drop in performance and should only be used when you are debugging a transformation

See also

The recipe named *Comparing two streams and generating differences* in this chapter. This recipe shows you a more advanced option for merging streams.

Comparing two streams and generating differences

Suppose that you have two streams with the same structure and want to find out the differences in the data. Kettle has a step meant specifically for that purpose: the *Merge Rows (diff)* step. In this recipe, you will see how it works.

Suppose that you have a file with information about the fastest roller coasters around the world. Now, you get an updated file and want to find out the differences between the files: There can be new roller coasters in the list; maybe some roller coasters are no longer among the fastest. Besides, you were told that in the old file, there were some errors about the location, country, and year information, so you are also interested in knowing if some of these have changed.

Getting ready

For this recipe, you will need two files with information about roller coasters. You can download them from the book's site.

Both files have the same structure and look like the following:

```
Roller_Coaster|Speed|park|location|country|Year
Kingda Ka|128 mph|Six Flags Great Adventure|Jackson, New Jersey||2005
Top Thrill Dragster|120 mph|Cedar Point|Sandusky, Ohio||2003
Dodonpa|106.8 mph|Fuji-Q Highland|FujiYoshida-shi|Japan|2001
Steel Dragon 2000|95 mph|Nagashima Spa Land|Mie|Japan|2000
Millennium Force|93 mph|Cedar Point|Sandusky, Ohio||2000
. . .
```

For the *There's more section,* you will also need a database with the first file already loaded in a table. You will find a script for creating and loading it also available for downloading.

How to do it...

Carry out the following steps:

1. Create a transformation.

2. Drag a **Text file input** step into the canvas and use it to read the file `top_roller_ coasters.txt`. As a separator, type `|`.

3. Do a preview to make sure that you are reading the file as expected.

4. Add a **Sort rows** step to sort the rows by `roller_coaster` and `park`.

5. Repeat the steps 2 to 4 to read the file named `top_roller_coasters_updates. txt` and sort the rows also by `roller_coaster` and `park`.

6. From the **Join** category, add a **Merge Rows (diff)** step and use it to join both streams as depicted in the following diagram:

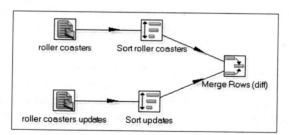

7. Double-click on the step you just added. In the **Reference rows origin:** select the name of the step coming from the stream that reads the `top_roller_coasters. txt` file.

8. In the **Compare rows origin:** select the name of the step coming from the stream that reads the `top_roller_coasters_updates.txt` file.

9. As **Flag fieldname**, type `flag`.

10. Fill the **Keys to match:** and **Values to compare:** grids as shown in the following screenshot:

Keys to match :			Values to compare :	
#. ▲	**Key field**		**#. ▲**	**Value field**
1	roller_coaster		1	location
2	park		2	country
			3	year

 You can save time by clicking on the **Get key fields** and **Get value fields** buttons to fill each grid respectively. Then just delete the fields that you don't need.

11. Close the window and do a preview; you should see the following:

Rows of step: merge and find diff. (17 rows)

	roller_coaster	speed	park	location	country	year	flag
1	Colossos	74.6 mph	Heide Park	Soltau	Germany	2001	deleted
2	Dodonpa	106.8 ...	Fuji-Q Highland	FujiYoshida-shi	Japan	2001	identical
3	Extreme Rusher	84 mph	Happy Valley	Beijing	China		new
4	Formula Rossa	149 mph	Ferrari World	Dubai	United Ara...	2010	new
5	Fujiyama	81 mph	Fuji-Q Highland	FujiYoshida-shi	Japan	1996	deleted
6	Furious Baco	84 mph	Port Aventura	Salou	Spain	2007	changed
7	Goliath	85 mph	Six Flags Magic ...	Valencia, California		2000	identical
8	Intimidator 305	90 mph	Kings Dominion	Doswell, Virginia		2010	identical
9	Kingda Ka	128 mph	Six Flags Great ...	Jackson, New Jersey		2005	identical
10	Millennium Force	93 mph	Cedar Point	Sandusky, Ohio		2000	identical
11	Phantom's Rev...	85 mph	Kennywood	West Mifflin, Pennsylv...		2001	identical

How it works...

The *Merge Rows (diff)* step is used for comparing two streams and finding out the differences between them. The output of the step is a single stream. The output stream contains a new field that acts as a flag indicating the kind of difference found as explained next.

 When you use the *Merge Rows (diff)* step, the two streams you are merging must have the same metadata, that is, the name, order, and type of the fields must be the same.

Let's call the streams being merged **reference stream** and **compare stream**. The first holds the old data while the second holds the new data. In the recipe, the old data is the data coming from the top_roller_coasters.txt file and the new data is the data coming from the top_roller_coasters_update.txt file.

Both streams must be sorted on the specified keys.

In order to perform the comparison, you have to tell Kettle how to detect that a row is the same in both streams, that is, you have to specify the key fields. You do it by entering them in the first grid. In the recipe, the key was made up by the roller coaster name and the park name (`roller_coaster` and `park` fields).

 If your data comes from a database, instead of using a *Sort rows* step for sorting the rows, you can sort them in the *Table input*. That will give you better performance.

Given the two streams, Kettle tries to match rows of both streams based on the key fields provided. Depending on the result, it sets a different value for the flag as explained in the following table:

Result of the comparison	Flag	Example
The key was only found in the reference stream	new	Formula Rossa roller coaster
The key was only found in the compared stream	deleted	Colossos roller coaster
The key was found in both streams and the fields typed in the **Value to compare** grid are equal	identical	Millennium Force roller coaster. The location (Sandusky, Ohio), country (empty), and year (2000) were the same in both streams.
The key was found in both streams but at least one of the fields typed in the **Value to compare** grid is different	changed	Furious Baco roller coaster. The location changed from Spain to Salou and the Country changed from empty to Spain.

Note that if a row is found in both streams with identical key fields and compare fields, it is marked as identical even if there are differences in other fields. For example, the Dodonpa roller coaster has a speed of 106.8 mph in the reference stream, but a speed of 106 mph in the compare stream. As you didn't put the speed in the values to compare list, the rows are marked as identical.

As a final remark, note that for the rows marked as new or changed, the values that pass to the output stream are those coming from the compare stream.

For the rows marked as identical or deleted, the values that are passed are those coming from the reference stream.

There's more...

The *Merge Rows* (*diff*) step is commonly used together with the *Synchronize after merge* step to keep a database table updated. The following section shows an example of how to do this.

Using the differences to keep a table up to date

Suppose that you have a table in a database with information about roller coasters, and that you have already inserted the data in the `top_roller_coasters.txt` file in that table.

Now, you have the `top_roller_coasters_updates.txt` file and want to update the table based on the differences.

 The table is totally de-normalized on purpose to keep the exercise simple.

Try the following:

1. After running the script mentioned in the introduction, modify the transformation in the recipe by replacing the first stream with a **Table Input** step, in order to read the table `rollercoasters`. Use the following statement:

```
SELECT    roller_coaster
        , speed
        , park
        , location
        , country
        , year
FROM      rollercoasters
ORDER BY  roller_coaster
        , park
```

2. You will have something like the following:

Rows of step: roller coasters (15 rows)

	roller_coaster	speed	park	location	country	year
1	Colossos	74.6 mph	Heide Park	Soltau	Germany	2001
2	Dodonpa	106.8 mph	Fuji-Q Highland	FujiYoshida-shi	Japan	2001
3	Fujiyama	81 mph	Fuji-Q Highland	FujiYoshida-shi	Japan	1996
4	Furious Baco	84 mph	Port Aventura	Spain		2007
5	Goliath	85 mph	Six Flags Magic Mou...	Valencia, California		2000
6	Intimidator 305	90 mph	Kings Dominion	Doswell, Virginia		2010
7	Kingda Ka	128 mph	Six Flags Great Adv...	Jackson, New Jersey		2005
8	Millennium Force	93 mph	Cedar Point	Sandusky, Ohio		2000
9	Phantom's Revenge	85 mph	Kennywood	West Mifflin, Pennsylvania		2001
10	Son of Beast	78.3 mph	Kings Island	Cincinnati, Ohio		2000

3. Do a preview on the last step, the **Merge Rows (diff)**. The output should be exactly the same as the output in the recipe.

4. Now, add a **Synchronize after merge** step. Select the connection to the database or create it if it doesn't exist and as **Target table**, type `rollercoasters`. Fill the grids as shown in the following screenshot:

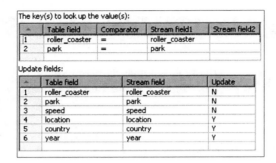

5. Select the **Advanced** tab and fill in the **Operation** frame as shown in the following screenshot:

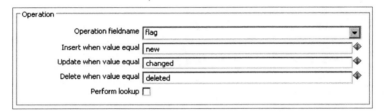

6. Close the window, save the transformation, and run it.

7. Execute a `SELECT` statement to see the data in the `rollercoaster` table. The roller coasters with the flag `deleted` should have been deleted from the table. The rows with the flag `new` should have been inserted in the table, and the rows with the flag `changed` should have been updated.

See also

The recipe named *Inserting, deleting, or updating a table depending on a field* in *Chapter 1, Working with Databases*. This recipe will help you understand the use of the *Synchronize after merge* step.

Generating all possible pairs formed from two datasets

This is a quick recipe that teaches you how to do a Cartesian product between datasets. By Cartesian product we mean taking all rows from one dataset, all rows from the other, and generate a new dataset with all the possible combinations of rows.

This particular recipe is in fact the implementation of the **CAG** or **Community Acronym Generator** as proposed by Nicholas Goodman (@nagoodman) on **twitter**:

> *@webdetails @pmalves @josvandongen How about CAG? Community Acronym Generator? A project to generate new acronyms for community projects?!*

There are already several community projects around Pentaho such as CDF, CDE, or CDA. Why don't we follow Nicholas's suggestion and develop the CAG as follows:

Given two lists of words, the Kettle transformation will generate all combinations of words that lead to potential community projects.

How to do it...

Carry out the following steps:

1. Create a new transformation and add two **Data Grid** steps from the **Input** category.

2. Use one of the **Data Grid** steps to create a dataset with a single **String** field named `middle_word`. Under the **Data** tab, enter a set of names for the middle word of the acronym. Here you have a sample list: `Dashboard, Data, Chart, Acronym, Cube, Report`.

3. Use the other **Data Grid** step to create a dataset with a single **String** field named `last_word`. Under the **Data** tab, enter a set of names for the last word of the acronym. Here you have a sample list: `Framework, Editor, Translator, Access, Generator, Integrator, Component`.

4. From the **Join** category, add a **Join Rows (Cartesian product)** step.

5. Create hops from the **Data Grid** steps toward this step. You will have something like the following:

middle word   middle and last word combinations   last word

6. From the **Scripting** category, add a **User Defined Java Expression** step (**UDJE** for short).

7. Use the **UDJE** to add two `String` fields. Name the first `new_component`, and as **Java Expression** type `"Community "+middle_word+" "+last_word`. Name the second field `acronym` and as **Java Expression** type `"C"+middle_word.substring(0,1)+last_word.substring(0,1)`.

8. Do a preview on this last step. You will see a list of candidate community projects as shown in the following screenshot:

#	middle_word	last_word	new_component	acronym
1	Dashboard	Framework	Community Dashboard Framework	CDF
2	Dashboard	Editor	Community Dashboard Editor	CDE
3	Dashboard	Translator	Community Dashboard Translator	CDT
4	Dashboard	Access	Community Dashboard Access	CDA
5	Dashboard	Generator	Community Dashboard Generator	CDG
6	Dashboard	Integrator	Community Dashboard Integrator	CDI
7	Dashboard	Component	Community Dashboard Component	CDC
8	Data	Framework	Community Data Framework	CDF
9	Data	Editor	Community Data Editor	CDE
10	Data	Translator	Community Data Translator	CDT
11	Data	Access	Community Data Access	CDA
12	Data	Generator	Community Data Generator	CDG

Rows of step: new_component (42 rows)

How it works...

The **Join Rows (Cartesian product)** step has the task of performing the Cartesian product of all streams coming to it. In this case, you had two streams but you could have had more. The step received those two streams and created all combinations of rows.

Then with the **UDJE**, you simply build the strings with the name of the candidate community projects and their acronyms, as for example, **Community Chart Framework (CCF)**. The real purpose of the generated potential projects is up to your imagination and out of the scope of the book.

There's more...

In the recipe, you used the *Join Rows (Cartesian product)* step for joining two datasets. You could join more datasets if you want to; however that is not a common requirement.

There are a couple of settings in the step that you didn't use in the recipe. They are explained in the following subsections.

Getting variables in the middle of the stream

This section describes one of the most common situations in which you may see the *Join Rows (Cartesian product)* step in action. Back to the recipe. Suppose that you have a **named parameter** named VERSION, which can be CE (representing Community Edition) or EE (representing Enterprise Edition). After generating the names of the candidate projects and their acronyms, you want to add the version. You can add the version to your stream by using a **Get Variable** step from the **Job** category. However, instead of getting the variable for each row, it's recommended to get it outside the main stream and then join both streams, as shown in the following screenshot:

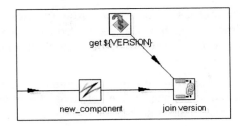

As the stream coming out of the *Get Variable* step has a single row, the Cartesian product will have all the possible combinations of N rows of the main stream with a single row, that is, N rows. In this case, it is important that in the *Main step to read from* option, you select the main stream, the stream coming from the *UDJE*. Doing so, you tell Kettle that most of the data will come from this step and Kettle will cache or spool to disk the data coming from the *Get Variable* step.

Limiting the number of output rows

With a *Join Rows (Cartesian product)* step, you can limit the number of output rows by entering a simple or complex condition in its setting window. The rows that don't meet the condition are discarded.

Back to the recipe. As you might have noticed, it is possible for the transformation to generate acronyms that already exist, for example, **CDF**. In the previous subsection, you added a second *Join Rows (Cartesian product)* step. In this step, you could add a condition to discard the rows with acronyms that already exist, excepting when the product is Enterprise Edition. The condition area in the setting window of the step would look like the one shown in the following screenshot (except for the exact list of acronyms which might have changed by the time you're reading this):

If you do a preview on this step, you will see something like the following:

Rows of step: join version (34 rows)

#. ▲	middle_word	last_word	new_component	acronym	version
1	Dashboard	Translator	Community Dashboard Translator	CDT	CE
2	Dashboard	Generator	Community Dashboard Generator	CDG	CE
3	Dashboard	Integrator	Community Dashboard Integrator	CDI	CE
4	Dashboard	Component	Community Dashboard Component	CDC	CE
5	Data	Translator	Community Data Translator	CDT	CE
6	Data	Generator	Community Data Generator	CDG	CE
7	Data	Integrator	Community Data Integrator	CDI	CE
8	Data	Component	Community Data Component	CDC	CE
9	Chart	Framework	Community Chart Framework	CCF	CE
10	Chart	Editor	Community Chart Editor	CCE	CE

If you take a look at the **Step Metrics** tab of the **Execution Results** window, you will notice that the number of written rows is less than Cartesian product of incoming rows. Note that the GUI for entering the condition is the same as the one in the **Filter rows** step.

 As you may pick fields from more than one stream in the condition of the *Join Rows (Cartesian product)* step, it is therefore required that the picked fields have unique names in the streams.

See also

▸ The recipe named *Joining two or more streams based on giving conditions* in this chapter. This recipe shows you an alternative step to the *Join Rows (Cartesian product)* step, with better performance.

▸ The recipe named *Splitting a stream into two or more streams based on a condition* in this chapter. This recipe helps you configure the filter area in the **Join Rows (Cartesian product)** setting window.

Joining two or more streams based on given conditions

There are occasions where you will need to join two datasets. If you are working with databases, you could use SQL statements to perform this task, but for other kinds of input (XML, text, Excel), you will need another solution.

Kettle provides the *Merge Join* step to join data coming from any kind of source.

Let's assume that you are building a house and want to track and manage the costs of building it. Before starting, you prepared an Excel file with the estimated costs for the different parts of your house. Now, you are given a weekly file with the progress and the real costs. So, you want to compare both to see the progress.

Getting ready

To run this recipe, you will need two Excel files, one for the budget and another with the real costs. The budget.xls has the estimated starting date, estimated end date, and cost for the planned tasks. The costs.xls has the real starting date, end date, and cost for tasks that have already started.

You can download the sample files from the book's site.

How to do it...

Carry out the following steps:

1. Create a new transformation.

2. Drop two **Excel input** steps into the canvas.

3. Use one step for reading the budget information (budget.xls file) and the other for reading the costs information (costs.xls file).

4. Under the **Fields** tab of these steps, click on the **Get fields from header row...** button in order to populate the grid automatically. Apply the format dd/MM/yyyy to the fields of type **Date** and $0.00 to the fields with costs.

5. Add a **Merge Join** step from the **Join** category, and create a hop from each **Excel input** step toward this step. The following diagram depicts what you have so far:

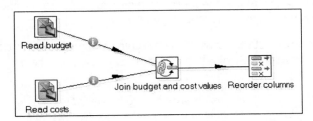

6. Configure the **Merge Join** step, as shown in the following screenshot:

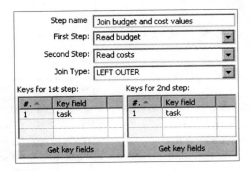

7. If you do a preview on this step, you will obtain the result of the two Excel files merged. In order to have the columns more organized, add a **Select values** step from the **Transform** category. In this new step, select the fields in this order: task, starting date (est.), starting date, end date (est.), end date, cost (est.), cost.

8. Doing a preview on the last step, you will obtain the merged data with the columns of both Excel files interspersed, as shown in the following screenshot:

	task	starting date (est.)	starting date	end date (est.)	end date	cost (est.)	cost
1	foundations	01/12/2010	01/12/2010	31/12/2010	10/01/2011	$45000.00	$52000.00
2	walls	01/01/2011	11/01/2011	25/01/2011	15/02/2011	$280000.00	$259000.00
3	roof	26/01/2011		14/02/2011		$150000.00	
4	swimming pool	01/01/2011	07/01/2011	05/02/2011		$98000.00	$77000.00
5	electrical work	01/03/2011		10/03/2011		$66500.00	
6	plumbing	01/03/2011		25/03/2011		$48000.00	
7	painting	15/04/2011		25/04/2011		$34000.00	
8	kitchen	01/04/2011		30/04/2011		$124500.00	
9	bathrooms	01/04/2011		30/04/2011		$92800.00	
1.	laundry	01/04/2011		30/04/2011		$55000.00	

How it works...

In the example, you saw how to use the *Merge Join* step to join data coming from two Excel files. You can use this step to join any other kind of input.

In the *Merge Join* step, you set the name of the incoming steps, and the fields to use as the keys for joining them. In the recipe, you joined the streams by just a single field: the `task` field.

 The rows are expected to be sorted in an ascending manner on the specified key fields.

There's more...

In the example, you set the **Join Type** to LEFT OUTER JOIN. Let's see explanations of the possible join options:

Join	Description	In the example
INNER	The result contains only the rows with the same key in both sources	You will obtain only the tasks that have estimated and real information.
LEFT OUTER	The result contains all the rows from the first source, and the correspondent values for second source (or empty values for non-matching keys)	You will obtain all the tasks from the budget, and the real costs related to these tasks (with empty values for the tasks that still haven't any associated costs).
RIGHT OUTER	The result contains all the rows from the second source, and the corresponding values for the first source (or empty values for non-matching keys)	You will obtain all the real tasks' costs and their related information from the budget. If there is a cost for a task that hadn't been estimated, the estimated cost will be empty.
FULL OUTER	The result contains all the rows from both sources (with empty values for non-matching keys)	You will obtain all the tasks from the budget and the real costs. This was the case in the recipe.

The recipe named *Reading an Excel file* in *Chapter 2, Reading and Writing Files*. In this recipe, you can learn the details of reading Excel files with Kettle.

Interspersing new rows between existent rows

In most Kettle datasets, all rows share a common meaning; they represent the same kind of entity, for example:

- In a dataset with sold items, each row has data about one item
- In a dataset with the mean temperature for a range of days in five different regions, each row has the mean temperature for a different day in one of those regions
- In a dataset with a list of people ordered by age range (0-10, 11-20, 20-40, and so on), each row has data about one person

Sometimes, there is a need of interspersing new rows between your current rows. Taking the previous examples, imagine the following situations:

- In the sold items dataset, every 10 items, you have to insert a row with the running quantity of items and running sold price from the first line until that line.
- In the temperature's dataset, you have to order the data by region and the last row for each region has to have the average temperature for that region.
- In the people's dataset, for each age range, you have to insert a header row just before the rows of people in that range.

In general, the rows you need to intersperse can have fixed data, subtotals of the numbers in previous rows, header to the rows coming next, and so on. What they have in common is that they have a different structure or meaning compared to the rows in your dataset.

Interspersing these rows is not a complicated task, but is a tricky one. In this recipe, you will learn how to do it.

Suppose that you have to create a list of products by category. For each category, you have to insert a header row with the category description and the number of products inside that category.

The final result should be as follows:

desc_product	qty_prod
CATEGORY: SLEEPING BAGS	6
Teton Sports Celsius XL 0-Degree Sleeping Bag	
Suisse Sport Adult Adventurer Mummy Ultra-Compactable Sleeping Bag	
Stansport Redwood Ultra Light Sleeping Bag (Green, 45-Degree)	
Eureka! Lady Bug Sleeping Bag	
Eureka Grasshopper Kids 30-Degree Sleeping Bag	
Coleman Palmetto Cool-Weather Sleeping Bag	
CATEGORY: TENTS	12
Wenzel Twin Peaks Sport Dome Tent, Red/Black	
Wenzel Pine Ridge 10-by-8 Foot Four-to-Five-Person 2-Room Dome T...	
Wenzel Alpine 8.5 X 8-Feet Dome Tent (Light Grey/Blue/Gold)	
Kelty Grand Mesa 2-Person Tent (Ruby/Tan)	
Eureka Solo Backcountry 1 Tent	
Eureka Apex 2XT Adventure 7' 5" by 4' 11" Two-Person Tent	
Coleman WeatherMaster 8 Tent	
Coleman Sundome Tent (10-Feet x 10-Feet)	
Coleman SunDome 7-Foot by 7-Foot 3-Person Dome Tent (Orange/Gr...	

Getting ready

This recipe uses an outdoor database with the structure shown in *Appendix, Data Structures*. As source, you can use a database like this or any other source, for example a text file with the same structure.

How to do it...

Carry out the following steps:

1. Create a transformation, drag into the canvas a **Table Input** step, select the connection to the outdoor database, or create it if it doesn't exist. Then enter the following statement:

   ```
   SELECT category
        , desc_product
   FROM   products p
        ,categories c
   WHERE p.id_category = c.id_category
   ORDER by category
   ```

2. Do a preview of this step. You already have the product list!

3. Now, you have to create and intersperse the header rows. In order to create the headers, do the following: From the **Statistics** category, add a **Group by** step and fill in the grids, as shown in the following screenshot:

The fields that make up the group:

	Group field	
1	category	

Aggregates :

	Name	Subject	Type	Value
1	qty_prod	desc_product	Number of Values (N)	

4. From the **Scripting** category, add a **User Defined Java Expression** step, and use it to add two fields: The first will be a **String** named `desc_product`, with value `("Category: " + category).toUpperCase()`. The second will be an **Integer** field named `order` with value 1.

5. Use a **Select values** step to reorder the fields as `category`, `desc_product`, `qty_product`, and `order`. Do a preview on this step; you should see the following result:

Rows of step: Select values (5 rows)

	category	desc_product	qty_prod	order
1	kitchen	CATEGORY: KITCHEN	24	1
2	lights	CATEGORY: LIGHTS	15	1
3	sleeping bags	CATEGORY: SLEEPING BAGS	6	1
4	tents	CATEGORY: TENTS	12	1
5	tools	CATEGORY: TOOLS	10	1

6. Those are the headers. The next step is mixing all the rows in the proper order. Drag an **Add constants** step into the canvas and a **Sort rows** step. Link them to the other steps as shown:

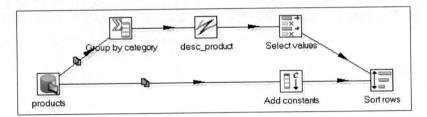

7. Use the **Add constants** to add two **Integer** fields: `qty_prod` and `order`. As **Value**, leave the first field empty, and type 2 for the second field.

8. Use the *Sort rows* step for sorting by `category`, `order`, and `desc_product`.

9. Select the last step and do a preview. You should see the rows exactly as shown in the introduction.

How it works...

When you have to intersperse rows between existing rows, there are just four main tasks to do, as follows:

1. Create a secondary stream that will be used for creating new rows. In this case, the rows with the headers of the categories.

2. In each stream, add a field that will help you intersperse rows in the proper order. In this case, the key field was named `order`.

3. Before joining the two streams, add, remove, and reorder the fields in each stream to make sure that the output fields in each stream have the same metadata.

4. Join the streams and sort by the fields that you consider appropriate, including the field created earlier. In this case, you sorted by `category`, inside each category by the field named `order` and finally by the products description.

Note that in this case, you created a single secondary stream. You could create more if needed, for example, if you need a header and footer for each category.

See also

The recipe named *Merging the rows of two streams with the same or different structure* in this chapter. This recipe will help you with the task of merging streams.

Executing steps even when your stream is empty

As you must know, a Kettle transformation is a group of linked steps through which data flows. Each step is meant to receive rows of data, process the data somehow, and deliver those rows to the next step or steps. If you agree with this definition, then you must realize that if there are no rows coming to the step, the step will not be executed.

This seems reasonable, but on occasion, it can be a problem. To get an idea of that kind of situation, look at the following scenarios:

- You have a very simple transformation that reads a file, does some calculations, and finally updates a table with the system date and the number of processed rows. If the file doesn't exist or if it is empty, then no rows will go out from the file input step. Consequently and contrary to what you need to do, the step that updates the table will never be executed.

- You need to set some variables with values that are supposed to be in a file. If the file exists and has the values, you are able to do it. If not, the step that sets the variables will not be executed. It would be good if it sets the variables with at least some default values.

▶ You have a database with products and want to generate a list of products whose descriptions match a given text. For example, if the text is `lamp`, your file will have all products that contain `lamp` in their descriptions. If there are no lamps, you want to generate a file with a single row recording the situation. The problem is that, if there are no lamps, no row will come out of the input step. Consequently the output step, as in the first example, will never be executed.

For situations like these, there is a way to overcome the problem: the use of the *Detect empty stream* step. This recipe shows you how to use it. It implements the last of the examples: The generation of the file with a list of products.

Getting ready

For this recipe, you will need a database with outdoor products with the structure defined in *Appendix, Data Structures*.

How to do it...

Carry out the following steps:

1. Create a transformation and drag a **Table Input** step.

2. Double-click on the step and select the connection to the `outdoors` database or create it if it doesn't exist. Then, enter the following statement:

```
SELECT
      category
   , id_product
   , desc_product
   , price
FROM products p
   ,categories c
WHERE p.id_category = c.id_category
AND desc_product like '%${PROD_FILTER}%'
ORDER by category, desc_product
```

3. Check the **Replace variables in script?** option.

4. Add an **Excel output** step. Configure the step to generate a file with all fields coming from the **Table Input** step.

5. From the **Flow** category, add a **Detect empty stream** step. Also, add a **User Defined Java Expression** or **UDJE** step, and link all steps as follows:

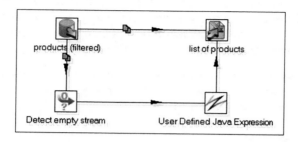

6. Use the **UDJE** step and fill it in, as shown in the following screenshot:

Fields:

	New field	Java expression	Value type	Length	Precision	Replace value
1	category	"criteria doesn't match any product"	String			category

That's all! Let's test the transformation:

1. Press *F9* to run it; give the **PROD_FILTER** variable the value `lamp` (or any value that you know is part of the description of some of your products). You do this by typing the value into the grid named **Variables**. Click on **Launch**.

2. Open the generated file. It should look like the one shown in the following screenshot:

	A	B	C	D
1	category	id_product	desc_product	price
2	lights	34	Petzl E41 PBY Tikkina 2-LED Headlamp, Black and Yellow	19,00
3	lights	36	Petzl E49P TacTikka Plus 4-LED Headlamp, Black	43,00
4	lights	26	Petzl E97 PP Tikka Plus 2 Headlamp, Pistachio	39,00
5				

3. Run the transformation again, but this time, type a value that you know isn't part of the descriptions of your products, for example `motorcycle`.

4. Open the file. This time it should have the content as shown in the following screenshot:

	A	B	C	D
1	category		id_product	desc_prod	price
2	criteria doesn't match any product			
3				

How it works...

When a step doesn't return data, the flow ends. None of the steps that follow that step are executed because they don't receive data for processing. The *Detect empty stream* step, as the name suggests, detects that situation. As a consequence, it generates a stream with the same metadata as the expected stream, and a single row with null values. This way, you avoid the stream to "die".

In order to understand what the step does in a better way, try the following:

1. In the transformation that you just created, select the **Detect empty stream** step.
2. Press *F9* to do a preview, give to the variable **PROD_FILTER** the value `lamp`, and click on **Launch**.
3. You will see a message informing you that there are no rows to preview. That's because the main stream had rows and they went toward the Excel step.
4. Try the same procedure again, but this time, enter an invalid value, for example, `motorcycle`. You will see a single row with the columns `category`, `id_product`, `desc_product`, and `price`, all with null values.

In the recipe, in the step that follows the **Detect empty stream** step, you replaced the null value in the `category` column with the message you wanted to write in the file, and sent the data toward the Excel file.

The *Excel output* step doesn't care if the data came from the main stream or the alternative one that you created for the empty stream. It simply sends the columns to the Excel file.

Finally, it's worth mentioning why we used the *UDJE* step. The selection of this step is smart because it replaces the value of the `category` field. Most steps add new fields, but are not able to manipulate existing ones.

There's more...

You can use the *Detect empty stream* step in the same way you would implement error handling. The difference is that here there are no errors; you simply have an exceptional situation.

As you would do when handling errors, you can fix or manipulate the stream and send it back to the main stream, as you did in the recipe, or you could completely ignore the metadata generated by the *Detect empty stream* step and simply use that step as the beginning of a new independent stream. For example, instead of generating the Excel file when there are no rows, you could write a message to the log, such as `criteria doesn't match any product`.

Processing rows differently based on the row number

There will be some situations where you will need to process the data differently depending on the position or number of each row.

Let's assume that you have a bookstore and want to know the top five bestsellers books, the following 10 bestsellers, and the rest of the books for different purposes (for example, to do a differentiated marketing promotion for each group). To do this, you will divide the list of books into different groups depending on their sales.

Getting ready

You need an Excel spreadsheet file containing a list of books with the following columns:

- `title`
- `id_author`
- `price, id_title`
- `genre`
- `sales`

This last column represents the quantity of books sold in the last period.

You can download a sample file from the book's website.

How to do it...

Carry out the following steps:

1. Create a new transformation and drag an **Excel Input** step from the **Input** category.
2. Under the **Files** tab, browse to and select the `sales_books.xls` file.
3. Complete the **Fields** tab with the following values:

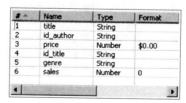

#	Name	Type	Format
1	title	String	
2	id_author	String	
3	price	Number	$0.00
4	id_title	String	
5	genre	String	
6	sales	Number	0

4. Add a **Sort rows** step from the **Transform** category. Complete the step grid with the `sales` **Fieldname**. Type N in the **Ascending** column.

5. Add an **Add sequence** step from the **Transform** category. Type `rank` in the **Name of value** textbox.

6. By previewing this step, you will obtain a list of books ranked by their sales.

7. Add two **Filter rows** steps and three **Dummy** steps (all from the **Flow** category) and create the hops, as depicted in the following diagram:

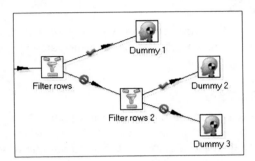

8. In the first **Filter rows**, set the following condition: `rank <= 5`.

9. In the last **Filter rows** step add the condition `rank <= 15`.

10. The **Dummy 1** step represents the 5 best-selling books. For example:

	title	id...	price	id_title	genre	sales	rank
1	Rich Dad, Poor Dad	A0...	$19,90	323-602	Business	570	1
2	Pet Sematary	A0...	$41,00	123-351	Fiction	478	2
3	Harry Potter and the Death...	A0...	$38,00	423-007	Children	470	3
4	The Obama Diaries	A0...	$28,90	223-301	Non-fiction	456	4
5	Who Took My Money	A0...	$21,00	323-603	Business	450	5

Rows of step: top 5 (5 rows)

11. The **Dummy 2** step represents the next 10 best-selling books.

12. The rest of the books can bee seen in the **Dummy 3** step.

13. You can do a preview of each of these **Dummy** steps and verify the results.

How it works...

This recipe reads the `sales_books.xls` file to create a dataset of the book titles along with their sales information. The *Sort rows* step is necessary to order the books by sales starting with the best seller.

Then, you dropped an *Add sequence* step to enumerate the rows. In this case, the field you added represents the ranking value. The best selling book will have the number one.

At this moment, you have the list of books ranked by their sales. Now, you only have to filter the books based on their ranks. You do it by using the *Filter rows* step.

The first *Filter rows* step uses the condition `rank <= 5` to get the top five best-selling books. The rest of the books will be filtered again, now with the condition `rank <= 15`; this will bring the rows ranked from 6 to 15. The remaining books, those with a rank greater than 15, will go to the last *Dummy* step.

There's more...

In the recipe, you enumerated the rows and then you did different things based on the row number. There are also some specific use cases, which are explained in the following subsections.

Identifying specific rows

Suppose that you only want to keep the books with rank 15 to 20 and discard the rest. In this case, you don't have to add the *Add sequence* step and the *Filter rows* step afterward. There is a simpler way of doing that. There is also a step named **Sample rows** in the **Statistics** category that allows picking specific rows from a dataset. For example, filling the **Lines range** textbox with `1..5,9,15..20`, you will get:

- ▸ The rows 1 to 5
- ▸ The row 9
- ▸ The rows 15 to 20

The rest of the lines will be discarded. For the preceding example, you should just type `15..20`.

Identifying the last row in the stream

Suppose that you want to know which book sold the least. In this case, you cannot filter by row number because you don't know how many books there are. In this case, instead of enumerating the rows, you can use the **Identify last row in a stream** step from the **Flow** category.

In this step, you only have to type a value for the **Result fieldname** textbox. When you execute the transformation, this new field will return `Y` for the last row and `N` otherwise. In the example, you can know which the least sold book was, by filtering the row where the field is equal to `Y`.

Avoiding using an Add sequence step to enumerate the rows

If you need to enumerate the rows just after reading the data, then you don't need to add an *Add sequence* step. In several of the input steps, such as **Text file input** or **Get data from XML**, you have a checkbox named **Rownum in output?** under the **Content** tab. This allows you to create a new field with a sequence for the rows. The name of this new field must be typed in the **Rownum fieldname** textbox.

This also applies when you need to rank the rows as in the recipe, and your input data is already ordered.

See also

The recipe named *Splitting a stream into two or more streams based on a condition* in this chapter. This recipe has all the details about the *Filter row* step.

7
Executing and Reusing Jobs and Transformations

In this chapter, we will cover:

- ▸ Executing a job or a transformation by setting static arguments and parameters
- ▸ Executing a job or a transformation from a job by setting arguments and parameters dynamically
- ▸ Executing a job or a transformation whose name is determined at runtime
- ▸ Executing part of a job once for every row in the dataset
- ▸ Executing part of a job several times until a condition is true
- ▸ Creating a process flow
- ▸ Moving part of a transformation to a subtransformation

Introduction

A transformation by itself rarely meets all the requirements of a real-world problem. It's common to face some of the following situations:

- ▸ You need to execute the same transformation over and over again
- ▸ You need to execute a transformation more than once, but with different parameters each time

- ► You decide at runtime which job to run from a group of jobs
- ► You have to reuse part of a transformation in a different scenario

Kettle is versatile enough to allow you to do that kind of thing. However, you may get confused trying to do some of them without guidance.

This chapter contains quick recipes just meant to teach you the basics. The transformations and jobs used are simple enough to serve as templates for you to modify for your own needs.

Before starting on the recipes, let's take a look at the following subsections:

- ► **Sample transformations**: As the name suggests, this section explains the sample transformations that will be used throughout the chapter.
- ► **Launching jobs and transformations**: This section quickly introduces Kitchen and Pan, the tools for launching jobs and transformations from the command line.

Sample transformations

The recipes in this chapter show you different ways of running Kettle transformations and jobs. In order to focus on the specific purposes of the recipes rather than on developing transformations, we've created some sample transformations that will be used throughout the chapter.

The transformations are described in the following subsections. You can download them from the book's website.

These transformations generate files in a directory pointed to by a variable named ${OUTPUT_FOLDER}. In order to run the transformations, this variable must be predefined.

Remember that you have several ways of defining variables: as a named parameter, in the Kettle properties file, in a previous job or transformation (if this transformation is going to be called from a job) or in the **Variables** section of the **Execute a transformation** window (the window that shows up when you run the transformation from **Spoon**).

Sample transformation: Hello

This transformation receives the name of a person as the first command-line argument and generates a file saying hello to that person.

The transformation looks like the one shown in the following diagram:

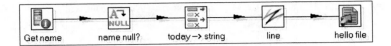

| Get name | name null? | today -> string | line | hello file |

A sample output file is as follows:

```
Hello, Eva! It's January 09, 09:37.
```

Sample transformation: **Random list**

This transformation generates a file with a list of random integers. The quantity generated is defined as a **named parameter** called QUANTITY, with a default value of 10.

The transformation looks like the one depicted in the following diagram:

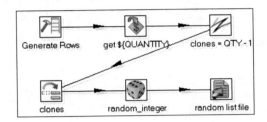

A sample output file is as follows:

```
-982437245
1169516784
318652071
-576481306
1815968887
```

Sample transformation: **Sequence**

This transformation generates a file with a list of numbers. The transformation receives two command-line arguments representing FROM and TO values. It also has a **named parameter** called INCREMENT with a default of 1. The transformation generates a list of numbers between FROM and TO, with increments of INCREMENT.

The transformation looks like the one shown in the following diagram:

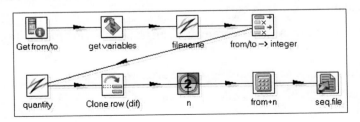

A sample output file using `from=0, to=6, increment=2` is as follows:

```
0
2
4
6
```

Sample transformation: File list

This transformation generates a file containing the names of the files in the current directory.

The transformation looks like the one depicted in the following diagram:

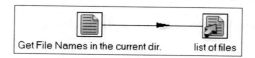

A sample output file is as follows:

```
gen_random.ktr
gen_sequence.ktr
get_file_names.ktr
hello.ktr
```

Launching jobs and transformations

As said, the recipes in this chapter are focused on different ways of running Kettle transformations and jobs. Ultimately, you will end up with a main job. In order to test your job with different inputs or parameters, you can use Spoon as usual, but it might be useful or even simpler to use **Kitchen**, a command-line program meant to launch Kettle jobs. If you're not familiar with Kitchen, this section gives you a quick review.

In order to run a job with Kitchen:

1. Open the terminal window
2. Go to the Kettle installation directory
3. Run `kitchen.bat /file:<kjb file name>` (Windows system) or `kitchen.sh /file:<kjb file name>` (Unix-based system), where `<kjb file name>` is the name of your job, including the complete path. If the name contains spaces, you must surround it with double quotes.

If you want to provide command-line parameters, just type them in order as part of the command.

If you want to provide a named parameter, use the following syntax:

```
/param:<parameter name>=<parameter value>
```

For example, `/param:INCREMENT=5`

Additionally, you can specify the logging level by adding the following option:

```
/level:<logging level>
```

The logging level can be one of the following: `Error`, `Nothing`, `Minimal`, `Basic` (this is the default level), `Detailed`, `Debug`, or `Rowlevel`.

If you intend to run a transformation instead of a job, use **Pan**: Just replace `kitchen.bat/kitchen.sh` with `pan.bat/pan.sh`, and provide the name of the proper `.ktr` file.

While you use Spoon for developing, debugging and testing transformations and jobs, Kitchen and Pan are most commonly used for running jobs and transformations in production environments. For a complete list of available options and more information on these commands, visit the Pan documentation at the following URL:

```
http://wiki.pentaho.com/display/EAI/Pan+User+Documentation
```

For Kitchen documentation, visit the following URL:

```
http://wiki.pentaho.com/display/EAI/Kitchen+User+Documentation
```

Executing a job or a transformation by setting static arguments and parameters

When you develop a transformation which reads command-line arguments or defines named parameters, you usually intend to call it more than once with different values for those parameters or arguments. If you know the values beforehand, then there is an easy way to call the transformation, as you will see in this recipe.

Suppose that you want to create the following three files:

1. First file: Numbers from 1 to 10, incrementing by 1, as in 0, 1,..., 10.
2. Second file: Numbers from 0 to 100, incrementing by 20, as in 0, 20, 40,..., 100.
3. Third file: Numbers from 100 to 500, incrementing by 100, as in 100, 200,..., 500.

You have a transformation that generates sequences like these. You just have to call it three times with the proper arguments and parameters.

Getting ready

You need the sample transformation that generates a file with a sequence described in the introduction.

Make sure you have defined the variable $\${OUTPUT\_FOLDER}$ with the name of the destination folder. Also, make sure that the folder exists.

How to do it...

Carry out the following steps:

1. Create a job.

2. Drag a **Start** job entry and three **Transformation** job entries into the canvas. Link all the entries, one after the other.

3. Double-click on the first **Transformation** entry.

4. As **Transformation filename**, browse to and select the sample transformation gen_ sequence.ktr.

5. Select the **Argument** tab and fill the grid with a 1 in the first row and a 10 in the second row.

6. Double-click on the second **Transformation** entry.

7. As **Transformation filename**, select the sample transformation gen_sequence.ktr.

8. Select the **Argument** tab and fill the grid with a 0 in the first row and a 100 in the second.

9. Select the **Parameters** tab. In the first row of the grid, type INCREMENT under **Parameter** and 20 under **Value**.

10. Double-click on the last **Transformation** entry.

11. As **Transformation filename**, select the sample transformation gen_sequence.ktr.

12. Select the **Argument** tab and fill the grid with a 50 in the first row and a 500 in the second.

13. Select the **Parameters** tab. In the first row of the grid, type INCREMENT under **Parameter** and 50 under **Value**.

14. Save and run the job.

15. Check the output folder. You will find the following three files:

    ❑ sequence_1_10_1.txt

    ❑ sequence_0_100_20.txt

    ❑ sequence_50_500_50.txt

16. Edit the files. You will see that they contain the sequences of numbers 0, 1,..., 10 in the first file, 0, 20, 40,..., 100 in the second, and 100, 200,..., 500 in the third, just as expected.

How it works...

When you run a transformation from a job, you have to specify at least the name and location of the transformation. There are however, a couple of extra settings that may be useful. In this recipe, you saw the use of the **Argument** and the **Parameters** tabs.

The **Argument** tab is used for sending command-line arguments to the transformation.

The grid in the **Argument** tab is equivalent to the **Arguments** grid you see when you run a transformation from Spoon. Each row belongs to a different command-line argument.

In this case, your transformation expected two command-line arguments: the limits `from` and `to` of the sequence. In the recipe, you set values for those arguments the **Argument** tab of each **Transformation** entry setting window.

The **Parameters** tab is used for setting values for the named parameters defined in the transformation. The grid under the **Parameters** tab is equivalent to the **Parameters** grid you see when you run a transformation from Spoon. Each row belongs to a different named parameter. You only have to provide values if they are different to the default values.

In this case, your transformation defined one named parameter: `INCREMENT` with a default value of `1`. Therefore, you skipped the setting of this parameter in the first **Transformation** entry, but set values in the others.

> Note that if you set arguments or parameters in the **Transformation** entry setting window, the corresponding argument or parameters sent from the command line will be ignored if you run the job with Kitchen.

There's more...

All that was said for the **Transformation** job entry is also valid for **Job** job entries. That is, you can use the **Argument** and **Parameters** tab in a **Job** entry to send fixed values for command-line arguments or named parameters to the job.

See also

The recipe named *Executing a job or a transformation from a job by setting arguments and parameters dynamically* in this chapter. Here you will find directions on setting arguments and parameters at runtime.

Executing a job or a transformation from a job by setting arguments and parameters dynamically

Suppose that you developed a transformation which reads command-line arguments or defines named parameters. Now you want to call that transformation from a job, but you don't know the values for the arguments or the parameters; you have to take them from some media, for example, a file or a table in a database. This recipe shows you how to get those values and pass them to the transformation at runtime.

For this recipe, suppose that you want to create a file with a sequence of numbers. You have a transformation that does it. The problem is that the limits `from` and `to` and the `increment` value are stored in a properties file. This represents an obstacle to calling the transformation directly, but can be done with Kettle in a very simple way.

Getting ready

You need a sample transformation that generates a file with a sequence as described in the introduction. Make sure you have defined the variable `${OUTPUT_FOLDER}` with the name of the destination folder. Also, make sure that the folder exists.

You also need a file named `sequence.properties` with the following content:

```
from=0
to=90
increment=30
```

With those values, your transformation should generate the values 0, 30, 60, 90.

How to do it...

Carry out the following steps:

1. Create a transformation.

2. From the **Input** category, drag a **Property Input** step into the canvas, and use it to read the properties file. Under the **File** tab, enter the name and location of the file. Under the **Fields** tab, click on **Get Fields** to fill the grid with the fields: Key and Value.

3. From the **Transform** category, add a **Row denormalizer** step and create a hop from the input step toward this one.

4. Double-click on the step. For the **key field**, select Key. Fill the **Target fields:** grid, as shown in the following screenshot:

Target fields:

#	Target fieldname	Value fieldname	Key value	Type	Format	Length
1	from_value	Value	from	String		
2	to_value	Value	to	String		
3	increment_value	Value	increment	String		

5. After that step, add a **Copy rows to result** step. You will find it under the **Job** category.

6. Do a preview on the last step. You should see the following screen:

Rows of step: Copy rows to result (1 rows)

#.	from_value	to_value	increment_value
1	0	90	30

7. Save the transformation and create a job.

8. Drag a **Start** job entry and two **Transformation** job entries into the canvas. Link the entries, one after the other.

9. Double-click on the first **Transformation** entry and for **Transformation filename**, select the transformation you just created.

10. Close the window and double-click on the second **Transformation** entry.

11. For **Transformation filename**, select the sample transformation `gen_sequence.ktr`.

12. Select the **Advanced** tab and check the first three options: **Copy previous results to args?**, **Copy previous results to parameters?**, and **Execute for every input row?**

13. Select the **Parameters** tab. For the first row in the grid, type INCREMENT under **Parameter** and `increment_value` under **Stream column name**.

14. Close the window.

15. Save and run the job.

16. As a result, you will have a new file named `sequence_0_90_30.txt`. The file will contain the sequence of numbers 0, 30, 60, 90, just as expected.

How it works...

The transformation you ran in the recipe expects two arguments: `from` and `to`. It also has a named parameter: INCREMENT. There are a couple of ways to pass those values to the transformation:

▶ Typing them at the command line when running the transformation with **Pan** or **Kitchen** (if the transformation is called by a job).

▶ Typing them in the transformation or job setting window when running it with Spoon.

- In a static way by providing fixed values in the **Transformation** entry setting window, as in the previous recipe.

- Dynamically by taking the values from another source as you did in this recipe.

If the values for the arguments or parameters are stored in another media, for example, a table, an Excel sheet, or a properties file, you can easily read them and pass the values to the transformation. First, you call a transformation that creates a dataset with a single row with all required values. Then, you pass the values to the transformation by configuring the **Advanced** tab properly. Let's see an example.

In the recipe, you created a transformation that generates a single row with the three needed values: `from_value`, `to_value`, and `increment_value`. By adding a **Copy rows to result** step, that row became available for use later.

In the main job, you did the trick: By checking the **Copy previous results to args?** and **Execute for every input row?** options, you take that row and pass it to the transformation as if the fields were command-line arguments. That is, the values of the fields `from_value`, `to_value`, and `increment_value`—namely 0, 90, and 30—are seen by the transformation as if they were the command-line arguments 1, 2, and 3 respectively. Note that in this case, the transformation only read two of those arguments, the third one was ignored.

With regard to the named parameter, `INCREMENT`, you passed it to the transformation by checking the **Copy previous results to parameters?** option and adding a row in the **Parameters** tab grid. Here you entered the map between the named parameter `INCREMENT` and the incoming stream field `increment_value`.

There's more...

All that was said for the **Transformation** job entry is also valid for **Job** entries. That is, you can set the **Advanced** tab in a **Job** entry to copy the previous results as arguments or as parameters to the job that is going to be executed.

See also

- The recipe named *Executing a job or a transformation by setting static arguments and parameters* in this chapter. This is useful if you know the values for the arguments and parameters beforehand.

- The recipe named *Executing a job or a transformation once for every row in dataset* in this chapter. With this recipe, you can go further and learn how to run a transformation several times, with a different set of arguments or parameters.

Executing a job or a transformation whose name is determined at runtime

Suppose that you have a couple of transformations, but you do not want to run all of them. The transformation to be executed will depend on conditions only known at runtime. If you have just two transformations, you could explicitly call one or the other in a simple fashion. On the other hand, if you have several transformations or if you do not even know the names of the available transformations, you must take another approach. This recipe shows you how.

Suppose that you want to run one of the three sample transformations described in the introduction. The transformation to run will be different depending on the time of day:

- Before 8:00 in the morning, you will call the `Hello` transformation
- Between 8:00 and 20:00, you will call the transformation that generates random numbers
- From 20:00 to midnight, you will call the transformation that lists files

Here's how to do it.

Getting ready

You will need the transformations described in the introduction. Make sure you have defined the variable $\{OUTPUT\_FOLDER\}$ with the name of the destination folder. Also, make sure that the folder exists.

Also, define a variable named $\{COMMON\_DIR\}$ with the path to the folder where you have the sample transformations, for example, `c:/my_kettle_work/common`.

How to do it...

Carry out the following steps:

1. Create the transformation that will pick the proper transformation to run.
2. Drag and drop a **Get System Info** step and use it to create a field named `now` with the system date.
3. Drag and drop a **Select Values** step and use it to get the current hour. Select the **Meta** tab; add the field named `now`, for **Type** select **String**, and for **Format**, type HH. Rename the field as `hour`.
4. Drag another **Select Values** step and use it to change the field `hour` to **Integer**.
5. After the last step, add a **Number range** step. You will find it in the **Transformation** category.

6. Double-click on the step. As **Input field:** select the field `hour` and as **Output field:** type `ktr_name`. Fill in the grid, as shown in the following screenshot:

Ranges (min <= x < max)			
#. ▲	Lower Bound	Upper Bound	Value
1		8.0	hello
2	8.0	20.0	gen_random
3	20.0		get_file_names

7. From the **Job** category, add a **Set Variables** step and use it to create a variable named `KTR_NAME` with the value of the field `ktr_name`. For **variable scope type**, leave the default **Valid in the root job**.

8. Save the transformation and do a preview on the last step. Assuming that it is 3:00 pm, you should see something like the following:

Rows of step: Set Variable ${KTR_NAME} (1 rows)		
#. ▲	hour	ktr_name
1	15	gen_random

9. Save the transformation and create a job.

10. Drag a **Start** job entry and two **Transformation** job entries into the canvas. Link the entries one after the other.

11. Configure the first **Transformation** entry to run the transformation just created.

12. Double-click on the second **Transformation** entry. For **Transformation filename:** type `${COMMON_DIR}/${KTR_NAME}.ktr` and close the window.

13. Run the job.

14. Supposing that it is 3:00 pm, the log should look like the following:

```
2010/12/04 15:00:01 - Spoon - Starting job...
...
... - Set Variable ${KTR_NAME}.0 - Set variable KTR_NAME to value
[gen_random]
...
... - run the transformation - Loading transformation from XML
file [C:/my_kettle_work/common/gen_random.ktr]
...
2010/12/04 15:00:02 - Spoon - Job has ended.
```

15. Browse the output folder (the folder defined in the variable `${OUTPUT_FOLDER}`). You should see a new file named `random.txt` with ten random numbers in it.

 Note that this file is generated whenever you run the transformation between 12:00 and 20:00. At a different time of the day, you will see a different output.

How it works...

When you execute a transformation from a job, you can either type the exact name of the transformation, or use a combination of text and variables instead.

In this recipe, you implemented the second option. As you did not know which of the three transformations you had to run, you created a transformation that set a variable with the proper name. Then, in the job, instead of typing the name of the transformation, you used that variable in combination with a variable representing the path to the `.ktr` file. When you ran the job, the first transformation set the name of the transformation to run depending on the current time. Finally, that transformation was executed.

There's more...

In the recipe, you were sure that no matter the value of the variable `${KTR_NAME}` that transformation exists. If you are not sure, it is recommended that you insert **File exist** entry before the second **Transformation** entry. With this entry, you should verify a file with the name of the transformation exists before trying to execute it. This way, you avoid your job crashing.

If instead of files you are working with a repository, you can also verify the existence of the transformation. Instead of verifying the existence of a file, you have to run a SELECT statement on the repository database to see if the transformation exists or not. If your transformation is in the root directory of the repository, then this is quite simple, but it can become a little more complicated if your transformation is deep in the transformations directory tree.

Finally, all said so far about transformations is valid for jobs as well. In order to run a job, you can either type its exact name or use a combination of text and variables, just as you did in the recipe for running a transformation.

See also

The recipe named *Getting information about transformations and jobs (repository based)* in *Chapter 9, Getting the Most Out of Kettle*. With this recipe, you will understand how to know if a transformation or job exists in a repository.

Executing part of a job once for every row in a dataset

Assume that you have a list of things or entities such as students, files, dates, products, and so on. Now, suppose that you want to execute a group of job entries once for every entity in that list.

Suppose that you have a file with a list of names, as for example:

```
name
Paul
Santiago
Lourdes
Anna
```

For each person, you want to:

- ▶ Generate a file saying hello to that person
- ▶ Wait for 2 seconds
- ▶ Write a message to the log

For a single person, these tasks can be done with a couple of entries. If you have a small known list of entities (persons in this example), then you could copy and paste that group of entries, once for each. On the other hand, if the list is long, or you do not know the values in advance, there is another way to achieve this. This recipe shows you how.

Getting ready

For this recipe, we will use the `Hello` transformation described in the introduction.

The destination folder for the file that is generated is in a variable named `${OUTPUT_FOLDER}` that has to be predefined. Make sure that the folder exists.

You will also need a sample file such as the one described.

Both the sample file and the transformation are available for download.

How to do it...

This recipe is split into three parts. The first part is the development of a transformation that generates the list of people:

1. Create a transformation. This transformation will read the list of people and send the rows outside the transformation for further processing.
2. Read the sample file with a **Text file input** step.
3. After reading the file, add a **Copy rows to result** step. You will find it under the **Job** category.
4. Do a preview on this step. You should see the following screen:

Rows of step: Copy rows to result (4 rows)		
#. ▲	**name**	
1	Paul	
2	Santiago	
3	Lourdes	
4	Anna	

5. Save the transformation.

Now, you will create a job that will generate a file for every person in the list; then deliberately wait for 2 seconds and write a message to the log.

1. Create a job. Add to the job a **START**, a **Transformation**, a **Wait for** (from the **Conditions** category), and a **Write To Log** (from the **Utility** category) entry. Link them one after the other in the same order.

2. Double-click on the **Transformation** entry and configure it to run the `Hello` transformation explained earlier.

3. Double-click on the **Wait for** entry and set the **Maximum timeout** to 2 seconds.

4. Double-click on the **Write To Log** entry. For **Log subject**, type `Information` and for **Log message**, type `A new file has been generated`.

5. The final job should look similar to the following diagram:

6. Save the job.

Finally, you will create the main job by carrying out the following steps:

1. Create another job. Add to the job a **START**, a **Transformation**, and a **Job** entry. Create a hop from the **START** to the **Transformation** entry, and another hop from this entry toward the **Job** entry.

2. Use the first entry to run the transformation that reads the file and copies the rows to result.

3. Double-click on the second entry. As **Job filename**, select the job that generates a file for a single person, that is, the job created above.

4. Select the **Advanced** tab and check the **Execute for every input row?** and **Copy previous results to args?** options.

5. Close the setting window and save the job.

6. Run the job. Under the **Job metrics** tab in the **Execution results** window, you will see something similar to the following:

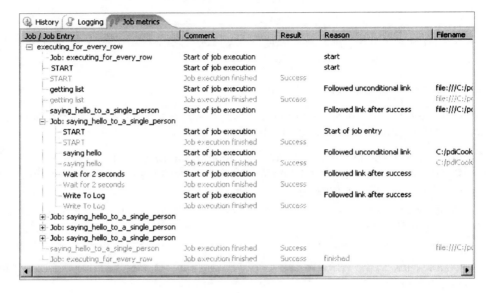

7. If you explore the output directory, you will find one file for every person in the list. The dates of the files will differ by 2 seconds one from another.

How it works...

You needed to execute a couple of entries for every person in the list. The first thing you did was to create a job (let's call it the subjob from now on) encapsulating the functionality you wanted for each person: generate the file, wait for 2 seconds, and write a message to the log.

In order to iterate the execution of the subjob over the list of people, you did the following:

▸ You created a transformation that built the list of people and copied the rows to result.

▸ You created a main job that called that transformation and then executed the subjob once for every person in the list. You did this by clicking on the **Execute for every input row?** option in the **Job** entry.

In the screenshot with the job metrics, you can see it: the execution of the transformation in the first place, followed by four executions of the subjob. Four is the number of people in our example list.

Finally, the **Copy previous results to args?** option that you checked in the **Job** entry caused the copied rows to become available (one at a time) to the subjob and in particular, to the Hello transformation inside the subjob, in the form of command-line arguments.

There's more...

When you have a set of entries that you want to execute once for every element in a list, you can do it with the following three steps:

1. Create a transformation that builds the list you need. The stream should end with a **Copy rows to result** step.

2. Create a job with the set of entries that you need to execute for every element in the list.

3. Create a job that first calls the transformation and then calls the job created above. In the **Job** entry settings window, check the **Execute for every input row?** option.

The **Copy rows to result** step causes the rows in the transformation to be copied to the outside.

The **Execute for every input row?** option causes the subjob to be executed as many times as the number of copied rows, unless an error occurs.

 If an error occurs while executing the subjob, then the iteration is aborted and the main job fails.

 If you want the iteration to continue even if the subjob fails for a single row, then modify the subjob by handling the errors properly, in order to avoid it failing.

With regard to the copied rows, they will be available one at a time to the subjob. The first execution of the subjob will see the first copied row, the second execution will see the second row, and so on. In the recipe, you accessed the copied rows by checking the **Copy previous results to args?** option, which made the rows available as command-line arguments to the subjob. There are other available options for accessing the copied rows in subsequent job entries, as you will see in the following subsection.

After that you will see particular use cases for executing entries for every element in a list.

Accessing the copied rows from jobs, transformations, and other entries

When you copy rows by using the **Copy rows to result** step, the copied rows become available to be used by the entries that are executed afterward.

There are four ways or procedures for accessing the fields of the copied row in subsequent entries:

Procedure	How to do it	Entries that support this procedure
Copying them to the arguments of an entry	Checking the **Copy previous results to args?** option	**Transformation, Job, Copy Files, Move Files, Delete files, Delete folders, Zip file, Unzip file, Truncate tables, Add filenames to result.**
Copying them as parameters	Checking the **Copy previous results to parameters?** option	**Transformation, Job**
Getting the rows from result	Using a **Get rows from result** step at the beginning of a transformation	**Transformation**
With JavaScript	Accessing the variable `row`. For example the following expression gets the value of the field `name` of the first row: `rows[0].getString("name", "")`	**JavaScript**

In the recipe, you used the first of these options: you checked the **Copy previous results to args?** option and that caused the rows to become available as the command-line arguments to the `Hello` transformation.

In this particular example, you could also have used the last method. In the `Hello` transformation, instead of reading the name as the command-line parameter 1, you could have used a **Get rows from result** step obtaining the same results. As implied from the preceding table, you don't have to check the **Copy previous results to args?** option in this case.

Executing a transformation once for every row in a dataset

If instead of a set of entries you just want to execute a single transformation once for every row in a dataset, then you don't have to move it to a subjob. Just leave the **Transformation** entry in the main job. Double-click on the entry, select the **Advanced** tab, and check the **Execute for every input row?** option. This will cause the transformation to be executed once for every row coming from a previous result.

Executing a transformation or part of a job once for every file in a list of files

If you want to execute part of a job (as a sub-job) or a transformation once for every file in a list of files, then the procedure is much the same. In the transformation that builds the list, use a **Get File Names** step from the **Input** category, in order to create the list of files. After modifying the dataset with the list of files as needed, add a **Copy rows to result** step just as you did in the recipe. The list of files will be sent outside for further processing.

Some novice users are tempted to use the **Set files in result** step instead.

 Do not use the **Set files in result** step for copying to result a row with a list of files. The **Set files in result**, has a completely different purpose compared to the **Copy rows to result** step: It adds files to a **result filelist**. Check the *See also* section below for further information about this.

See also

▶ The recipe named *Executing a job or a transformation from a job by setting arguments and parameters dynamically* in this chapter. This recipe explains the details of using the **Copy previous results to args?** and **Copy previous results to parameters?** options in a **Job** or **Transformation** entry.

▶ The recipe named *Working with ZIP files (Chapter 4)*. This recipe explains how to use the **Copy previous results to args?** in the **Zip file** entry. By following this recipe, you will get an idea of how to use it in other entries such as **Copy Files**, **Move Files**, and so on.

▶ The recipe named *Creating a process flow* in this chapter. This recipe explains the use of the couple of steps **Copy rows to result / Get rows from result**.

▶ The recipe named *Executing part of a job several times until a condition is true* in this chapter. If you wanted to access the copied row from a **JavaScript** entry, then take a look at this recipe in which this is explained.

▶ The recipe named *Copying or moving a custom list of files (Chapter 4)*. This recipe explains what the result filelist is about.

▶ The recipe named *Sending e-mails with attached files (Chapter 9, Getting the Most Out of Kettle)*. This recipe provides an example of how to use the **Set files in result** step.

Executing part of a job several times until a condition is true

Suppose that you have a list of tasks that have to be repeated while or until a condition is true (or false). If you know about programming languages, think of this as an analogy of a `while` or `repeat until` loop. Kettle allows you to implement these kinds of iterations and this recipe explains how to do it.

For the recipe, you will use one of the transformations described in the introduction of this chapter: the transformation that generates random numbers and writes them to a file. You will execute the transformation repeatedly and keep track of the number of lines written to those files. You will continue executing the transformation as long as the total number of written lines is less than 25.

Getting ready

You will need the transformation that generates random numbers described in the introduction. If instead of downloading the transformation you created it yourself, then you will have to do a quick fix in order to make Kettle save the number of written lines to the log (this has already been done in the transformation available on the book's site):

1. Edit the transformation.

2. Press *Ctrl-T* to bring the transformation's setting window.

3. Select the **Logging** tab and click on **Transformation**.

4. In the **Fields to log:** grid, search for the entry named **LINES_OUTPUT**. Under **Step name**, select the name of the step that generates the file of random numbers. The result is shown in the following screenshot:

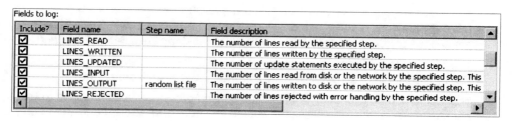

Fields to log:

Include?	Field name	Step name	Field description
☑	LINES_READ		The number of lines read by the specified step.
☑	LINES_WRITTEN		The number of lines written by the specified step.
☑	LINES_UPDATED		The number of update statements executed by the specified step.
☑	LINES_INPUT		The number of lines read from disk or the network by the specified step. This
☑	LINES_OUTPUT	random list file	The number of lines written to disk or the network by the specified step. This
☑	LINES_REJECTED		The number of lines rejected with error handling by the specified step.

5. Save the transformation.

How to do it...

Carry out the following steps:

1. Create a job.

2. From the **General** category, drag **START**, **Set variables**, and **Transformation** entries. Create a hop from the **START** entry toward the **Set variables** entry, and another from this entry toward the **Transformation** entry.

3. Double-click on the **Set variables** entry. Add a row in order to define the variable that will keep track of the number of lines written. Under **Variable name**, type total_lines, for **Value** type 0, and for **Variable scope type** select **Valid in the current job**.

4. Configure the **Transformation** entry to run the transformation that generates the random numbers.

5. From the **Scripting** category, add a **JavaScript** entry.

6. From the **Utility** category, drag two **Write To Log** entries.

7. Link the entries as shown in the following diagram:

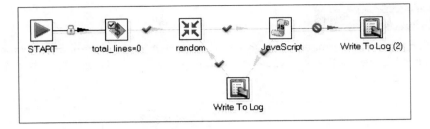

8. Double-click on the **JavaScript** entry. In the **JavaScript:** area, type the following code:

```
var total_lines = parseInt(parent_job.getVariable("total_lines"))
var new_total_lines = total_lines + previous_result.
getNrLinesOutput();
parent_job.setVariable("total_lines", new_total_lines);

new_total_lines < 25;
```

9. Double-click on the **Write To Log** entry that is executed after the success of the **JavaScript** entry (the entry at the end of the green hop). For **Log level**, select **Minimal logging**. For **Log subject**, type lines written=${total_lines}. For **Log message** type Ready to run again.

10. Double-click on the other **Write To Log** entry, the one that is executed after the failure of the **JavaScript** entry (the entry at the end of the red hop). For **Log level**, select **Minimal logging**. For **Log subject** type ${total_lines} lines have been written. For **Log message**, type The generation of random numbers has succeeded.

11. Save the job.

12. Press *F9* to run the job. For **Log level**, select **Minimal logging** and click on **Launch**.

13. In the **Logging** tab of the **Execution results** pane, you will see the following:

```
2011/01/11 22:43:50 - Spoon - Starting job...
2011/01/11 22:43:50 - main - Start of job execution
2011/01/11 22:43:50 - lines written=10 - Ready to run again ...
2011/01/11 22:43:50 - lines written=20 - Ready to run again ...
2011/01/11 22:43:51 - 30 lines have been written. - The generation
of random numbers has been successful.
2011/01/11 22:43:51 - main - Job execution finished
2011/01/11 22:43:51 - Spoon - Job has ended.
```

14. In order to confirm that 30 lines have actually been written, open the generated files.

How it works...

In order to run the transformation that generates a file with random numbers until the number of written lines is greater than 25, you implemented a loop. The following flow chart shows you the logic of this process:

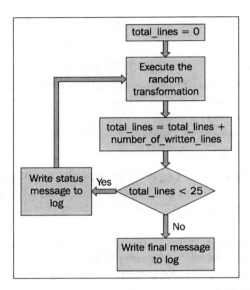

To control the execution of the transformation, you created a variable named `total_lines` and initialized this variable with the value `0`. After executing the transformation, you incremented the value of the variable using JavaScript code. If the value was less than `25`, you wrote a message to the log and re-ran the transformation. If not, you wrote a final message to the log.

The JavaScript code deserves a separate explanation:

`previous_result.getNrLinesOutput()` is the function that returns the number of lines that were written by the previous job entry. That is the value that you have to add to the `total_lines` variable, in order to keep the variable updated.

The couple of functions `parent_job.getVariable()` and `parent_job.setVariable()` are meant to get and set the value of the Kettle variable named `total_lines`. By default, the type of the Kettle variables is **String**. Therefore, in order to do the math, you had to use the `parseInt()` JavaScript function.

The second line in the JavaScript code evaluates to `True` or `False`. If it evaluates to `True`, the **JavaScript** entry follows the green arrow. If it evaluates to `False`, the **JavaScript** entry follows the red arrow.

There's more...

In this recipe, you built a loop and controlled the execution with the help of a **JavaScript** entry. The following subsections give you more information about these topics.

Implementing loops in a job

Suppose that you need to build a job in which one or more entries have to be executed repeatedly until a condition is met. People refer to these repetitive tasks as a **loop**. The first thing you have to have in mind is a clear understanding of the logic of this loop; that is, the condition that will cause the exit from the loop: You may want to exit the loop when:

 ▸ There are no more files for processing

 ▸ The number of errors exceeds a predefined threshold

 ▸ The job is taking more time than expected - maybe due to an unavailable service

 ▸ The number of records inserted into a table exceeded the expected value and so on

Once you understand this, you have to implement the logic. In the recipe, you implemented the logic with a **JavaScript** job entry. There are other entries that you can use for deciding whether to exit a loop or not. You will find useful entries for this purpose in the **Conditions** category: **Simple evaluation**, **Evaluate file metrics**, **Check webservice availability**, and so on. You can even implement the logic with an extra transformation that will succeed or fail according to your rules.

Make sure that the number of iterations is small. If you build an endless loop or a loop with many iterations, then you risk running out of heap space.

Here are a few tips to avoid errors:

If your loop is causing you troubles—for instance, you run out of memory—try to rethink the solution. The following are some alternatives you can think of:

 ▸ Solve the same problem by creating a list of elements and iterating over that list.

 ▸ Consider limiting the number of iterations to a maximum value N.

 ▸ In the logic that determines whether to exit the loop or not, add a condition for ensuring that the number of iterations remains below N.

Using the JavaScript step to control the execution of the entries in your job

The **JavaScript** entry is a useful step for controlling whether a job entry or a group of job entries should be executed or not. In particular, you used it in the recipe for deciding if the loop should end or not.

This entry works as follows: In its setting window, you should type JavaScript code that ends with an expression that evaluates to a **Boolean**. As with any job entry, the **Javascript** entry either succeeds or fails. Success or failure is decided by the result of evaluating that expression. Then, based on that value, Kettle knows which entry to execute next.

Within the code, you are free to use the `previous_result` element. The `previous_result` element is the representation of the **Result object**, an object that contains the result of the execution of the previous job entry. In the recipe, you used the `previous_result` element to ask for the number of written lines, but you can ask for the number of read lines, the number of errors, the number of executed job entries, and so on. You can find a complete description of the available `previous_result` options at the following URL: `http://wiki.pentaho.com/display/EAI/Evaluating+conditions+in+The+JavaScript+job+entry`

See also

The recipe named *Executing part of a job once for every row in dataset* in this chapter. This recipe will help you understand one of the alternative approaches for avoiding running out of memory.

Creating a process flow

Suppose that you have a dataset with a list of entities such as people, addresses, products, or names of files, just to give some examples. You need to take that data and perform some further processing such as cleaning the data, discarding the useless rows, or calculating some extra fields. Finally, you have to insert the data into a database and build an Excel sheet containing statistics about the just processed. All of this can be seen as a simple task flow or a **process flow**. With Kettle, you can easily implement a process flow like this.

Suppose that you have a file with a list of names and dates of birth, for example:

```
name,birthdate
Paul,31/12/1969
Santiago,15/02/2004
Santiago,15/02/2004
Lourdes,05/08/1994
Isabella
Anna,08/10/1978
Zoe, 15/01/1975
```

The file may have some duplicates (identical consecutive rows) and some birthdates may be absent. You want to keep only the unique rows and discard the entries of people whose date of birth is missing. Finally, you want to generate a file with the list of people you kept, along with their age sorted by date of birth.

Getting ready

You will need a sample file such as the one shown earlier in this recipe.

How to do it...

You will implement the task flow with two transformations. The first will read the data and clean it according to the earlier requirements and the second will calculate the age and generate the file. So carry out the following steps:

1. Create a transformation.

2. With a **Text file input**, read the sample file. Do a preview to make sure you are reading it properly.

3. After that step, add a **Filter rows** step (**Flow** category) and enter the condition `birthdate IS NOT NULL`.

4. Add **Unique rows** (**Transform** category).

5. Finally, add a **Copy rows to result** step. You will find it in the **Job** category. Your final transformation should look like the one in the following diagram:

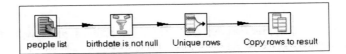

people list   birthdate is not null   Unique rows   Copy rows to result

6. Do a preview on the last step; you should see the following result:

# ▲	name	birthdate
1	Paul	31/12/1969
2	Santiago	15/02/2004
3	Lourdes	05/08/1994
4	Anna	08/10/1978
5	Zoe	15/01/1975

Rows of step: Copy rows to result (5 rows)

7. Now create the second transformation.

8. From the **Job** category, add a **Get rows from result** step.

9. Double-click on it and add two fields: a field named `name` (**String**) and a field named `birthdate` (**Date**).

The following steps are meant to calculate the age of a person at the present day, given the date of birth:

1. From the **Transform** category, add a **Calculator** step. Double-click on it and fill in the setting window as shown in the following screenshot:

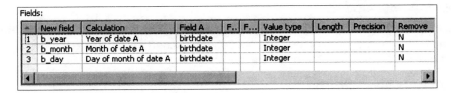

	New field	Calculation	Field A	F..	F..	Value type	Length	Precision	Remove
1	b_year	Year of date A	birthdate			Integer			N
2	b_month	Month of date A	birthdate			Integer			N
3	b_day	Day of month of date A	birthdate			Integer			N

2. From the **Scripting** category, add a **User Defined Java Expression** step (**UDJE** for short). Double-click on it and fill in the grid as shown in the following screenshot:

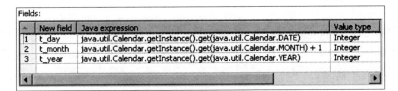

	New field	Java expression	Value type
1	t_day	java.util.Calendar.getInstance().get(java.util.Calendar.DATE)	Integer
2	t_month	java.util.Calendar.getInstance().get(java.util.Calendar.MONTH) + 1	Integer
3	t_year	java.util.Calendar.getInstance().get(java.util.Calendar.YEAR)	Integer

3. Add a fourth field named `calculated_age`. For **Value type**, select **Integer**. For **Java expression** type the following:

```
((b_month > t_month) ||
(b_month == t_month && b_day > t_day))?
(t_year - b_year - 1):(t_year - b_year)
```

 This expression is written over three lines for clarity. You should type the whole expression on a single line.

4. From the **Transform** category, add a **Sort rows** step. Use it to sort the rows by `birthdate`.

5. Finally, add a **Text file output** step and use it to generate the desired file. Provide a name for the file. For **Separator**, leave the default (;). Fill in the **Fields** grid as shown in the following screenshot:

	Name	Type	Format	L.	P.	C.	D.	G..	Trim Type	N..
1	name	String							both	
2	birthdate	Date	dd/MM/yyyy						both	
3	age	Integer	0						both	

6. Save the transformation.

Now you will create a job that will execute the transformations in order:

1. Create a job and add a **START** and two **Transformation** entries and link them one after the other.

2. Configure the entries to run the transformations you just created in the same order. First the transformation that gets the list of people and cleans the data; then the transformation that calculates the age and generates the file.

3. Save the job and run it.

4. Look at the output file. Assuming that today is January 18, 2011, the file should look like the following:

```
name;birthdate;age
Santiago;15/02/2004;6
Lourdes;05/08/1994;16
Anna;08/10/1978;32
Zoe;15/01/1975;36
Paul;31/12/1969;41
```

How it works...

You needed to perform a task defined by the following two subtasks:

1. Read and clean some data about people

2. Calculate their age and generate a sorted file

You implemented the task as a mini process flow made up of two transformations, one for each subtask then you embedded the transformations into a job that executed them one after the other. The flow of data between the first and the second transformation was determined by using the **copy/get rows mechanism**. With a **Copy rows to result** step, you sent the flow of data outside the first transformation, and with a **Get rows from result step** in the second transformation, you picked up that data to continue the process flow.

In the recipe, you did a preview on the **Copy rows to result** step and you were able to see the final data that would be sent outside the transformation. Normally you cannot preview the second transformation as is. The **Get rows from result** step is just a definition of the data that will be provided; it has no data for previewing.

 While you are designing a transformation starting with a **Get rows from result** step, you can provisionally replace that step with a step that provides some fictional data, for example, a **Text file input**, a **Generate rows**, a **Get System Info**, or a **Data Grid** step.

This fictional data has to have the same metadata as that defined in the **Get rows from result**. This will allow you to preview and test your transformation before using it as part of your process flow.

 Note that the tasks performed in this recipe could easily be done in a single transformation. We split it into two for demonstration purposes only.

The next section explains in detail when and why you should consider splitting a process into several transformations.

There's more...

There is no limit to the number of transformations that can be chained using this mechanism. You may have a transformation that copies the rows, followed by another that gets the rows and copies again, followed by a third transformation that gets the rows, and so on.

In most cases, it is possible to put them all into a single transformation. Despite this, there are still some reasons for splitting the tasks up and creating a process flow. Look at some examples:

- The transformation is so big that it's worthwhile splitting it into smaller transformations for simplicity.

- You want to separate different parts of the transformation for reuse. In the example, you might want to use the cleaned list of people for a purpose beyond that of generating a file with their ages. You can reuse the first transformation on another process without modifying it.

- You want to separate different parts of the transformation for maintainability. In the example, if you know new rules for cleansing the data (suppose that now you have to remove special characters such as quotes or brackets from the name field), then you just have to modify the first transformation leaving the second untouched.

The copy of the rows is made in memory. While this is useful when you have small datasets, for larger ones you should choose one of the following alternatives:

Serializing/De-serializing data

For transferring a dataset between transformations, there is an alternative approach - the **serialize/de-serialize mechanism**. There are two main differences between this and the **copy/get rows mechanism**, which are as follows:

1. With the serialize/de-serialize mechanism, the copy of the rows is made in files rather than in memory.

2. The serialize/de-serialize mechanism copies not only the data but the metadata as well.

Let's see it applied to our recipe.

To change the method from copy/rows to serialize/de-serialize, carry out the following steps:

1. In the first transformation, replace the **Copy rows to result** step with a **Serialize to file** step from the **Input** category.

2. Double-click on the step and provide a name for the file in the **Filename** textbox.

3. In the second transformation, replace the **Get rows from result** step with a **De-serialize from file** step, found in the **Output** category.

4. Double-click on the step and in the **Filename** textbox, type the same file name you typed in the **Serialize to file** step.

5. Execute the first transformation; a file with the given name should have been generated.

6. Do a preview in the **De-serialize from file** step; you will see the data copied from the first transformation.

7. If you run the job, you should obtain the same results as you obtained using the main recipe.

For large datasets this method is recommended over the previous one. This method is also practical for datasets that have many columns or where the number or order of columns changes over time. As the metadata is saved in the file along with the data, you are not required to specify the details in the second transformation.

 Note that the file generated with a **Serialize to file** step has a binary format and cannot be read with a text editor.

Other means for transferring or sharing data between transformations

As mentioned earlier, a simple way for transferring or sharing data between transformations is by the use of the copy/get rows mechanism. A step further is the use of the serialize/de-serialize method. Now, suppose that you need the data for some extra purpose besides transferring it between these two transformations. For example, suppose that you need to send it to someone by e-mail. None of those methods will work in this case. As said, the first copies the data via memory and the second saves the data to an unreadable file. In this case, you have other alternatives, such as saving the data in a text file or to a database table in the first transformation, and then creating the dataset from the file or table in the second transformation.

 The database method is also the preferred method in the case where you are dealing with large datasets. Staging large quantities of data on disk should be avoided if possible.

Moving part of a transformation to a subtransformation

Suppose that you have a part of a transformation that you will like to use in another transformation. A quick way to do that would be to copy the set of steps and paste them into the other transformation, and then perform some modifications, for example, changing the names of the fields accordingly.

Now you realize that you need it in a third place. You do that again: copy, paste, and modify.

What if you notice that there was a bug in that part of the transformation? Or maybe you'd like to optimize something there? You would need to do that in three different places! This inconvenience is one of the reasons why you might like to move those steps to a common place - a **subtransformation**.

In this recipe, you will develop a subtransformation that receives the following two dates:

1. A date of birth
2. A reference date

The subtransformation will calculate how old a person was (or will be) at the reference date if the date of birth provided was theirs.

For example, if the date of birth is December 30, 1979 and the reference date is December 19, 2010 the age would be calculated as 30 years.

Then, you will call that subtransformation from a main transformation.

Getting ready

You will need a file containing a list of names and dates of birth, for example:

```
name,birthdate
Paul,31/12/1969
Santiago,15/02/2004
Lourdes,05/08/1994
Anna,08/10/1978
```

How to do it...

This recipe is split into two parts.

First, you will create the subtransformation by carrying out the following steps:

1. Create a transformation.

2. From the **Mapping** category, add two **Mapping input specification** and one **Mapping output specification** steps. Rename this step `output`.

3. Also, add a **Join Rows (Cartesian product)** (**Join** category), a **Calculator** (**Transform** category), and a **User Defined Java Expression** or **UDJE** for short (**Scripting** category) step. Link the steps as shown in the following diagram:

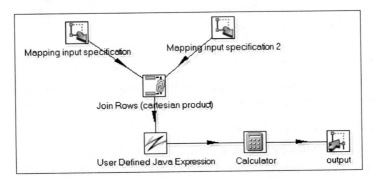

4. Double-click on one of the **Mapping input specification** steps. Add a field named `birth field`. For **Type**, select **Date**. Name the step `birthdates`.

5. Double-click on the other **Mapping input specification** step. Add a field named `reference_field`. For **Type**, select **Date**. Name the step `reference date`.

6. Double-click the **Join** step. For **Main step to read from**, select **birthdates**.

The following two steps perform the main task - the calculation of the age.

 Note that these steps are a slightly modified version of the steps you used for calculating the age in the previous recipe.

1. Double-click on the **Calculator** step and fill in the setting window, as shown in the following screenshot:

Fields:

	New field	Calculation	Field A	F.	F	Value type	L...	P..	Remove
1	b_year	Year of date A	birth_field			Integer			N
2	b_month	Month of date A	birth_field			Integer			N
3	b_day	Day of month of date A	birth_field			Integer			N
4	t_year	Year of date A	reference_field			Integer			N
5	t_month	Month of date A	reference_field			Integer			N
6	t_day	Day of month of date A	reference_field			Integer			N

2. Double-click on the **UDJE** step. Add a field named `calculated_age`. As **Value type**, select **Integer**. For **Java expression** type:

```
((b_month > t_month) ||
(b_month - t_month ==0  && b_day > t_day))?
(t_year - b_year - 1):(t_year - b_year)
```

 The expression is written over three lines for clarity. You should type the whole expression on a single line.

3. Save the transformation.

Now you will create the main transformation. It will read the sample file and calculate the age of the people in the file as at the present day.

1. Create another transformation.

2. Use a **Text file input** step to read the sample file. Name the step `people`.

3. Use a **Get System Info** step to get the present day: Add a field named `today`. For **Type**, select **Today 00:00:00**. Name the step `today`.

4. From the **Mapping** category, add a **Mapping (sub-transformation)** step. Link the steps as shown in the following diagram:

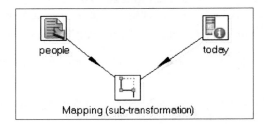

5. Double-click on the **Mapping** step. The following are the most important steps in this recipe!

6. In the first textbox, under the text **Use a file for the mapping transformation**, select the transformation created earlier.

7. Click on the **Add Input** button. A new **Input** tab will be added to the window. Under this tab, you will define a correspondence between the incoming step `people` and the subtransformation step `birthdates`.

8. In the **Input source step name**, type `people`, the name of the step that reads the file.

 Alternatively, you can select it by clicking on the **Choose...** button.

9. In the **Mapping target step name**, type `birthdates`, the name of the subtransformation step that expects the dates of birth.

10. Click on **Ask these values to be renamed back on output?**

11. Under the same tab, fill in the grid as follows: Under **Fieldname from source step** type `birthdate`, the name of the field coming out the **people** step containing the date of birth. Under **Fieldname to mapping input step**, type `birth_field`, the name of the field in the subtransformation step **birthdates** that will contain the date of birth needed for calculating the age.

 Alternatively, you can add the whole line by clicking on **Mapping...** and selecting the matching fields in the window that is displayed.

12. Add another **Input** tab. Under this tab, you will define a correspondence between the incoming step `today` and the subtransformation step `reference date`. Fill in the tab as follows:

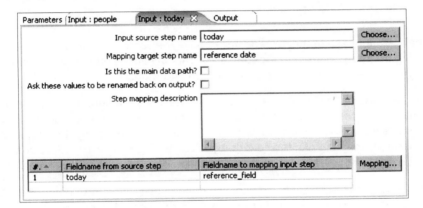

13. Finally, click on **Add Output** to add an **Output** tab. Under this tab, click on **Is this the main data path?**

14. Under the same tab, fill in the grid as follows: Under **Fieldname from mapping step,** type `calculated_age`. Under **Fieldname to target step,** type `age`.

15. Close the mapping settings window and save the transformation.

16. Do a preview on the last step; you should see the following screen:

Rows of step: calculating age (4 rows)

	name	birthdate	reference_field	b_year	b_month	b_day	t_year	t_month	t_day	age
1	Paul	31/12/1969	2011/01/15 0...	1969	12	31	2011	1	15	41
2	Santiago	15/02/2004	2011/01/15 0...	2004	2	15	2011	1	15	6
3	Lourdes	05/08/1994	2011/01/15 0...	1994	8	5	2011	1	15	16
4	Anna	08/10/1978	2011/01/15 0...	1978	10	8	2011	1	15	32

How it works...

The subtransformation (the first transformation you created) has the purpose of calculating the age of a person at a given reference date. In order to do that, it defines two entry points through the use of the **Mapping input specification** steps. These steps are meant to specify the fields needed by the subtransformation. In this case, you defined the date of birth in one entry point and the reference date in the other. Then it calculates the age in the same way you would do it with any regular transformation. Finally it defines an output point through the **Mapping output specification** step.

Note that we developed the subtransformation blindly, without testing or previewing. This was because you cannot preview a subtransformation. The **Mapping input specification** steps are just a definition of the data that will be provided; they have no data to preview.

 While you are designing a subtransformation, you can provisionally substitute each **Mapping input specification** step with a step that provides some fictional data, for example, a **Text file input**, a **Generate rows**, a **Get System Info**, or a **Data Grid** step.

This fictional data for each of these steps has to have the same metadata as the corresponding **Mapping input specification** step. This will allow you to preview and test your subtransformation before calling it from another transformation.

Now, let's explain the main transformation, the one that calls the subtransformation. You added as many input tabs as entry points to the subtransformation. The input tabs are meant to map the steps and fields in your transformation to the corresponding steps and fields in the subtransformation. For example, the field that you called `today` in your main transformation became `reference_field` in the subtransformation.

On the other side, in the subtransformation, you defined just one output point. Therefore, under the **Output** tab, you clicked on **Is this the main data path?** Checking it means that you don't need to specify the correspondence between steps. What you did under this tab was fill in the grid to ask the field `calculated_age` be renamed to `age`.

In the final preview, you can see all the fields you had before the subtransformation, plus the fields added by it. Among these fields, there is the `age` field which was the main field you expected to be added.

As you can see in the final dataset, the field `birthdates` kept its name, while the field `today` was renamed to `reference_field`. The field `birthdates` kept its name because you checked the **Ask these values to be renamed back on output?** option under the **people** input tab. On the other hand, the field `today` was renamed because you didn't check that option under the **today** input tab.

There's more...

Kettle subtransformations are a practical way to centralize some functionality so that it may be used in more than one place. Another use of subtransformations is to isolate a part of a transformation that meets some specific purpose as a whole, in order to keep the main transformation simple, no matter whether you will reuse that part or not.

Let's look at some examples of what you might like to implement via a subtransformation:

- Take some free text representing an address, parse it, and return the street name, street number, city, zip code, and state.
- Take some text, validate it according to a set of rules, clean it, for example by removing some unwanted characters and return the validated clean text along with a flag indicating whether the original text was valid or not.
- Take an error code and write a customized line to the Kettle log.
- Take the date of birth of a person and a reference date and calculate how old that person was at the reference date.

If you then wish to implement any of the following enhancements, you will need to do it in one place:

- Enhance the process for parsing the parts of an address
- Change the rules for validating the text
- Internationalize the text you write to the Kettle log
- Change the method or algorithm for calculating the age

From the development point of view, a subtransformation is just a regular transformation with some input and output steps connecting it to the transformations that use it.

Back in *Chapter 6, Understanding Data Flows*, it was explained that when a transformation is launched, each step starts a new thread; that is, all steps work simultaneously. The fact that we are using a sub transformation does not change that. When you run a transformation that calls a subtransformation, both the steps in the transformation and those in the subtransformation start at the same time, and run in parallel. The subtransformation is not an isolated process; the data in the main transformation just flows through the subtransformation. Imagine this flow as if the steps in the subtransformation were part of the main transformation. In this sense, it is worth noting that a common cause of error in the development of subtransformations is the wrong use of the **Select values** step.

 Selecting some values with a **Select values** step by using the **Select & Alter** tab in a subtransformation will implicitly remove not only the rest of the fields in the subtransformation, but also all of the fields in the transformation that calls it.

If you need to rename or reorder some fields in a subtransformation, then make sure you check the **Include unspecified fields, ordered by name** option in order to keep not only the rest of the fields in the subtransformation but also the fields coming from the calling transformation.

If what you need is to remove some fields, do not use the **Select & Alter** tab; use the **Remove** tab instead. If needed, use another **Select values** step to reorder or rename the fields afterward.

8
Integrating Kettle and the Pentaho Suite

In this chapter, we will cover:

- ▶ Creating a Pentaho report with data coming from PDI
- ▶ Configuring the Pentaho BI Server for running PDI jobs and transformations
- ▶ Executing a PDI transformation as part of a Pentaho process
- ▶ Executing a PDI job from the **PUC** (**Pentaho User Console**)
- ▶ Generating files from the PUC with PDI and the **CDA** (**Community Data Access**) plugin
- ▶ Populating a **CDF** (**Community Dashboard Framework**) dashboard with data coming from a PDI transformation

Introduction

Kettle, also known as PDI, is mostly used as a stand-alone application. However, it is not an isolated tool, but part of the **Pentaho Business Intelligence Suite**. As such, it can also interact with other components of the suite; for example, as the datasource for a report, or as part of a bigger process. This chapter shows you how to run Kettle jobs and transformations in that context.

The chapter assumes a basic knowledge of the **Pentaho BI platform** and the tools that made up the Pentaho Suite. If you are not familiar with these tools, it is recommended that you visit the wiki page (`wiki.pentaho.com`) or the **Pentaho BI Suite Community Edition** (**CE**) site: `http://community.pentaho.com/`.

As another option, you can get the Pentaho Solutions book (Wiley) by Roland Bouman and Jos van Dongen that gives you a good introduction to the whole suite.

A sample transformation

The different recipes in this chapter show you how to run Kettle transformations and jobs integrated with several components of the Pentaho BI suite. In order to focus on the integration itself rather than on Kettle development, we have created a sample transformation named `weather.ktr` that will be used through the different recipes.

The transformation receives the name of a city as the first parameter from the command line, for example `Madrid, Spain`. Then, it consumes a web service to get the current weather conditions and the forecast for the next five days for that city. The transformation has a couple of named parameters:

Name	Purpose	Default
TEMP	Scale for the temperature to be returned. It can be C (Celsius) or F (Farenheit)	C
SPEED	Scale for the wind speed to be returned. It can be Kmph or Miles	Kmph

The following diagram shows what the transformation looks like:

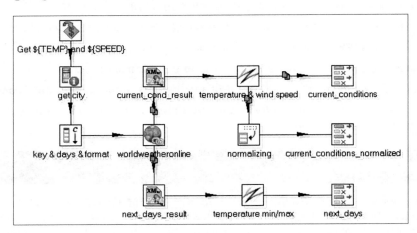

It receives the command-line argument and the named parameters, calls the service, and retrieves the information in the desired scales for temperature and wind speed.

You can download the transformation from the book's site and test it. Do a preview on the **next_days, current_conditions**, and **current_conditions_normalized** steps to see what the results look like.

The following is a sample preview of the **next_days** step:

Rows of step: next_days (6 rows)

	city	date	temperatureMin	temperatureMax
1	Madrid, Spain	2011-01-29	1	7
2	Madrid, Spain	2011-01-30	-2	6
3	Madrid, Spain	2011-01-31	-3	6
4	Madrid, Spain	2011-02-01	-3	8
5	Madrid, Spain	2011-02-02	-3	9
6	Madrid, Spain	2011-02-03	0	12

The following is a sample preview of the **current_conditions** step:

Rows of step: current_conditions (1 rows)

	city	observation_time	temperature	weatherDesc	windspeedMiles	windspeedKmph
1	Madrid, Spain	10:12 PM	4	Partly Cloudy	11	17

Finally, the following screenshot shows you a sample preview of the **current_conditions_ normalized** step:

Rows of step: current_conditions_normalized (11 rows)

#	FEATURE	VALUE
1	City	Madrid, Spain
2	Observation time	10:14 PM
3	Weather description	Partly Cloudy
4	Temperature	4
5	Wind speed	17
6	Wind direction	WSW
7	Precipitation	2.0
8	Humidity	81
9	Visibility	10
10	Pressure	1010
11	Cloud Cover	75

For details about the web service and understanding the results, you can take a look at the recipe named *Specifying fields by using XPath notation* (*Chapter 2, Reading and Writing Files*)

There is also another transformation named `weather_np.ktr`. This transformation does exactly the same, but it reads the city as a named parameter instead of reading it from the command line. The *Getting ready* sections of each recipe will tell you which of these transformations will be used.

Avoiding consuming the web service

It may happen that you do not want to consume the web service (for example, for delay reasons), or you cannot do it (for example, if you do not have Internet access). Besides, if you call a free web service like this too often, then your IP might be banned from the service. Don't worry. Along with the sample transformations on the book's site, you will find another version of the transformations that instead of using the web service, reads sample fictional data from a file containing the forecast for over 250 cities. The transformations are `weather (file version).ktr` and `weather_np (file version).ktr`. Feel free to use these transformations instead. You should not have any trouble as the parameters and the metadata of the data retrieved are exactly the same as in the transformations explained earlier.

If you use transformations that do not call the web service, remember that they rely on the file with the fictional data (`weatheroffline.txt`). Wherever you copy the transformations, do not forget to copy that file as well.

Creating a Pentaho report with data coming from PDI

The **Pentaho Reporting Engine** allows designing, creating, and distributing reports in various popular formats (HTML, PDF, and so on) from different kind of sources (JDBC, OLAP, XML, and so on).

There are occasions where you need other kinds of sources such as text files or Excel files, or situations where you must process the information before using it in a report. In those cases, you can use the output of a Kettle transformation as the source of your report. This recipe shows you this capability of the Pentaho Reporting Engine.

For this recipe, you will develop a very simple report: The report will ask for a city and a temperature scale and will report the current conditions in that city. The temperature will be expressed in the selected scale.

Getting ready

A basic understanding of the Pentaho Report Designer tool is required in order to follow this recipe. You should be able to create a report, add parameters, build a simple report, and preview the final result.

Regarding the software, you will need the Pentaho Report Designer. You can download the latest version from the following URL:

`http://sourceforge.net/projects/pentaho/files/Report%20Designer/`

You will also need the sample transformation `weather.ktr`.

The sample transformation has a couple of **UDJE** steps. These steps rely on the **Janino** library. In order to be able to run the transformation from Report Designer, you will have to copy the `janino.jar` file from the Kettle `libext` directory into the Report Designer `lib` directory.

How to do it...

In the first part of the recipe, you will create the report and define the parameters for the report: the city and the temperature scale.

1. Launch Pentaho Report Designer and create a new blank report.
2. Add two mandatory parameters: A parameter named `city_param`, with `Lisbon, Portugal` as **Default Value** and a parameter named `scale_param` which accepts two possible values: `C` meaning Celsius or `F` meaning Fahrenheit.

Now, you will define the data source for the report:

1. In the **Data** menu, select **Add Data Source** and then **Pentaho Data Integration**.
2. Click on the **Add a new query** button. A new query named `Query 1` will be added. Give the query a proper name, for example, `forecast`.
3. Click on the **Browse** button. Browse to the sample transformation and select it. The **Steps** listbox will be populated with the names of the steps in the transformation.
4. Select the step `current_conditions`. So far, you have the following:

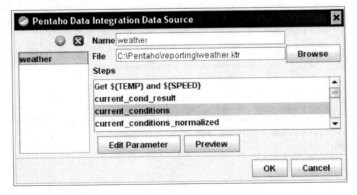

The specification of the transformation file name with the complete path will work only inside Report Designer. Before publishing the report, you should edit the file name (`C:\Pentaho\reporting\weather.ktr` in the preceding example) and leave just a path relative to the directory where the report is to be published (for example, `reports\weather.ktr`).

5. Click on **Preview**; you will see an empty resultset. The important thing here is that the headers should be the same as the output fields of the **current_conditions** step: city, observation_time, weatherDesc, and so on.

6. Now, close that window and click on **Edit Parameters**.

7. You will see two grids: **Transformation Parameter** and **Transformation Arguments**. Fill in the grids as shown in the following screenshot. You can type the values or select them from the available drop-down lists:

8. Close the **Pentaho Data Integration Data Source** window. You should have the following:

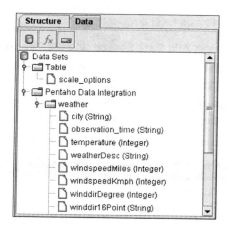

The data coming from Kettle is ready to be used in your report.

9. Build the report layout: Drag and drop some fields into the canvas and arrange them as you please. Provide a title as well. The following screenshot is a sample report you can design:

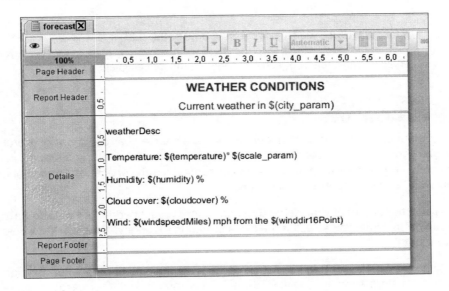

10. Now, you can do a **Print Preview**. The sample report above will look like the one shown in the following screenshot:

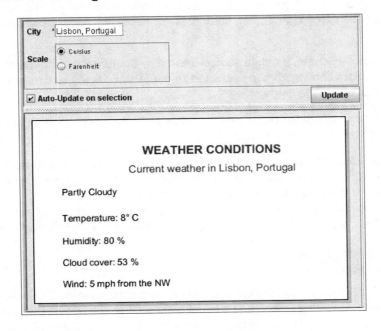

Note that the output of the **current_condition** step has just one row.

If for data source you choose the *next_days* or the *current_condition_normalized* step instead, then the result will have several rows. In that case, you could design a report by columns: one column for each field.

How it works...

Using the output of a Kettle transformation as the data source of a report is very useful because you can take advantage of all the functionality of the PDI tool. For instance, in this case you built a report based on the result of consuming a web service. You could not have done this with Pentaho Report Designer alone.

In order to use the output of your Kettle transformation, you just added a **Pentaho Data Integration** datasource. You selected the transformation to run and the step that would deliver your data.

In order to be executed, your transformation needs a command-line parameter: the name of the city. The transformation also defines two named parameters: the temperature scale and the wind scale. From the Pentaho Report Designer you provided both—a value for the city and a value for the temperature scale. You did it by filling in the **Edit Parameter** setting window inside the **Pentaho Data Integration Data Source** window. Note that you did not supply a value for the SPEED named parameter, but that is not necessary because Kettle uses the default value.

As you can see in the recipe, the data source created by the report engine has the same structure as the data coming from the selected step: the same fields with the same names, same data types, and in the same order.

Once you configured this data source, you were able to design your report as you would have done with any other kind of data source.

Finally, when you are done and want to publish your report on the server, do not forget to fix the path as explained in the recipe—the **File** should be specified with a path relative to the solution folder. For example, suppose that your report will be published in my_solution/reports, and you put the transformation file in my_solution/reports/resources. In that case, for **File**, you should type resources/ plus the name of the transformation.

There's more...

Pentaho Reporting is a suite of Java projects built for report generation. The suite is made up of the Pentaho Reporting Engine and a set of tools such as the Report Designer (the tool used in this recipe), Report Design Wizard, and Pentaho's web-based Ad Hoc Reporting user interface.

In order to be able to run transformations, the Pentaho Reporting software includes the Kettle libraries. To avoid any inconvenience, be sure that the versions of the libraries included are the same or newer than the version of Kettle you are using. For instance, Pentaho Reporting 3.8 includes Kettle 4.1.2 libraries. If you are using a different version of Pentaho Reporting, then you can verify the Kettle version by looking in the `lib` folder inside the reporting installation folder. You should look for files named `kettle-core-<version>.jar`, `kettle-db-<version>.jar`, and `kettle-engine-<version>.jar`.

Besides, if the transformations you want to use as data sources rely on external libraries, then you have to copy the proper jar files from the Kettle `libext` directory into the Report Designer `lib` folder, just as you did with the `janino.jar` file in the recipe.

For more information about Pentaho Reporting, just visit the following wiki website:

`http://wiki.pentaho.com/display/Reporting/Pentaho+Reporting+Community +Documentation`

Alternatively, you can get the book **Pentaho Reporting 3.5 for Java Developers** (*Packt Publishing*) by *Will Gorman*.

Configuring the Pentaho BI Server for running PDI jobs and transformations

The Pentaho BI Server is a collection of software components that provide the architecture and infrastructure required to build business intelligence solutions. With the Pentaho BI Server, you are able to run reports, visualize dashboards, schedule tasks, and more. Among these tasks, there is the ability to run Kettle jobs and transformations. This recipe shows you the minor changes you might have to make in order to be able to run Kettle jobs and transformations.

Getting ready

In order to follow this recipe, you will need some experience with the Pentaho BI Server.

For configuring the Pentaho BI server, you obviously need the software. You can download the latest version of the Pentaho BI Server from the following URL:

`http://sourceforge.net/projects/pentaho/files/Business%20 Intelligence%20Server/`

 Make sure you download the distribution that matches your platform.

If you intend to run jobs and transformations from a Kettle repository, then make sure you have the name of the repository and proper credentials (user and password).

How to do it...

Carry out the following steps:

1. If you intend to run a transformation or a job from a file, skip to the *How it works* section.

2. Edit the `settings.xml` file located in the `\biserver-ce\pentaho-solutions\system\kettle` folder inside the Pentaho BI Server installation folder.

3. In the `repository.type` tag, replace the default value `files` with `rdbms`. Provide the name of your Kettle repository and the user and password, as shown in the following example:

```
<kettle-repository>

   <!-- The values within <properties> are passed directly to the
Kettle Pentaho components. -->

   <!-- This is the location of the Kettle repositories.xml file,
leave empty if the default is used: $HOME/.kettle/repositories.xml
-->

   <repositories.xml.file></repositories.xml.file>

   <repository.type>rdbms</repository.type>

   <!--  The name of the repository to use -->
   <repository.name>pdirepo</repository.name>

   <!--  The name of the repository user -->
   <repository.userid>dev</repository.userid>

   <!--  The password -->
   <repository.password>1234</repository.password>

</kettle-repository>
```

4. Start the server. It will be ready to run jobs and transformations from your Kettle repository.

How it works...

If you want to run Kettle transformations and jobs, then the Pentaho BI server already includes the Kettle libraries. The server is ready to run both jobs and transformations from files. If you intend to use a repository, then you have to provide the repository settings. In order to do this, you just have to edit the `settings.xml` file, as you did in the recipe.

There's more...

To avoid any inconvenience, be sure that the version of the libraries included are the same or newer than the version of Kettle you are using. For instance, Pentaho BI Server 3.7 includes Kettle 4.1 libraries. If you are using a different version of the server, then you can verify the Kettle version by looking in the following folder:

`\biserver-ce\tomcat\webapps\pentaho\WEB-INF\lib`

This folder is inside the server installation folder. You should look for files named `kettle-core-TRUNK-SNAPSHOT.jar`, `kettle-db-TRUNK-SNAPSHOT.jar`, and `kettle-engine-TRUNK-SNAPSHOT.jar`.

Unzip any of them and look for the `META-INF\MANIFEST.MF` file. There, you will find the Kettle version. You will see a line like this: `Implementation-Version: 4.1.0`.

There is even an easier way: In the **Pentaho User Console** (**PUC**), look for the option **2. Get Environment Information** inside the **Data Integration with Kettle** folder of the **BI Developer Examples** solution; run it and you will get detailed information about the Kettle environment.

> For your information, the transformation that is run behind the scenes is `GetPDIEnvironment.ktr` located in the `biserver-ce\pentaho-solutions\bi-developers\etl` folder.

See also

- ▶ The recipe named *Executing a PDI transformation as part of a Pentaho process* in this chapter.
- ▶ The recipe named *Executing a PDI job from the PUC (Pentaho User Console)* in this chapter.

Executing a PDI transformation as part of a Pentaho process

Everything in the Pentaho platform is made of action sequences. An **action sequence** is, as its name suggests, a sequence of atomic actions that together accomplish small processes. Those atomic actions cover a broad spectrum of tasks, for example, getting data from a table in a database, running a piece of JavaScript code, launching a report, sending e-mails, or running a Kettle transformation.

For this recipe, suppose that you want to run the sample transformation to get the current weather conditions for some cities. Instead of running this from the command line, you want to interact with this service from the PUC. You will do it with an action sequence.

Getting ready

In order to follow this recipe, you will need a basic understanding of action sequences and at least some experience with the Pentaho BI Server and **Pentaho Design Studio**, the action sequences editor.

Before proceeding, make sure that you have a Pentaho BI Server running. You will also need Pentaho Design Studio. You can download the latest version from the following URL:

```
http://sourceforge.net/projects/pentaho/files/Design%20Studio/
```

Finally, you will need the sample transformation `weather.ktr`.

How to do it...

This recipe is split into two parts: First, you will create the action sequence, and then you will test it from the PUC. So carry out the following steps:

1. Launch Design Studio. If this is your first use, then create the solution project where you will save your work.
2. Copy the sample transformation to the solution folder.
3. Create a new action sequence and save it in your solution project with the name `weather.xaction`.
4. Define two inputs that will be used as the parameters for your transformation: `city_name` and `temperature_scale`.
5. Add two **Prompt/Secure Filter** actions and configure them to prompt for the name of the city and the temperature scale.
6. Add a new process action by selecting **Get Data From | Pentaho Data Integration**.
7. Now, you will fill in the **Input Section** of the process action configuration. Give the process action a name.
8. For **Transformation File**, type `solution:weather.ktr`. For **Transformation Step**, type `current_conditions_normalized` and for **Kettle Logging Level**, type or select **basic**.
9. In the **Transformation Inputs**, add the inputs `city_name` and `temperature_scale`.
10. Select the **XML source** tab.
11. Search for the `<action-definition>` tag that contains the following line:
    ```
    <component-name>KettleComponent</component-name>
    ```

12. You will find something like this:

```
<action-definition>
  <component-name>KettleComponent</component-name>
  <action-type>looking for the current weather</action-type>

    <action-inputs>
      <city_name type="string"/>
      <temperature_scale type="string"/>
    </action-inputs>
    <action-resources>
      <transformation-file type="resource"/>
    </action-resources>
    <action-outputs/>
    <component-definition>
      <monitor-step><![CDATA[current_conditions]]></monitor-step>
      <kettle-logging-level><![CDATA[basic]]></kettle-logging-
        level>
    </component-definition>
</action-definition>
```

13. Below `<component-definition>`, type the following:

```
<set-parameter>
    <name>TEMP</name>
    <mapping>temperature_scale</mapping>
</set-parameter>

<set-argument>
    <name>1</name>
    <mapping>city_name</mapping>
</set-argument>
```

 In fact, you can type this anywhere between `<component-definition>` and `</component-definition>`. The order of the internal tags is not important.

14. Go back to the tab named **2. Define Process**.

15. Now, fill in the **Output Section** of the **Process Data Integration** process action. For **Output Rows Name**, type `weather_result` and for **Output Rows Count Name**, type `number_of_rows`.

16. Below the **Process Data Integration** process action, add an **If Statement**. As the condition, type `number_of_rows==0`.

17. Within the **If Statement**, add a **Message Template** process action.

18. In the **Text** frame, type `No results for the city {city_name}`. For **Output Name**, type `weather_result`.

19. Finally, in the **Process Outputs** section of the action sequence, add **weather_result** as the only output.

20. Your final action sequence should look like the one shown in the following screenshot:

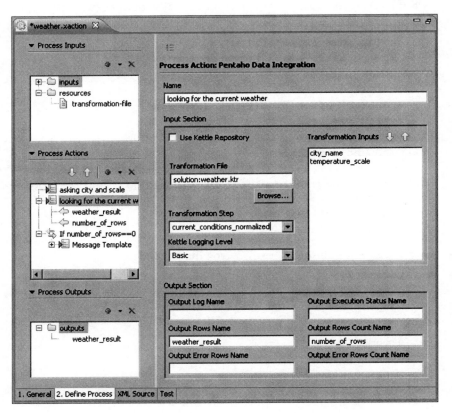

21. Save the file.

Now, it is time to test the action sequence that you just created.

1. Login to the PUC and refresh the repository, so that the `weather.xaction` that you just created shows up.

2. Browse the solution folders and look for the **xaction** and double-click on it.

3. Provide a name of a city and change the temperature scale, if you wish.

4. Click on **Run**; you will see something similar to the following:

FEATURE	VALUE
	Weather conditions ⊗
	Action Successful
City	Rome, Italy
Observation time	05:37 PM
Weather description	Partly Cloudy
Temperature	45
Wind speed	31
Wind direction	N
Precipitation	14.0
Humidity	93
Visibility	8
Pressure	1008
Cloud Cover	75

5. You can take a look at the Pentaho console to see the log of the transformation running behind the scenes.

6. Run the action sequence again. This time, type the name of a fictional city, for example, my_invented_city. This time, you will see the following message

```
Action Successful
weather_result=No results for the city my_invented_city
```

How it works...

You can run Kettle transformations as part of an action sequence by using the **Pentaho Data Integration process action** located within the **Get Data From** category of process actions.

The main task of a PDI process action is to run a Kettle transformation. In order to do that, it has a list of checks and textboxes where you specify everything you need to run the transformation and everything you want to receive back after having run it.

The most important setting in the PDI process action is the name and location of the transformation to be executed. In this example, you had a .ktr file in the same location as the action sequence, so you simply typed solution: followed by the name of the file.

Then, in the **Transformation Step** textbox, you specified the name of the step in the transformation that would give you the results you needed. The PDI process action (just as any regular **process action**) is capable of receiving input from the action sequence and returning data to be used later in the sequence. Therefore, in the drop-down list in the **Transformation Step** textbox, you could see the list of available action sequence inputs. In this case, you just typed the name of the step.

> If you are not familiar with action sequences, note that the drop-down list in the **Transformation Step** textbox is not the list of available steps. It is the list of available action sequence inputs.

You have the option of specifying the Kettle log level. In this case, you selected **Basic**. This was the level of log that Kettle wrote to the Pentaho console. Note that in this case, you also have the option of selecting an action sequence input instead of one of the log levels in the list.

As said earlier, the process action can use any inputs from the action sequence. In this case, you used two inputs: `city_name` and `temperature_scale`. Then you passed them to the transformation in the XML code:

▶ By putting `city_name` between `<set-parameter></set-parameter>`, you passed the `city_name` input as the first command-line argument.

▶ By putting `temperature_scale` between `<set-argument></set-argument>`, you passed the `temperature_scale` to the transformation as the value for the named parameter `TEMP`.

As mentioned, the process can return data to be used later in the sequence. The textboxes in the **Output Section** are meant to do that. Each textbox you fill in will be a new data field to be sent to the next process action. In this case, you defined two outputs: `weather_result` and `number_of_rows`. The first contains the dataset that comes out of the step you defined in **Transformation Step**; in this case, `current_conditions_normalized`. The second has the number of rows in that dataset.

You used those outputs in the next process action. If `number_of_rows` was equal to zero, then you would overwrite the `weather_result` data with a message to be displayed to the user.

Finally, you added the `weather_result` as the output of the action sequence, so that the user either sees the current conditions for the required city, or the custom message indicating that the city was not found.

There's more...

The following are some variants in the use of the Pentaho Data Integration process action:

Specifying the location of the transformation

When your transformation is in a file, you specify the location by typing or browsing for the name of the file. You have to provide the name relative to the solution folder. In the recipe, the transformation was in the same folder as the action sequence, so you simply typed `solution:` followed by the name of the transformation including the extension `ktr`.

If instead of having the transformation in a file it is located in a repository, then you should check the **Use Kettle Repository** option. The **Transformation File** textbox will be replaced with two textboxes named **Directory** and **Transformation File**. In these textboxes, you should type the name of the folder and the transformation exactly as they are in the repository. Alternatively, you can select the names from the available drop-down lists.

In these drop-down lists, you will not see the available directories and transformations in the repository. The lists are populated with the available action sequence inputs. This also applies to specifying the location of a job in an action sequence.

Supplying values for named parameters, variables and arguments

If your transformation defines or needs named parameters, Kettle variables or command-line arguments, you can pass them from the action sequence by mapping **KettleComponent** inputs.

First of all, you need to include them in the **Transformation Inputs** section. This is equivalent to typing them inside the KettleComponent action-definition XML element.

Then, depending on the kind of data to pass, you have to define a different element:

Element in the transformation	Element in the action sequence
Command line parameter	`<set-argument></set-argument>`
Variable	`<set-variable></set-variable>`
Named parameter	`<set-parameter></set-parameter>`

In the recipe, you mapped one command line argument and one named parameter.

With the following lines, you mapped the input named `temperature_scale` with the named parameter `TEMP`:

```
<set-parameter>
    <name>TEMP</name>
    <mapping>temperature_scale</mapping>
</set-parameter>
```

In the case of a variable, the syntax is exactly the same.

In the case of arguments instead of a name, you have to provide the position of the parameter: 1, 2, and so on.

> Design Studio does not implement the capability of mapping inputs with variables or named parameters. Therefore, you have to type the mappings in the XML code. If you just want to pass command-line arguments, then you can skip this task because by default, it is assumed that the inputs you enter are command-line arguments.
>
> This way of providing values for named parameters, variables, and command-line arguments also applies to jobs executed from an action sequence.

Keeping things simple when it's time to deliver a plain file

Reporting is a classic way of delivering data. In the PUC, you can publish not only Pentaho reports, but also third-party ones, for example, Jasper reports. However, what if the final user simply wants a plain file with some numbers in it? You can avoid the effort of creating it with a reporting tool. Just create a Kettle transformation that does it and call it from an action, in the same way you did in the recipe. This practical example is clearly explained by *Nicholas Goodman* in his blog post *Self Service Data Export using Pentaho*. The following is the link to that post, which also includes sample code for downloading:

```
http://www.nicholasgoodman.com/bt/blog/2009/02/09/self-service-data-export-using-pentaho/
```

See also

▸ The recipe named *Configuring the Pentaho BI Server for running PDI jobs and transformations* in this chapter. It is recommended that you see this recipe before trying to run a transformation from the PUC.

▸ The recipe named *Executing a PDI job from the Pentaho User Console* in this chapter. See this recipe if you want to run a job instead of a transformation.

Executing a PDI job from the Pentaho User Console

The **Pentaho User Console** (**PUC**) is a web application included with the Pentaho Server conveniently built for you to generate reports, browse cubes, explore dashboards, and more. Among the list of tasks, you can do is the ability of running Kettle jobs. As said in the previous recipe, everything in the Pentaho platform is made up of action sequences. Therefore, if you intend to run a job from the PUC, you have to create an action sequence that does it.

For this recipe, you will use a job which simply deletes all files with extension tmp found in a given folder. The objective is to run the job from the PUC through an action sequence.

Getting ready

In order to follow this recipe, you will need a basic understanding of action sequences and at least some experience with the Pentaho BI Server and **Pentaho Design Studio**, the action sequences editor.

Before proceeding, make sure you have a Pentaho BI Server running. You will also need Pentaho Design Studio; you can download the latest version from the following URL:

```
http://sourceforge.net/projects/pentaho/files/Design%20Studio/
```

Besides, you will need a job like the one described in the introduction of the recipe. The job should have a named parameter called TMP_FOLDER and simply delete all files with extension .tmp found in that folder.

You can develop the job before proceeding (call it delete_files.kjb), or download it from the book's site.

Finally, pick a directory on your computer (or create one) with some tmp files for deleting.

How to do it...

This recipe is split into two parts: First, you will create the action sequence and then you will test the action sequence from the PUC.

1. Launch Design Studio. If it is the first time you do it, create the solution project where you will save your work.

2. Copy the sample job to the solution folder.

3. Create a new action sequence and save it in your solution project with the name delete_files.xaction.

4. Define an input that will be used as the parameter for your job: folder. As **Default Value**, type the name of the folder with the .tmp files, for example, c:\myfolder.

5. Add a process action by selecting **Execute | Pentaho Data Integration Job**.

6. Now, you will fill in the **Input Section** of the process action configuration. Give the process action a name.

7. As **Job File**, type solution:delete_files.kjb.

8. In the **Job Inputs**, add the only input you have: folder.

9. Select the **XML source** tab.

10. Search for the <action-definition> tag that contains the following line:

```
<component-name>KettleComponent</component-name>
```

11. You will find something similar to the following:

```
<action-definition>
    <component-name>KettleComponent</component-name>
    <action-type>Pentaho Data Integration Job</action-type>
    <action-inputs>
      <folder type="string"/>
    </action-inputs>
    <action-resources>
      <job-file type="resource"/>
    </action-resources>
    <action-outputs/>
    <component-definition/>
</action-definition>
```

12. Replace the `<component-definition/>` tag with the following:

```
<component-definition>
  <set-parameter>
    <name>TMP_FOLDER</name>
    <mapping>folder</mapping>
  </set-parameter>
</component-definition>
```

13. Save the file.

Now, it is time to test the action sequence that you just created.

1. Login to the Pentaho BI Server and refresh the repository.
2. Browse the solution folders and look for the `delete_files` action you just created. Double-click on it.
3. You should see a window with the legend **Action Successful**.
4. You can take a look at the Pentaho console to see the log of the job.
5. Take a look at the folder defined in the input of your action sequence. There should be no `tmp` files.

How it works...

You can run Kettle jobs as part of an **action sequence** by using the **Pentaho Data Integration Job process action** located within the **Execute** category of process actions.

The main task of a PDI Job process action is to run a Kettle job. In order to do that, it has a series of checks and textboxes where you specify everything you need to run the job, and everything you want to receive back after having run it.

The most important setting in the PDI process action is the name and location of the job to be executed. In this example, you had a `.kjb` file in the same location as the action sequence, so you simply typed `solution:` followed by the name of the file.

You can specify the Kettle log level, but it is not mandatory. In this case, you left the log level empty. The log level you select here (or `Basic`, by default) is the level of log that Kettle writes to the Pentaho console when the job runs.

Besides the name and location of the job, you had to provide the name of the folder needed by the job. In order to do that, you created an input named `folder` and then you passed it to the job. You did it in the XML code by putting the name of the input enclosed between `<set-parameter>` and `</set-parameter>`.

When you run the action sequence, the job was executed deleting all `.tmp` files in the given folder.

> Note that the action sequence in this recipe has just one process action (the PDI Job). This was made on purpose to keep the recipe simple, but it could have had other actions as well, just like any action sequence.

There's more...

The main reason for embedding a job in an action sequence is for scheduling its execution with the Pentaho scheduling services. This is an alternative approach to the use of a system utility such as **cron** in Unix-based operating systems or the **Task Scheduler** in Windows.

See also

▶ The recipe named _Configuring the Pentaho BI Server for running PDI jobs and transformations_ of this chapter. It is recommended that you see this recipe before trying to run a job from the PUC.

▶ The recipe named _Executing a PDI transformation as part of a Pentaho process_ in this chapter. The topics explained in the _There's more_ section apply equally to transformations and jobs. If you want to run a job from a repository, or if you want to know how to pass command-line arguments or variables to a job, then read this section.

Generating files from the PUC with PDI and the CDA plugin

As you know, PDI allows you to generate Excel, CSV, and XML files and starting with the latest version, also JSON files. You do it with a transformation that has to be executed from Spoon or the command line. There is a quicker way to generate those kinds of files in an interactive fashion from the **Pentaho User Console** (**PUC**). This recipe teaches you how to do it by using the **Community Data Access** (**CDA**) plugin.

You will experiment the **CDA Editor** and the **CDA Previewer** for querying the current weather conditions in a given city. Then, you will learn how to export the results to different formats. You will do that from the PUC.

Getting ready

In order to follow this recipe, you will need some experience with the Pentaho BI Server.

Regarding the software, you will need a Pentaho BI Server running. You will also need the CDA plugin. You can download the installer from `http://cda.webdetails.org` or the source code from `http://code.google.com/p/pentaho-cda/`

> The **Community Dashboard Editor** (**CDE**) includes CDA. Therefore, if you have CDE installed, just skip the CDA installation.

Finally, you will need the sample transformation `weather_np.ktr`.

How to do it...

This recipe is split in two parts: In the first part, you will create a CDA file for getting the data you need. In the second part, you will export the results.

So, carry out the following steps in order to complete the first part:

1. Create the solution project where you will save your work.

2. Inside the folder of your project, copy the `weather_np.ktr` transformation into your project directory.

3. Also inside that folder, create an empty file with `cda` extension. Name it `weather. cda`.

4. Log in to the Pentaho User Console and refresh the repository. You should see the solution folder with the file that you just created.

5. Right-click on the file and select **Edit**. A new tab window should appear with the CDA Editor ready to edit your CDA file, as shown in the following screenshot:

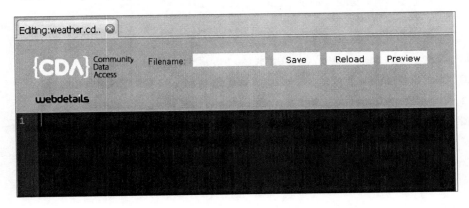

6. The black area is where you will type the CDA file content. Type the skeleton of the file:

```
<?xml version="1.0" encoding="UTF-8"?>
<CDADescriptor>
   <DataSources>
   </DataSources>
</CDADescriptor>
```

7. Inside the `<DataSources>` tag, type the connection to the Kettle transformation:

```
<Connection id="weather" type="kettle.TransFromFile">
  <KtrFile>weather_np.ktr</KtrFile>
  <variables datarow-name="CITY"/>
  <variables datarow-name="Scale" variable-name="TEMP"/>
</Connection>
```

8. Now you will define a data access to that datasource. In CDA terminology, this is a **query** over the preceding connection. Below the closing tag `</DataSources>`, type the following:

```
<DataAccess access="public"
            cache="true"
            cacheDuration="3600"
            connection="weather"
            id="current"
            type="kettle">
   <Columns/>
   <Parameters>
     <Parameter default="Lisbon, Portugal"
                name="CITY"
                type="String"/>
     <Parameter default="C"
                name="Scale"
```

```
                                type="String"/>
            </Parameters>
            <Query>current_conditions_normalized</Query>
            <Output indexes="0,1"/>
        </DataAccess>
```

9. Click on the **Save** button located at the top of the editor window.

10. Click on **Preview** and a new window is displayed with the **CDA Previewer**.

11. In the drop-down list, select the data access that you just defined.

12. Take a look at the Pentaho server console. You should see how the `weather_np` transformation is being executed. The following is an excerpt of that log:

```
... - weather_np - Dispatching started for transformation
[weather_np]
... - Get ${TEMP}, ${SPEED} and ${CITY} - Finished processing
(I=0, O=0, R=1, W=1, U=0, E=0)
... - key & days & format - Finished processing (I=0, O=0, R=1,
W=1, U=0, E=0)
... - worldweatheronline - Finished processing (I=0, O=0, R=1,
W=2, U=0, E=0)
... - ...
... - current_conditions_normalized - Finished processing (I=0,
O=0, R=11, W=11, U=0, E=0)
```

13. In the previewer, you will see the results of the CDA query, as shown in the following screenshot:

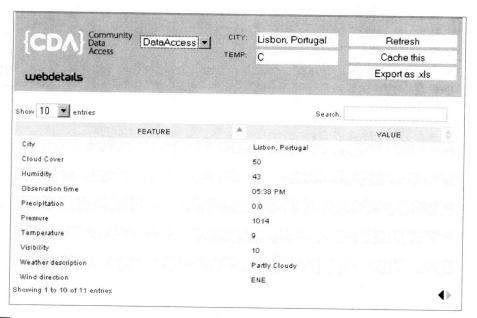

14. Try changing the values for the parameters: `city` and `temperature` scale. Click on **Refresh** and the data should be refreshed accordingly.

    Now that you have a CDA file with a connection and a data access, let's export some results to `.csv` format.

15. Copy the URL of the previewer and paste it into a new tab window of your browser. Assuming that you are running the server on localhost, and your solution is in the folder `pdi_cookbook/CDA`, the complete URL should look like the following:

    ```
    http://localhost:8080/pentaho/content/cda/previewQuery?path=pdi_
    cookbook/CDA/weather.cda
    ```

 By *double-clicking* on the CDA file, the editor opens in a tab inside the PUC. This prevents you from copying the URL.

 In order to be able to copy the URL, double-click on the tab that contains the CDA Editor. Alternatively, you can right-click on the CDA file and select **Open in New Window**.

16. In the URL, replace `previewQuery` with `doQuery`.

17. At the end of the URL, add the following:

    ```
    &dataAccessId=current
    &paramCITY=›Buenos Aires, Argentina›
    &paramScale=F
    &outputType=csv
    ```

 These parameters are written in four lines for simplicity. You should type all in a single line one next to the other.

18. Press *Enter*. A `csv` will be generated that should look like the following:

    ```
    FEATURE;VALUE
    City;Buenos Aires, Argentina
    Observation time;06:25 PM
    Weather description;Moderate or heavy rain in area
    Temperature;91
    Wind speed;24
    Wind direction;W
    Precipitation;0.2
    Humidity;53
    Visibility;3
    Pressure;9982
    Cloud Cover;100
    ```

How it works...

In this recipe, you exported the results of a Kettle transformation to a `.csv` file from the PUC. In order to do that, you used CDA.

First, you created a CDA file. You edited it with the CDA Editor. The purpose of this file was to firstly define a connection to the Kettle transformation and then a query over that connection. Let's explain them in detail.

The connection or CDA DataSource is the definition of the source of your data, in this case a Kettle transformation. The following is the definition of your connection:

```
<Connection id="weather" type="kettle.TransFromFile">
  <KtrFile>weather_np.ktr</KtrFile>
  <variables datarow-name="CITY"/>
  <variables datarow-name="Scale" variable-name="TEMP"/>
</Connection>
```

The `id` must be unique in the CDA file. `type="kettle.TransFromFile"` identifies this as a connection to a Kettle transformation. You provide the name of the Kettle transformation inside the tags `<KtrFile></KtrFile>`.

Then you have the variables. The variables are the means for passing parameters from CDA to Kettle; `datarow-name` is the name you use in the CDA file, while `variable-name` is the name of the Kettle named parameter. For example, the named variable `TEMP` defined in the transformation is referred to as `Scale` inside the CDA file.

If both names coincide, then you can just put the `datarow-name` and omit the `variable-name`, as in the case of the `CITY` variable.

Each variable you define in a CDA connection of type `kettle`, `TransFromFile` must be defined as a named parameter in the transformation. That was the reason for using the transformation `weather_np.ktr` instead of `weather.ktr`.

Now, let's see the CDA query. A CDA DataAccess is a query over a CDA Datasource. In the case of Kettle, a CDA DataAccess has the details of a Kettle transformation execution. A CDA query is enclosed inside a tag named `DataAccess`:

```
<DataAccess access="public"
            cache="true"
            cacheDuration="3600"
            connection="weather"
            id="current"
            type="kettle">
```

```
    . . .
</DataAccess>
```

Here you define a unique data access id (id="current"), the data access type
(type="kettle"), and the connection (connection="weather"). The connection must
be declared earlier in the same file.

The <columns></columns> tag is useful if you want to rename the columns or perform
operations between them, which was not the case here. Therefore, you left it empty.

Then you have a parameters section:

```
<Parameters>
    <Parameter default="Lisbon, Portugal"
               name="CITY"
               type="String"/>
    <Parameter default="C"
               name="Scale"
               type="String"/>
</Parameters>
```

Here you define one <Parameter> tag for each parameter you want to pass to the
transformation. The parameters you type here will be available in the CDA Previewer
for you to change.

 In order to be able to pass the parameters, they have to be defined in the
DataSource as explained earlier.

Inside <Query></Query> tag, you type the name of the transformation step that returns
the data you need. The sample transformation has three steps that return data: current_
conditions, current_conditions_normalized, and forecast. You typed the second
of these steps.

Finally, the <Output> tag is meant to indicate which columns you want and in which order.
The output fields of the current_conditions_normalized step are FEATURE and
VALUE. You wanted both fields and in the same order, therefore, you typed indexes="0,1".

 You can edit the CDA files in any text editor. Just remember that if you do
not use the CDA Editor, then you should periodically refresh the solution
repository in order to be able to preview them.

Once you created the contents of the file, you saved it, and previewed the results with the CDA
Previewer. This previewer shows the results as a table.

After previewing the results, you experimented with the **doQuery** feature of the **CDA API**.

The `doQuery` function allows you to export the results of a DataAccess to different formats. In order to run a `doQuery`, you have to provide the following parameters:

Parameter	Description	Example
`dataAccessId`	ID of the DataAccess to run	`dataAccessId=current`
`param + <name of param.>`	One of this for each parameter you want to pass to the transformation	`paramCITY='Buenos Aires, Argentina'`
`outputType`	Desired output type. Available output types: `Json` (default if the parameter is omitted), `csv`, `Excel`, and `XML`.	`outputType=csv`

The parameters you provided in the recipe (shown in the preceding table) meant: Run the DataAccess with ID `current`, supplying the parameter `CITY` with values `Buenos Aires, Argentina` and `Scale` with value `F`, and give me a `csv` file with the results.

There's more...

CDA is a plugin for the Pentaho BI Suite developed by **Webdetails**, one of the main Pentaho Community Contributors.

CDA was designed as an abstraction tool between sources of information, for example, Kettle transformations, databases, or **Mondrian** cubes, and the CDF. As such, it is mainly used in the context of Pentaho Dashboards.

However, it also serves for exporting data to different formats from the PUC. That was exactly what you did in the recipe.

If you are interested in knowing more about CDA, then you will find the complete documentation at the following URL: `http://cda.webdetails.org`.

Populating a CDF dashboard with data coming from a PDI transformation

A dashboard is in its broad sense is an application that shows you visual indicators, for example, bar charts, traffic lights, or dials. A **CDF** dashboard is a dashboard created with the **Community Dashboard Framework**. CDF accepts many kinds of data sources being the output of a Kettle transformation being one of them.

In this recipe, you will create a very simple dashboard that shows this capability. You will type the name of a city and the dashboard will display graphically the 5-days forecast for that city. The forecast information will be obtained with the sample transformation explained in the introduction.

Getting ready

In order to follow this recipe, you will need a minimal experience with the Pentaho BI Server. Some experience with the **Community Dashboard Editor** (**CDE**) is also desirable.

Before proceeding, make sure you have a Pentaho BI Server running. You will also need the CDE. You can download it from `http://cde.webdetails.org`. To install it, simply unzip the downloaded material and follow the instructions in the `INSTALL.txt` file.

Finally, you will need the sample transformation `weather_np.ktr`.

How to do it...

Carry out the following steps:

1. Log into the Pentaho User Console.
2. Create the solution folder where you will save your work.
3. Copy the sample transformation to the solution folder and refresh the repository.
4. From the **File** menu, select **New | CDE Dashboard** or click on the CDE icon in the toolbar.
5. Save the dashboard in the solution folder that you just created, close the dashboard window, and refresh the repository. A new file with extension `wcdf` will appear in the solution folder.
6. Go to the solution folder, right-click on the dashboard file and select **Edit**. The dashboard editor will appear. Maximize the window, so that you can work more comfortably.
7. Define the dashboard layout by adding rows and columns from the layout toolbar, until you get the following screen:

Now, let's add the visual elements of the dashboard.

1. Click on **Components** from the menu at the top-right area of the editor.
2. From the **Generic** category, add a **Simple parameter**. Name it `city_param` and type `Lisbon, Portugal` for **Property value**.

3. From the **Selects** category, add a **TextInput Component**. Name it `city_textbox`. For **Parameter**, select `city_param` and for **HtmlObject**, select `filter_panel`.

4. Click on **Save** on the menu at the top of the editor.

5. Click on **Preview**; you will see the dashboard with a textbox prompting for the `city_name` parameter, showing the default value `Lisbon, Portugal`.

6. Close the preview window.

7. Now, you will add the chart that will display the forecast. From the **Charts** category, add a **CCC Bar Chart**.

8. Fill in the properties as follows:

   ❏ For **Name**, type `forecast_bars`

   ❏ For **Width**, type `350`

   ❏ For **Height**, type `250`

   ❏ For **Datasource**, type `forecast`

   ❏ For **Crosstab mode**, select **True**

   ❏ For **Title**, type `5-days forecast`

   ❏ For **HtmlObject**, select `chart_panel`

   ❏ For **Listeners**, select `city_param`

9. Click on the **Parameters** property and in the window that displays, add one parameter. For **Arg0**, type `CITY` and for **Val0**, type `city_param`, and then Click on **Ok**.

Finally, you have to create the datasource for that chart: `forecast`. The following steps will do it:

1. Click on **Data Sources** from the menu at the top-right area of the editor. In the list of available data sources, click on **KETTLE Queries** and select **kettle over kettleTransFromFile**. A new datasource will be added.

2. Fill in the list of properties as explained in the following steps:

3. For **Name**, type `forecast`.

4. For **Kettle Transformation File**, type `weather_np.ktr`.

5. Click on **Variables** and in the window that displays, click on **Add**. For **Arg0**, type `CITY` and click on **Ok**.

6. Click on **Parameters** and in the window that displays, click on **Add**.

   ❏ For **Arg0**, type `CITY`

   ❏ For **Val0** type **Lisbon, Portugal**

   ❏ For **Type0** leave the default **String** and click on **Ok**.

7. Click on **Output Options** and in the window that shows up, click on **Add** three times. For **Arg0**, **Arg1**, and **Arg2**, type 1, 2, and 3 respectively and click on **Ok**.

8. Click on **Column Configurations** and in the window that displays, click on **Add** twice. In the first row, type 2 for **Arg0** and MIN for **Val0**. In the second row, type 3 for **Arg1** and MAX for **Val1**.

9. Click on the little square to the next of the **Query** property. The **Sql Wizard** shows up. In the editing area, type next_days and click on **Ok**.

10. Save the dashboard by clicking on **Save** and click on **Preview** to see the dashboard. You should see a result similar to that shown in the following screenshot:

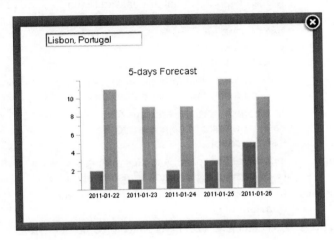

11. If you take a look at the Pentaho console, then you will see the log of the Kettle transformation that is executed.

12. Try changing the value for the city and press *Enter*. The chart should be refreshed accordingly.

How it works...

In this recipe, you created a very simple dashboard. The dashboard allows you to enter the name of a city and then refreshes a bar chart displaying the 5-days forecast for that city. The special feature of this dashboard is that it gets data from a web service through the execution of a Kettle transformation.

In order to use the output of your Kettle transformation as data source, you just have to add a new datasource from **KETTLE Queries | kettle over kettleTransFromFile** and configure it properly. This configuration involves providing the following properties:

Property	Meaning / Purpose	Example
Name	Unique datasource name inside the dashboard	`forecast`
Kettle Transformation File	Name of the transformation file	`weather_np.ktr`
Variables	Name of variables that are passed to the transformation. You have to provide it in pairs (`<CDE parameter>`,`<Kettle named parameter>`) or (`<CDE parameter>`,`""`) if both coincide.	`"CITY",""`
Access Level	`Public` (available from outside) / `Private` (available only from other data sources)	`Public`
Parameters	Name, default value, and type for each parameter to be passed to the transformation	`"CITY", "Lisbon, Portugal", "String"`
Output Options (opt)	Indexes of the columns to pick among the fields coming out from the transformation	`1,2,3`
Column Configurations (opt)	Renaming the columns coming out from the transformation	`2,"MIN"`
Column Configurations II (opt)	Calculating new columns based on other columns	`AVG, (MAX + MIN)/2`
Query	Name of the step that delivers the data	`next_days`
Cache	Keep results in cache (True/False)	`TRUE`
Cache Duration	Time to keep the results in cache in seconds	`3600`

Once you configured your Kettle transformation as a datasource, it was ready to be used in the components of your dashboard.

There's more...

CDF is a community project whose objective is mainly to integrate dashboards in the Pentaho's solution repository structure. In the recipe, you used the CDE, which is a graphical editor that complements the power of the CDF engine. With CDE, you can create dashboards without having to get involved in the low-level details of the CDF files, thus focusing on the business requirements.

Kettle is just one of several kinds of data sources accepted by CDF. Behind the scenes, most of the data sources definitions are saved in a CDA file.

If you already have a CDA file that has a data access for your transformation, then you can avoid configuring the data source twice and use the **Community Data Access | CDA Datasource** instead.

CDF is bundled with the Pentaho BI Suite, but maintained by **Webdetails** with the help of the community. For more information about CDF, see the full documentation here: http://cdf.webdetails.org. For more on CDE visit http://cde.webdetails.org.

See also

The recipe named _Generating files from the PUC with PDI and the Community Data Access_ _(CDA) plugin_ in this chapter. This recipe explains about CDA.

9
Getting the Most Out of Kettle

In this chapter, we will cover:

- ▶ Sending e-mails with attached files
- ▶ Generating a custom log file
- ▶ Programming custom functionality
- ▶ Generating sample data for testing purposes
- ▶ Working with JSON files
- ▶ Getting information about transformations and jobs (file-based)
- ▶ Getting information about transformations and jobs (repository-based)

Introduction

The recipes in this chapter cover a variety of topics that don't fit into any of the previous categories. The topics range from customizing a Kettle log to understanding the structure of a Kettle database repository. Feel free to browse the pages and see if there is a recipe that fits your needs.

Sending e-mails with attached files

Nowadays, it is very common to use e-mails to exchange digital messages from one author to several recipients. These e-mails can also have a list of files attached that will be sent along with the message.

Kettle offers job entries and transformation steps that allow the sending of e-mails with attached files. In this recipe, you will use the **Email job** entry to send an e-mail with a set of files attached with a particular condition: the files must have been modified after a given date.

Getting ready

You need a directory named `filesToAttach` containing sample files. You will also need access to an SMTP server. You can use the `smtp.gmail.com` server. You also need at least one valid account to play with.

How to do it...

Carry out the following steps:

1. Create a new transformation.

2. Drop a **Get Files Names** from the **Input** category.

3. Under the **File** tab, type or browse for the `filesToAttach` folder in **the File or directory** textbox. Type `.*` in the **Regular Expression** textbox and click on the **Add** button to populate the **Selected files** grid.

4. Under the **Filter** tab, uncheck on the **Add filename to result** checkbox.

5. Add a **Filter rows** step from the **Flow** category. Here, add a new condition, select the field `lastmodifiedtime`, the operator `'`, and enter a constant value date to compare with, for example, `2010/11/01`. Don't forget to select the **Conversion format** expression to match the date format.

6. Add a **Set files in result** step (**Job** category).

7. Create a hop from the **Filter rows** step towards this step. When asked for the kind of hop, select **Main output of step**. The transformation will look similar to the one shown in the following diagram:

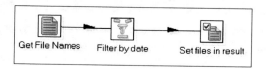

8. Double-click on the **Set file in result** step. Select `filename` in the **Filename** field, and `General` in the **Type of file to** prompt.

9. Create a new job, and drop a **START** job entry into the canvas.

10. Add a **Transformation** job entry from the **General** category.

11. Double-click on this job entry and type the complete path of the previously created transformation (or browse for it) in the **Transformation filename** textbox.

12. Add a **Mail validator** job entry from the **email** category. In this step, type the destination account in the **Email address** textbox.

13. Add a **Mail** job from the **Mail** category.

14. Under the **Addresses** tab, fill in the **Destination address** textbox and the **Sender address** textbox with two valid e-mail addresses (they can be the same if you only have one account to play with). In addition, you need to complete the **Sender name** textbox. For example, you can type your name.

 You can specify more than one account using a space as a separator in the **Destination address** of the **email** and **Mail validator** job entries.

15. Complete the **Server** tab as shown in the following screenshot:

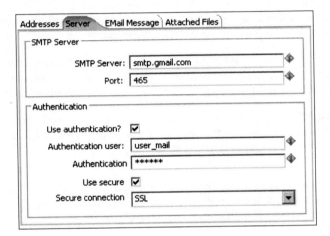

 You need to fill the **Authentication user** and **Authentication** textboxes with a valid user and password. If your account is user@gmail.com, then you have to type user in the **Authentication user** textbox, and your e-mail password in the **Authentication** textbox.

The default **Port** for the **SMTP Server** is 465, but if you use a secure connection through TLS, then the default is 587.

16. Under the **Email Message** tab, complete the **Subject** textbox and the **Comment** area with sample text. Also, check the **Only send comment in the mail body?** checkbox.

17. Select the **Attached Files** tab and check the option **Attach file(s) to message?**

18. Select the option General in the **Select file type** listbox.

19. Check the **Zip files to single archive?** checkbox. Type a filename in the **Name of zip archive** textbox (for example, files.zip).

20. Running the job, an e-mail will be sent to the destination address (if it is valid). It will include an attached ZIP file with all of the files from the `filesToAttach` folder that fulfill the date condition.

How it works...

The first task in the example was to create a transformation that gets the files that will be sent as an attachment with the e-mail. For this, you used the **Get Files Names** step to get the files inside the `filesToAttach` folder, and then the **Filter rows** step to filter the files with a `lastmodifiedtime` greater than a specific date, in this case `2010/11/01`. Only the files that pass this condition will be set in the result. Remember to uncheck the **Add filename to result** checkbox in the **Get Files Names** step, because you don't want all the files, only the result after the row filtering.

The job run this transformation, and then executes the *email* job entry. This job is quite self-explanatory. Under the **Addresses** tab, you must complete the destination and sender e-mails addresses, and the e-mail content under the **Email Message** tab.

The example uses Gmail's SMTP server (`smtp.gmail.com`), but you can use any e-mail server as long as you have access to the information required in the **Server** tab. Take a look at the firewall configuration if you have problems reaching the specified address.

Under the **Attached Files** tab, you selected the file type option named `General`; this indicates that all the files included in the result list will be attached to the e-mail. In addition, you configured the entry to zip all files into a single file.

 If the previous jobs or transformations also added files to results, then those files will be attached as well. Therefore, a *Delete filenames from result* job entry might be required at the beginning of this job.

You used the *Mail validator* job entry to verify the e-mail address structure. If the structure is not correct, then the *email* job entry will not run. You could use the **SMTP check?** checkbox here, if you want to validate the existence of the accounts.

There's more...

You will find more features about sending e-mails in the following subsections:

Sending logs through an e-mail

Let's assume that you want to include the log of the transformation inside the attached ZIP file. This is very simple; just double-click on the **Transformation** entry job and set the log file under the **Logging settings** tab, as shown in the following screenshot:

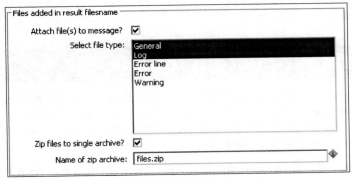

You can specify a more detailed level of log in the **Loglevel** listbox if you want.

Then, you need to include this file as an attached file. Double-click on the **email** job entry, select the **Attached Files** tab, and select the Log item in the **Select file type** listbox. As you need to select both General and Log items, you have to do it by pressing the *Ctrl* key.

After running the job, an e-mail will still be sent, but this time, the ZIP file attached will also contain a new file named logFile.log with the log information.

Sending e-mails in a transformation

There is a transformation step named **Mail**, in the **Utility** category, which is very similar to the **Mail** job entry. The main difference is that the **Mail** step sends one e-mail for each existent row.

Its configuration has listboxes instead of textboxes to refer to different settings (addresses, server configuration, subject, body, and so on). Here you should refer to existing fields instead of typing them.

In some cases, you could use either the step or the job entry with similar results, but there are particular scenarios where one approach is better than the other. For example:

▶ If you need to send several e-mails to different destination addresses, and/or with different content, and/or with different attached files, then it is better to use the **Mail** transformation step.

- If you need to send an e-mail with some information about the executed process—for example, the time that it took to execute it—you must use the **Mail** job entry.

- If you need to send only one e-mail with attached files coming from different jobs or transformations, then you should use the **Mail** job entry.

For an advanced example of using the **Mail** step for mailing, you can follow this link: `http://kjube.blogspot.com/2011/01/mailing-new-years-cards.html`. The blog post by **KJube** explains a transformation that sends best wishes for the New Year to a list of people. The following two considerations arise about the example provided:

- The transformation uses the **Excel Writer** plugin step. If you are working with Kettle 4.1, then you should install the plugin in order to open the transformation. That's not the case for Kettle 4.2, in which the plugin is already included as an **Experimental** step.

- The values for the **Server** configuration and the **Sender name** and **Sender address** are stored in Kettle variables; they don't change from row to row. However, as explained earlier, you cannot type the values directly in the step configuration window. You should refer to existing fields instead. Therefore, it is necessary to get those variables in a previous step.

Generating a custom log file

When you run a transformation or a job, all of what is happening in the process is shown in the **Execution Results** window, which has a tab named **Logging** where you can check the execution of your transformation step by step. By default, the level of the logging detail is **Basic**, but you can change it to show different levels of detail.

Under the **Logging** tab, you can see information about how the step is performing, for example, the number of rows coming from previous steps, the number of rows read, the number of rows written, errors in execution, and so on. All this data is provided by the steps automatically, but what if you want to write your custom messages to the **Logging** information? To do this, there is a step and an entry named *Write to log*, in the **Utility** folder.

To put them into practice, let's take a simple transformation that reads a text file with book novelties and splits them into two Excel files depending on their price. The objective here is to include, in the **Logging** window, custom messages about the incoming number of books and also how many of these books are cheap or expensive.

Getting ready

For checking this recipe, you will need a text file that includes information about book titles novelties. For example:

```
title;author_id;price;title_id;genre
Bag of Bones;A00002;51,99;123-353;Fiction
```

```
Basket Case;A00003;31,00;123-506;Fiction
Carrie;A00002;41,00;123-346;Fiction
Cashflow Quadrant;A00007;55,00;323-604;Business
Harry Potter and the Half-Blood Prince;A00008;61,00;423-005;Childrens
Harry Potter and the Prisoner of Azkaban;A00008;29,00;423-
003;Childrens
Power to the People;A00005;33,00;223-302;Non-fiction
Who Took My Money;A00007;21,00;323-603;Business
```

You can download the sample file from the book's website.

How to do it...

Carry out the following steps:

1. Create a new transformation.
2. Drop a **Text file input** step into the canvas. Set the file to read under the **File** tab, and type ; as the character **Separator** under the **Content** tab. Finally, use the **Get Fields** button under the **Fields** tab to populate the grid automatically.

Previewing this step, you will obtain the data of the books from the text file. Now, let's add the steps for counting the books and writing the information.

1. Add a **Group by** step from the **Statistics** folder. Create a hop from the text file to this step. In the **Aggregates** grid at the bottom, add a new field named qty, choose a field (for example, title_id) in the **Subject** column, and select the **Number of Values (N)** option in the **Type** column.
2. Add a **User Defined Java Expression** (**UDJE** for short) from the **Scripting** category and link it to the previous step. Create a new field named line of String type with the following Java expression:

   ```
   "Book news = " + Java.lang.Long.toString(qty)
   ```

3. From the **Utility** folder, add a **Write to log** step and create a hop from the previous step towards this one; name it Write books counting. Add the line field to the **Fields** grid. Choose Basic logging in the **Log level** listbox.

Run the transformation using **Basic logging** and check the **Logging** tab for the results.

You can verify the basic logging information where you should see the following line:

```
2011/01/25 10:40:40 - Write books counting.0 - Book news = 8
```

Now, you will generate two Excel files and write the information about cheap and expensive books to the log.

1. Drop one **Filter rows**, two **Excel output**, two **Group by**, two **UDJE**, two **Block this step until steps finish** (from **Flow** category), and two **Write to log** steps into the canvas. Link the steps, as shown in the following diagram:

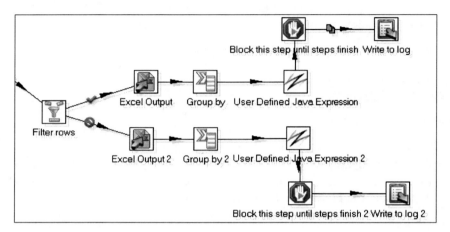

2. Create a hop from the **Text file input** step to the **Filter rows** step. Here, set the condition price ' 50. We will use an arbitrary price of $50 to determine if a book is cheap or expensive.

3. Point one **Excel Output** step filename to cheapBooks.xls, and use the **Get Fields** button to populate the grid under the **Fields** tab.

4. In the **Group by** step, add a new field named qty in the **Aggregates** grid, choose the field title_id in the **Subject** column, and select the **Number of Values (N)** option in the **Type** column.

5. Add a field named line of String type in the **UDJE** step with the following **Java expression**:

   "Cheap books = " + Java.lang.Long.toString(qty)

6. In the **Block this step until steps finish** steps, select the step named Write books counting in the **step name** column of the grid.

7. Finally, in the **Write to log** step, add the line field to the **Fields** grid and choose Basic logging in the **Log level** listbox.

8. Now, repeat the last five steps in order to configure the lower stream. This time use the **Excel Output** step (named Excel Output 2) to generate the expensiveBooks.xls file and replace the text Cheap for Expensive in the other **UDJE** step.

Running the transformation using **Basic logging**, you can verify that your custom messages have been written to the log under the **Logging** tab. Here's an example:

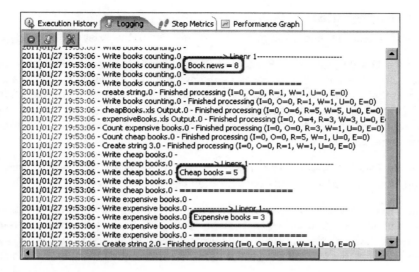

How it works...

The main objective in this recipe is to explain how you can write personalized messages to the logging windows. The task of the transformation is simple—it reads a text file at the beginning, uses a **Filter rows** step to split the list of books into cheap and expensive ones, and then writes two Excel spreadsheets with these details.

Now, let's analyze the task of customizing the log. In the first part of the recipe you wrote into the log the number of books:

- The *Group by* step does the counting
- The *UDJE* step creates the personalized string in a new field
- Finally, the *Write to log* step write this string to the log

After each of the *Excel output* steps, there is the same sequence of steps (*Group by*, *UDJE*, and *Write to log*), in order to write a message with the number of cheap books and the number of expensive books into the log.

There is also a *Block this step until steps finish* step in this sequence before the *Write to log* step, this is because you want to be sure that the total number of books will be written first.

There's more...

This recipe showed you the classic way for adding messages to the log. The following subsections show you some variants or alternative approaches.

Filtering the log file

Instead of adding text to the log, you may want to filter text in the existing log.

If you select the **Logging** tab in the **Execution Results** window, then you will see a toolbar. Under that toolbar, there is a button named **Log settings** that allows you to apply a filter. If you type some text into the **Select filter** textbox, then the log of the subsequent executions of the transformation will only show the lines that contain that text. For example, you could use the same text prefix in all of your custom messages, and then apply a filter using this fixed text to see only those messages.

This also works if you run the transformation from a job, and even if you restart Spoon because the filter is saved in a Kettle configuration file.

This is valid only in Spoon. If you intend to run a job or a transformation with Pan or Kitchen and you need to filter a log, for example, by keeping only the lines that contain certain words, then you have to take another approach. One way for performing that would be to save the job or transformation log in a file and then run another transformation that parses and filters that log file.

Creating a clean log file

The **Logging** window shows not only your messages, but also all of the information written by the steps. Sometimes you need a clean log file showing only your custom messages and discarding the rest.

There is another problem related to that - when you configure the **Write to log** step, you need to specify a level for your log. (In the recipe, you used `Basic logging`). If you run your transformation using a different log level, then you will not see any of your personalized messages.

One alternative would be using a *Text file output* instead of the *Write to log* step. With this, you will produce a new text file with only your desired messages. Be sure to point all of the **Text file output** steps to the same **Filename** under the **File** tab, and use the **Append** checkbox under the **Content** tab, in order to avoid overwriting the file with each run.

Isolating log files for different jobs or transformations

It is possible that you want to see different log levels depending on the job or transformation, or that you simply want to isolate the log for a particular job or transformation. This is a simple task to accomplish. In the main job, right-click on the **Job** or **Transformation** entry of interest; under the **Logging settings** tab check the **Specify logfile?** option and you will be able to specify a name for the log file as well as the log level desired. In this way, you can create different log files with different log levels for each of the **Jobs** and **Transformations** that are part of your main job.

See also

- ▶ The recipe named *Sending e-mails with attached files* in this chapter. In this recipe, you learn how to send logs through e-mail.

- ▶ The recipe named *Programming custom functionality* in this chapter. This recipe shows you how to send custom messages to the **Logging** window from the *User Defined Java Class* and *Modified Java Script Values* steps.

Programming custom functionality

In Kettle, you have a lot of functionality provided by the built-in steps, but if that is not enough for you, there is a step named **User Defined Java Class** (**UDJC** for short) where you can program custom functionality with Java code. In this way, you can accomplish complex tasks, access Java libraries, and even access the Kettle API. The code you type into this step is compiled once and executed at runtime for each passing row.

Let's create a simple example of the use of the *UDJC* step. Assume that you have a text file containing sentences; you want to count the words in each row and split the flow of data into two streams depending on the number of words per sentence.

Note that in order to develop a more interesting exercise, we added some extra considerations, as follows:

- ▶ There are several characters as separators, not only the blank spaces
- ▶ Sometimes, you can have a sequence of separators together
- ▶ Some sentences have a special character at the end, and some don't

Getting ready

You need a text file containing sentences, for example:

```
This is a sample text.
Another text with special characters, , ,   END OF FILE
hello,man
I wish you a happy new year:2011
The,last.but,not;the.least
```

You can download the sample file from the book's website.

How to do it...

Carry out the following steps:

1. Create a new transformation.

2. Drop a **Text file input** step from the **Input** category. Browse to your file under the **Files** tab, and press the **Add** button to populate the selected files grid. For example: `${Internal.Transformation.Filename.Directory}\samplefile.txt`.

3. Under the **Content** tab, uncheck the **Header** checkbox, and type ##### in the **Separator** textbox.

4. Under the **Fields** tab, add a field named **line** of `String` type.

5. Add a **UDJC** step from the **Scripting** category. Also, drop two **Dummy** steps from the **Flow** category and name them: `short sentences` step and `long sentences` step.

6. Create the hops between the steps as per the ones shown in the following diagram:

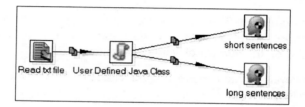

7. Double-click on the **UDJC** step.

8. Under the **Fields** tab of the bottom grid, add a new field named `qty`. Select **Integer** in the **Type** listbox.

9. Under the **Target** steps tab, create two tags and name them: `shortOnes` and `longOnes`. Then, select the steps as shown in the following screenshot:

Target steps:

#. ▲	Tag	Step	Description
1	shortOnes	short sentences	
2	longOnes	long sentences	

10. In the **Classes and code fragments** section on the left, open the **Code Snippets** folder. Expand the **Common use** option and drop the **Main** item to the editing area on the right. A fragment of Java code will be written for the function `processRow()`.

11. Replace or complete this fragment with the following code:

```
private RowSet shortSentences = null;
private RowSet longSentences = null;

public boolean processRow(StepMetaInterface smi,
    StepDataInterface sdi) throws KettleException
```

```
{
   Object[] r = getRow();
   if (r == null) {
      setOutputDone();
      return false;
   }
   if (first)  {
       first = false;
       shortSentences = findTargetRowSet("shortOnes");
       longSentences = findTargetRowSet("longOnes");
   }
   r = createOutputRow(r, data.outputRowMeta.size());
   String linein;
   linein = get(Fields.In, "line").getString(r);
   long len = linein.length();
   long qty = 0;
   boolean currentSpecialChar = false;
   for (int i=0;i'len;i++) {
      char ch = linein.charAt(i);
      switch(ch) {
         case ',':
         case '.':
         case ' ':
         case ';':
         case ':':
             if (!currentSpecialChar) qty++;
             currentSpecialChar = true;
             break;
         default:
             currentSpecialChar = false;
             break;
      }
   }
   if (!currentSpecialChar) qty++;
   get(Fields.Out, "qty").setValue(r, qty);
   if (qty ' 7) {
      putRowTo(data.outputRowMeta, r, shortSentences);
      }
   else {
    putRowTo(data.outputRowMeta, r, longSentences);
   }
   return true;
}
```

> The code snippet added with the **Main** item generates a row with this line:
> ```
> r = createOutputRow(r, outputRowSize);
> ```
> This line must be replaced with the following code to compile correctly:
> ```
> r = createOutputRow(r, data.outputRowMeta.size());
> ```

12. This code adds the desired functionality. If you preview this step, then you will obtain a new field named `qty` with the number of words in each sentence. The results for the file used as an example would be:

#. ▲	line	qty
1	This is a sample text.	5
2	Another text with special characters, , , END OF FILE	8
3	hello,man	2
4	I whish you a happy new year:2011	8
5	The,last.but,not;the.least	6

13. This **UDJC** step also redirects the rows to the short sentences step or the long sentences step depending on the field `qty`. You can preview both steps and verify that the sentences with exactly 7 or more than 7 words flow to the long sentences step, and those with fewer words flow to the short sentences step.

How it works...

The first step in the recipe has the task of reading the text file. You have used ##### as separator characters because that string is not present in the file. This assures you that the field `line` will contain the entire line of your file.

Now, you need to develop some custom code that counts the words in the `line` field. This task can't be accomplished using standard Kettle steps, so you have programmed the necessary functionality in Java code inside a *UDJC* step.

Let's explore the dialog for the *UDJC* step, which is shown in the following screenshot:

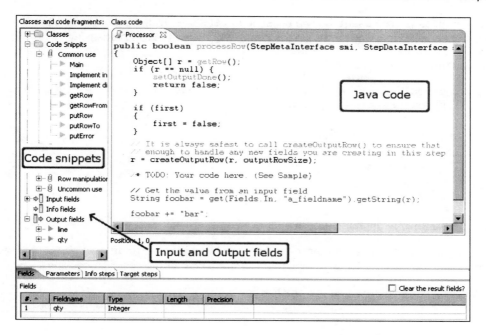

Most of the window is occupied by the editing area. Here you write the Java code using the standard syntax of that language. On the left, there is a panel with many code fragments ready to use (**Code Snippets**), and a section with sets and gets for the input and output fields. To add a code fragment to your script either double-click on it, drag it to the location in your script where you wish to use it, or just type it in the editing area.

The **Input** and **Outputs** fields appear automatically in the tree when the Java code compiles correctly; you can use the **Test class** button to verify that the code is properly written. If an error occurs, then you will see an error window otherwise, you will be able to preview the results of the transformation step.

The **Fields** tab on the bottom is to declare the new fields added by the step. In this case, you declared the field `qty` of **Integer** type. This field will be the output variable that will return the word count.

Under the **Target steps** tab, you can declare the steps where the rows will be redirected. In the recipe, you pointed to the two target **Dummy** steps; one for the short sentences, and the other for the long ones.

Let's see the Java code in detail:

At the beginning, there is a section with the variable declarations:

```
private RowSet shortSentences = null;
private RowSet longSentences = null;
```

These variables will represent the two possible target steps. They are declared at the beginning because this way they keep their values between the row processing.

Then, you have the main function:

```
public boolean processRow(StepMetaInterface smi, StepDataInterface
sdi) throws KettleException
{
    Object[] r = getRow();
    if (r == null) {
        setOutputDone();
        return false;
    }
}
```

The `processRow()` function process a new row.

The `getRow()` function gets the next row from the input steps. It returns an object array with the incoming row. A `null` value means that there are no more rows for processing.

The following code only executes for the first row:

```
if (first)  {
        first = false;
        shortSentences = findTargetRowSet("shortOnes");
        longSentences = findTargetRowSet("longOnes");
    }
```

You can use the flag `first` to prepare a proper environment before processing the rows. In this case, you set the target steps into two variables for further use.

The next code use the `get()` method to set the internal variable `linein` with the value of the `line` field.

```
r = createOutputRow(r, data.outputRowMeta.size());
String linein;
linein = get(Fields.In, "line").getString(r);
```

Here is the main cycle:

```
long len = linein.length();
long qty = 0;
boolean currentSpecialChar = false;

for (int i=0;i'len;i++) {
    char ch = linein.charAt(i);
    switch(ch) {
        case ',':
        case '.':
        case ' ':
```

```
        case ';':
        case ':':
            if (!currentSpecialChar) qty++;
            currentSpecialChar = true;
            break;
        default:
            currentSpecialChar = false;
            break;
    }
}
```

It parses the entire sentence looking for characters used as separators. If one of these separators is found, then it will increment the qty variable by one and set the flag currentSpecialChar to true, in order to not increment the value if the next character is also a separator.

The next line is to count the last word of the sentence only if it wasn't counted in the main cycle:

```
    if (!currentSpecialChar) qty++;
```

Here we set the new field named qty with the value of the internal variable qty, which has the word count:

```
    get(Fields.Out, "qty").setValue(r, qty);
```

Finally, if the word count is lower than 7 (arbitrary value), then the row will be passed to the short sentences step; otherwise the target will be the long sentences step.

```
    if (qty ' 7) {
        putRowTo(data.outputRowMeta, r, shortSentences);
        }
    else {
     putRowTo(data.outputRowMeta, r, longSentences);
    }

    return true;
}
```

 If you only have one target step, then you can use the simpler putRow() method.

There's more...

To learn about the syntax of the Java language, visit the following URL:

http://download.oracle.com/javase/tutorial/

As mentioned earlier, you can access the Kettle API from inside the UDJC code. To learn the details of the API, you should check the source. For instructions on getting the code, follow this link: `http://community.pentaho.com/getthecode/`.

Let's see some more information to take advantage of this very useful step:

Data type's equivalence

The code you type inside the UDJC step is pure Java. Therefore, the fields of your transformation will be seen as Java objects according to the following equivalence table:

Data type in Kettle	Java Class
String	Java.lang.String
Integer	Java.lang.Long
Number	Java.lang.Double
Date	Java.util.Date
BigNumer	BigDecimal
Binary	byte[]

The opposite occurs when you create an object inside the Java code and want to expose it as a new field to your transformation. For example, in the Java code, you defined the variable `qty` as `long` but under the **Fields** tab, you defined the new output field as `Integer`.

Generalizing you code

You can generalize your code by using parameters. You can add parameters and their values using the grid located under the **Parameters** tab at the bottom of the **UDJC** window.

In our example, you could have defined a parameter named `qtyParameter` with the value `7`. Then, in the Java code, you would have obtained this value with the following line of code:

```
long qty = getParameter("qtyParameter");
```

Looking up information with additional steps

You can also have additional steps that provide information to be read inside your Java code. They are called **Info steps**. You declare them in the grid located under the **Info step** tab at the bottom of the **UDJC** window.

In our recipe, suppose that you have the list of separators defined in a *Data Grid* step. In order to pick the separators from that list, you have to create a hop from the **Data Grid** towards the **UDJC** step and fill the **Info step** grid. You must provide a **Tag** name (for example, `charsList`) and select the name of the incoming step. Then, in the Java code, you can use the `findInfoRowSet()` method to reference the info step, and the `getRowFrom()` method to read the rows in a cycle. Check the code:

```
RowSet data = findInfoRowSet("charsList");
Object[] dataRow = null;
while((dataRow = getRowFrom(data)) != null){
//Do something
}
```

Customizing logs

You can add your custom messages for different levels of logging very easily. You can select the fragment of necessary code from the **Step logging** node in the `Code Snippets` folder, or just type the method in the edition area. For example:

```
if (qty ' 10) logBasic("Long sentence found!");
```

Scripting alternatives to the UDJC step

As an alternative to the **UDJC** step, there is another step named **User Defined Java Expression** (**UDJE**) also in the **Scripting** category. This step allows you to create new fields in an easy way by typing Java expressions. This step doesn't replace the functionality of that one, but it is more practical when the task you have to accomplish is simple.

 For examples on how to use this step, browse the different recipes in the book. There are several examples that use the *UDJE* step.

If you are more familiar with **JavaScript** language, instead of **UDJC** you could use the **Modified Java Script Value** (**MJSV**) step. Take into account that the code in the *JavaScript* step is interpreted, against the **UDJC** that is compiled; this means that a transformation that uses the *UDJC* step will have much better performance.

The UI for the **MJSV** step is very similar to the UI for the **UDJC** step; there is a main area to write the JavaScript code, a left panel with many functions as snippets, the input fields coming from the previous step, and the output fields.

You can learn more about JavaScript here: `http://www.w3schools.com/js`. As an additional resource, you can get *Pentaho 3.2 Data Integration: Beginner's Guide , María Carina Roldán, Packt Publishing*. There is a complete chapter devoted to the use of the *Modified Java Script Value* step.

Finally, if you prefer scripting to Java programming, there is a new Kettle plugin named **Ruby Scripting** developed by Slawomir Chodnicki, one of the most active Kettle contributors. As the name suggest, the step allows you develop custom functionality by typing Ruby code. The UI for the Ruby plugin is very similar to the UI for the *UDJC* step. In this case, you don't have snippets but you have many sample transformations that demonstrate the capabilities of the plugin. Along with the samples, you have a couple of links to Ruby resources on the web. The plugin is available at the following URL:

`https://github.com/type-exit/Ruby-Scripting-for-Kettle`

Generating sample data for testing purposes

Having sample data to test your transformations is very useful and allows you to move faster through your development and testing process. There are several cases where you will want to generate sample data, for example:

▶ To quickly populate datasets with random data

▶ Manually generate specific information

▶ Generate large volumes of custom data

▶ Take a subset from a large volume of data

In this recipe, you will learn how to generate a dataset with 100 random rows in different formats (integer, string, and dates). Then, in the *There's more* section, you will find alternative solutions for generating data for testing.

How to do it...

Carry out the following steps:

1. Create a new transformation.

2. Drop a **Generate rows** step from the **Input** category. Here, set the **Limit** textbox to 100.

3. Add a **Generate random value** step from the **Input** category. Add two elements to the grid: randomInteger of random integer type, and randomString of random string type.

4. Doing a preview on this last step, you will obtain a list of 100 random strings and integers. One example of this values would be: 1925608989 (integer) and 1jhn0udelvmpe (string)

All the integer values have a large number of digits. What if, for some particular purpose, you want an integer with few digits or an integer in a specific range of values? Let's create a random integer in another way.

1. Drop a **User Defined Java Expression** from the **Scripting** category. Add a new field named shortInteger and type the following text in the **Java expression** column: (int)Math.floor(Math.random()*3650). Also, select Integer in the **Value type** column.

2. Do a preview and check the new shorInteger field; it will have values between 0 and 3649.

Now, let's do a simple trick to create a random date.

1. In its **Field's** grid of the **Generate rows** step, create a new field named aDate, select Date in the **Type** listbox, use MM/dd/yyyy as the **Format**, and type 01/01/2000 in the **Value** column.

2. Add a **Calculator** step from the **Transform** category and complete the grid, as shown in the following screenshot:

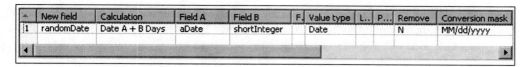

	New field	Calculation	Field A	Field B	F.	Value type	L..	P...	Remove	Conversion mask
1	randomDate	Date A + B Days	aDate	shortInteger		Date			N	MM/dd/yyyy

3. Finally, if you run a preview on this last step, you will have your desired random values in different formats. Check on the following screenshot, as an example:

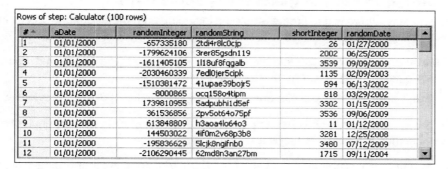

Rows of step: Calculator (100 rows)

#	aDate	randomInteger	randomString	shortInteger	randomDate
1	01/01/2000	-657335180	2tdi4r8lc0cjp	26	01/27/2000
2	01/01/2000	-1799624106	3rer85gsdn119	2002	06/25/2005
3	01/01/2000	-1611405105	1l18uf8fqgalb	3539	09/09/2009
4	01/01/2000	-2030460339	7edl0jer5cipk	1135	02/09/2003
5	01/01/2000	-1510381472	41upae39bojr5	894	06/13/2002
6	01/01/2000	-8000865	ocq158o4tipm	818	03/29/2002
7	01/01/2000	1739810955	5adpubhi1d5ef	3302	01/15/2009
8	01/01/2000	361536856	2pv5ot64o75pf	3536	09/06/2009
9	01/01/2000	613848809	h3aoa4lo64o3	11	01/12/2000
10	01/01/2000	144503022	4if0m2v68p3b8	3281	12/25/2008
11	01/01/2000	-195836629	5lcjk8ngifnb0	3480	07/12/2009
12	01/01/2000	-2106290445	62md8n3an27bm	1715	09/11/2004

How it works...

In this recipe, you have learnt the use of the _Generate random value_ step in order to generate random integer and string values.

The _Generate rows_ step, at the beginning, has the purpose of generating 100 blank rows, which will be filled later with random values. You can vary the **Limit** textbox if you desire a different number of rows.

Also, you have used the random function inside a Java expression, in order to generate a short integer by taking advantage of the _User Defined Java Expression_ step. In this way, you can also set the range for your random numbers.

Notice that in the _Generate rows_ step, you have declared a new field named aDate with the value 01/01/2000. This date will then be used in the _Calculator_ step. You generated a random date using a calculation that adds a random integer to the original date 01/01/2000. The integer has a value between 0 and 3649, which represents about 10 years, so the random date will be between 01/01/2000 and 28/12/2010.

There's more...

From the *Generate random value* step, you can also generate the following:

- Random numbers: Float values between 0 and 1
- **Universally Unique Identifier (UUID)**: Identifier standard such as b8f395d5-1344-11e0-af0b-6319f7359ecb
- Random message authentication code (**HMAC**): Typically, used in cryptography. For example, d59ee7a0e026aa1edc5c3398531d4452

In the following subsections, you will find more ways to generate data for testing in other scenarios.

Using Data grid step to generate specific data

The *Data grid* step allows you to create a dataset including both metadata and values inside the transformation. The step has the following two tabs:

- **Meta**: Under this tab, you add the fields and define their type and format. You can define fields using any of the Kettle data types.
- **Data**: Under this tab, you can enter the values for the fields defined previously.

This step is very useful when you need to populate a short list of rows with particular fields and/or values, thus avoiding creating a text file for that purpose.

Let's look at a practical example of the use of the *Data grid*. Suppose that you have created a regular expression and want to be sure that it is properly written. You can populate a data grid with a single String field. As values, you can type the list of values against which you want to test the regular expression, including values that should match the expression and values that shouldn't. After the *Data grid*, just add a *Regexp Evaluation* step, enter your regular expression, and do a preview on this step. That is a very easy and quick way of testing with the help of a *Data grid*.

The *Data grid* step was developed by **KJube** as part of its **Kettle Franchising Factory (KFF)** and contributed towards the standard PDI release. You can read more about KFF at the following URL:

```
http://kff.kjube.be/
```

Working with subsets of your data

On many occasions, you have to develop transformations that will process huge volumes of information. However, working with that volume during the development process is not a good idea: it slows down your development process, and makes testing what you are doing difficult. It's better to work with a small sample of that information.

There is a step named _Reservoir Sampling_ in the `Statistic` folder that allows you to return a subset of your incoming stream. In this step, you must set the number of rows to get in the **Sample size** textbox, and also set the **Random seed**, used internally in the step to produce a random sample of your data.

In the same category, you can find the _Sample rows_ step. This step also generates a subset of your incoming stream but, in this case, the rows are not chosen in a random way, you must specify the range as explained in _Chapter 6, Understanding Data Flows_.

See also

The recipe named _Doing different things based on the row number_ in _Chapter 6, Understanding Data Flows._ In the _There's more_ section of this recipe, you can see an example of the use of the _Sample rows_ step.

Working with Json files

JavaScript Object Notation (**Json**) is a lightweight language-independent data interchange format. It uses conventions similar to the C or JavaScript languages with some rules for the representation of structured data. The object is represented as a collection of `name_of_field:value_of_field` pairs and you can have an array of these elements using the `[]` characters.

PDI allows reading and writing these kind of files using the **Json input** and **Json output** steps from the **Input** category.

Let's see an example of reading a Json file. Let's assume that you have a file named `museums.js` that you want to read for further processing. The file has the following information:

```
{"data": {
   "museum": [
     {
     "country": "Italy",
     "city": "Venice",
     "id_museum": "109"
     "name": "Palazzo Ducale"},
     {
     "country": "Mexico",
     "city": "Mexico City",
     "id_museum": "36"
     "name": "Museo de Arte Contemporaneo de Monterrey"},
     {
     "country": "Italy",
     "city": "Florence",
```

```
      "id_museum": "47"
      "name": "Museo di San Marco"}
      ]
    }
  }
```

In addition, you want to read it for further processing.

Getting ready

To run this recipe, you need the `museums.js` file with the museum information shown earlier. You can also download the file from the book's site.

How to do it...

Carry out the following steps:

1. Create a new transformation.

2. Drop a **Json input** step from the **Input** category.

3. Type the name of the file with its complete path in the **File or directory** textbox located under the **File** tab. For example, `${Internal.Transformation. Filename.Directory}\museums.js`. Click on the **Add** button.

4. Complete the **Fields** tab as shown in the following screenshot:

	Name	Path	Type	F..	L...	P	C...	D..	G.	Trim ...	Repeat
1	country	$...country	String							none	N
2	city	$...city	String							none	N
3	id_museum	$...id_museum	String							none	N
4	name	$...name	String							none	N

5. Previewing the transformation, you will obtain a dataset with the museum information from the `museums.js` Json source file.

How it works...

The **Json input** step reads and interprets the `museum.js` Json data using the **Path** column under the **Files** tab. Here, you must use a JsonPath expression, in a similar way the XPath expressions are used in XML files.

A basic overview of the JsonPath syntax elements is shown in the following table:

JsonPath	Description
$	Root object
.	Child operator
[]	Array operator
[,]	Union operator in XPath

The child operator is used to access to different levels inside the Json structure, for example, `$...city` means "the `city` element inside the `museum` element inside the `data` element from the root".

If you want to access to a particular element, then you should use `$.data.museum[1].city`, that means "the `city` of the second `museum` element inside the `data` element from the root".

 Note that in Json, the lists are zero-based.

There's more...

You can find more information about Json language at the following URL:

`http://www.json.org/`

In the following subsections, you will find some considerations about reading and writing Json files:

Reading Json files dynamically

In this recipe, you used the **Json input** step to read the `museum.js` Json file, but you can also read the Json data from a field by checking the **Source is defined in a field?** checkbox and selecting the field in the **Get source from field** listbox.

Another option is when the name of the Json file is in a field. In this case, instead of typing the name of the file, you must check both the **Source is defined in a field?** and **Source is a filename?** checkboxes and select the field that contains the name of the Json file in the **Get source from field** listbox.

Writing Json files

If you need to create a file or a field in Json format, then you can use the **Json output** step from the **Output** category. Under the **General** tab of this step, there is a listbox named **Operation** where you can choose either a file or field destination.

If you choose a file destination, you need to fill the **Output File** section with information about the file to be generated. If you choose **Output value** operation, you must type the name of the new field in the **Output Value** textbox.

Then, under the **Fields** tab, you need to populate the grid with the source fields coming from the datasource, and the element name for the Json structure.

For example, assume that you are using a datasource with authors' information like the following:

```
"lastname","firstname","country","birthyear"
"Larsson","Stieg","Swedish",1954
"King","Stephen","American",1947
"Hiaasen","Carl ","American",1953
"Handler","Chelsea ","American",1975
"Ingraham","Laura ","American",1964
"Ramsey","Dave ","American",1960
"Kiyosaki","Robert ","American",1947,"A00007"
"Rowling","Joanne ","English",1965
"Riordan","Rick ","American",1964
```

If you add a **Json output** step and an **Output value** operation, then you will obtain a new field with each row in Json format, with a value as follows:

```
{"data":[{"lastname":"Larsson"},{"firstname":"Stieg"},{"country":"Swed
ish"},{"birthyear":1954}]}
```

Previewing the step, the result should be similar to the following:

	lastname	firstname	country	birthyear	outputValue
1	Larsson	Stieg	Swedish	1954	{"data":[{"lastname":"Larsson"},{"firstname":"Stieg"},{"co...
2	King	Stephen	American	1947	{"data":[{"lastname":"King"},{"firstname":"Stephen"},{"co...
3	Hiaasen	Carl	American	1953	{"data":[{"lastname":"Hiaasen"},{"firstname":"Carl "},{"co...
4	Handler	Chelsea	American	1975	{"data":[{"lastname":"Handler"},{"firstname":"Chelsea "},{...
5	Ingrah...	Laura	American	1964	{"data":[{"lastname":"Ingraham"},{"firstname":"Laura "},{"...
6	Ramsey	Dave	American	1960	{"data":[{"lastname":"Ramsey"},{"firstname":"Dave "},{"c...
7	Kiyosaki	Robert	American	1947	{"data":[{"lastname":"Kiyosaki"},{"firstname":"Robert "},{"...
8	Rowling	Joanne	English	1965	{"data":[{"lastname":"Rowling"},{"firstname":"Joanne "},{"...
9	Riordan	Rick	American	1964	{"data":[{"lastname":"Riordan"},{"firstname":"Rick "},{"cou...

Getting information about transformations and jobs (file-based)

The transformations and jobs are files with `.ktr` and `.kjb` extensions, but are, in fact, well-formed XML documents. You can open these files with a text editor to see their structures.

You could take advantage of this feature to process some information within these files. Let's look at an example: assume that you want to lookup the _Modified Java Script Value_ steps. You want to know where and how many of these steps are there because you want to replace them with a _User defined Java Class_ step, which provides better performance.

Getting ready

In order to use this recipe, you need a directory with a set of transformations, some of them including _Modified Java Script Value_ steps. The example points to the Kettle sample transformation directory.

How to do it...

Carry out the following steps:

1. Create a new transformation.

2. Drop a **Get data from XML** step from the **Input** category into the canvas.

3. Type or browse for the source transformations directory under the **File** tab, for example, `C:\Pentaho\pdi-ce-4.1\samples\transformations`. Type `.*\.ktr` in the **Regular Expression** textbox. Click on the **Add** button to populate the **Selected files** grid.

4. Select the **Content** tab and type `/transformation/step` in the **Loop XPath** textbox.

5. Complete the **Fields** tab as shown in the following screenshot:

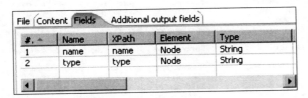

6. Under the **Additional output fields** tab, type `filename` in the **Short filename field**.

7. If you preview this step, you will obtain a list of all the steps from the transformations source directory, including information about what kind of step is it. Here's an example:

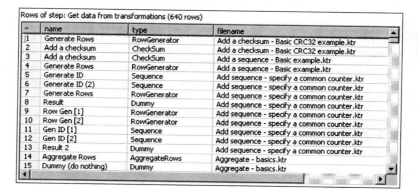

8. Add a **Filter rows step** from the **Flow** category. Add the following condition: `Type = ScriptValueMod`.

9. Now, previewing the step you will obtain only the name of the **Modified Java Script Value** steps included in the transformations, as well as the transformation filenames where these steps were found.

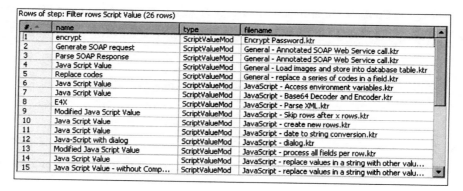

How it works...

In this recipe, you used the *Get data from XML* step to read the transformation files located in the directory `C:\Pentaho\pdi-ce-4.1\samples\transformations`.

By using the `/transformation/step` XPath node, you are getting a new row for each step in the transformations. As fields, you picked from that node the name of the step and its type.

Then, you used a *Filter rows* step to keep only the rows where the type of the step was equal to `ScriptValueMod`. This means, the *Modified Java Script Value* steps.

In the *Get data from XML* step, you also included the short filename of the transformation because you wanted to identify the source file of the transformations that had those steps.

There's more...

Here you can learn about the most important nodes in the transformation and job XML files.

Transformation XML nodes

LoopXPath	Information
/transformation	Root node for each transformation.
/transformation/info	One node for each transformation file. Here, you have the name and description of the transformation, its parameters, and the creation dates among others.
/transformation/notepads	From here you can get the notepads.
/transformation/info/log	You can get information about the transformation logging configuration.
/transformation/connection	One node for each database connection used in the transformation (or one for each database connection defined, if you didn't check the **Only save used connections to XML?** option)
/transformation/step	One node for each step of the transformation. You have the entire configuration of the step in this node; the most important elements here are the name of the step and its type.
/transformation/step/file	One node for each file or folder pointed to from a step. It includes data about the name of the file or folder, the mask typed, subfolders, and so on.
/transformation/step/field	One node for each field declared under the **Fields** tab of a step. You can get all the information about the fields, such as the name, its type, or the format configuration.
/transformation/order/hop	One node for each hop. Here you have the links between the steps.

Job XML nodes

LoopXPath	Information
/job	One node for each job. From here, you can get the name of the job and the parameters among other things.
/job/notepads	From here you can get the notepads.
/job/connection	One node for each database connection used in the job (or one for each database connection defined if you didn't check the **Only save used connections to XML?** option)
/job/job-log-table	These nodes have the job logging configuration.
/job/jobentry-log-table	
/job/channel-log-table	
/job/entries/entry	One node for each job entry. You can look here for the name of the entries, their type, and the entire configuration fields for the entries.
/job/hops/hop	One entry for each link between job entries.

Steps and entries information

You can check the name and the type of all steps in the **Step Information...** option from the **Help** menu of Spoon, as shown in the following screenshot:

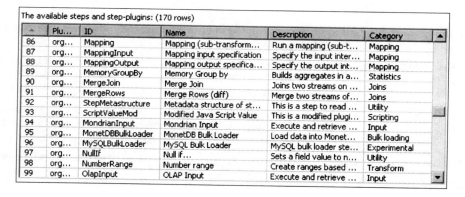

The **ID** column represents the steps identification, the **Name** column is how it appears in **Spoon**, and the **Description** column is the tool tip. You also can see the category of the step in the Category column.

In the recipe, you compared the **type** field in the transformation against the **ID** column in this list.

The **Job Entry Information...** option shows similar information, but for the job entries.

See also

The recipe named *Getting information about transformations and jobs (repository-based)* in this chapter. See this recipe if you are working with a database repository.

Getting information about transformations and jobs (repository-based)

In the previous recipe, you learned to read the `.ktr` and `.kjb` files to get information from the transformation and job files respectively. Spoon also allows for storing this data in tables in a relational database when using a repository-based configuration.

So, let's do the same task that we did in the previous recipe, but this time connect to a Kettle repository. The objective is to search for the *Modified Java Script Value* steps inside a set of transformations.

Getting ready

For running this recipe, you must have a Kettle repository and a set of transformations stored in it. If you don't have a list of sample transformations to play with, then you can connect to the repository and import them from the PDI samples directory.

How to do it...

Carry out the following steps:

1. Create a new transformation.
2. Drop a **Table input** step from the **Input** category into the canvas.
3. Create a connection to your repository database.
4. Type the following **SQL** statement:

```
SELECT  R_TRANSFORMATION.NAME AS transformation_name,
        R_STEP.NAME AS step_name,
        R_STEP_TYPE.CODE as step_type
FROM    R_STEP
INNER JOIN R_STEP_TYPE ON R_STEP.ID_STEP_TYPE =
        R_STEP_TYPE.ID_STEP_TYPE
INNER JOIN R_TRANSFORMATION ON R_STEP.ID_TRANSFORMATION =
        R_TRANSFORMATION.ID_TRANSFORMATION
WHERE   R_STEP_TYPE.CODE = 'ScriptValueMod'
```

5. Previewing this step, you will obtain a dataset with one row for each **Modified Java Script Value** step. In this dataset, you have the name of the transformation (in the **transformation_name** field) and the name of the Java script step (in the **step_name** field), as shown in the following screenshot:

Rows of step: Modified Java Script Value steps (29 rows)

#. ▲	transformation_name	step_name	step_type ▲
8	JavaScript Base64 Decoder and Encoder	Java Script Value	ScriptValueMod
9	JavaScript create new rows	Java Script Value	ScriptValueMod
10	JavaScript - date to string conversion	Java Script Value	ScriptValueMod
11	JavaScript dialog	Java-Script with dialog	ScriptValueMod
12	Hex convertor	Java Script Value	ScriptValueMod
13	example e4x	E4X	ScriptValueMod
14	JavaScript process all fields per row	Modified Java Script Value	ScriptValueMod
15	JavaScript - replace values in a string ...	Java Script Value	ScriptValueMod
16	JavaScript - replace values in a string ...	Java Script Value - without Compati...	ScriptValueMod
17	JavaScriptMod - skip rows after x rows	Modified Java Script Value	ScriptValueMod
18	JavaScript truncate a date	Modified Java Script Value	ScriptValueMod
19	Transformation 1	One line javascript step to convert ...	ScriptValueMod
20	example_uniq_rows_validation	Get two random numbers 1 - 10	ScriptValueMod
21	Easter-js	Modified Java Script Value	ScriptValueMod
22	XML Add - creating multi level XML files	Fill the placeholder	ScriptValueMod
23	XML Add - creating multi level XML files	Fill the placeholder 2	ScriptValueMod
24	XML Add - creating multi level XML files	Fill the placeholder 3	ScriptValueMod

How it works...

This recipe shows you how to read the transformation tables when you are working with a repository-based configuration.

The only thing to do here is to create a connection to the database where you have the repository and write the correct SQL Statement. In this case you must read the table that contains the steps (R_STEP) and filter those with match a **Modified Java Script Value** step (R_STEP_TYPE.CODE = 'ScriptValueMod'). If you open the R_STEP_TYPE table, then you can see the list of steps and verify that the ScriptValueMod code corresponds to a **Modified Java Script Value** step.

The SQL statement also includes a join with the R_TRANSFORMATION table in order to get the name of the transformation.

There's more...

A Kettle repository is made up of several tables where Kettle stores all the information related to transformations and jobs. The next subsections explain the most significant tables found in a repository

Transformation tables

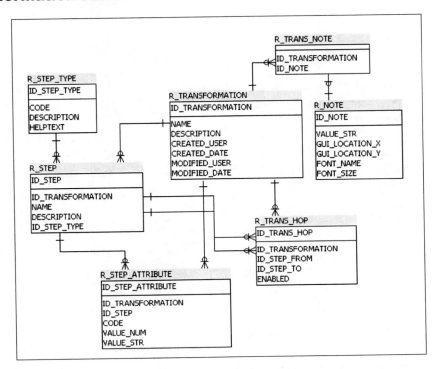

Table	Information
R_TRANSFORMATION	Here we have the basic information for the transformation, such as the transformation name or its creation date.
R_STEP	One record for each step. You can get the name of the step and the identification of its type.
R_STEP_TYPE	The list of step types. Here you can get the name, the description, and the tooltip for each kind of step.
R_TRANS_HOP	One record for each hop. It provides the information related to the link between steps.
R_STEP_ATTRIBUTE	Settings for the step. Each feature you define in a step is saved in the columns CODE and VALUE_NUM if the feature is a number, or CODE and VALUE_STR otherwise. For example, if the step represents the name of a file, then you will have CODE=filename and VALUE_STR=c:/files/sample.xls
R_TRANS_NOTE	Here are the notes from the transformation. There is a note identification field linked to the table R_NOTE, where you have the description of the note.

Job tables

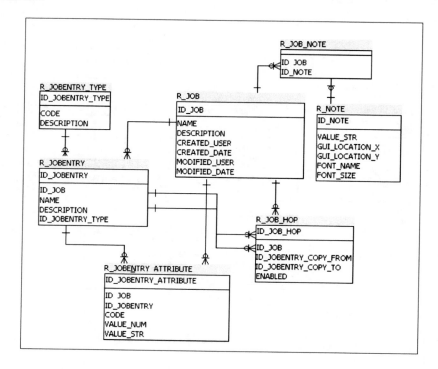

Table	Information
R_JOB	Basic information on the job. For example, its name or creation date.
R_JOBENTRY	One record for each job entry. Here you get the name and the type of the job entries.
R_JOBENTRY_TYPE	The list of the job entries (identification, name, and description)
R_JOB_HOP	One record for each hop. With this information, you know how the job entries are linked.
R_JOBENTRY_ATTRIBUTE	Settings for the step. Each feature you define in a step is saved in the columns CODE and VALUE_NUM if the feature is a number, or CODE, and VALUE_STR otherwise. See R_STEP_ATTRIBUTE in the previous table for an example.
R_JOB_NOTE	Here are the notes from the job. There is a note identification field linked to the table R_NOTE, where you have the description of the note.

Database connections tables

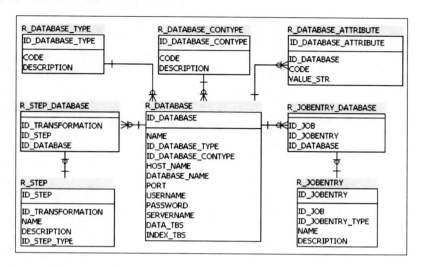

Table	Information
R_DATABASE	Here we have the settings for the database connections used in the steps or entries
R_STEP_DATABASE	One record for each step that uses a database connection. It links the step with the database identification.
R_JOBENTRY_DATABASE	One record for each entry job that uses a database connection. It links the entry job with the database identification.
R_DATABASE_TYPE	List of database engines. For example, MYSQL, ORACLE, DB2, MSSQL, among others.
R_DATABASE_CONTYPE	Type of access to the database: Native, ODBC, OCI, Plugin, JNDI.
R_DATABASE_ATTRIBUTE	Here, you have the settings for each database connection. In the CODE column, you have the name of the variable whereas in the VALUE_STR column, you have the value.

Data Structures

This appendix describes some structures used in several recipes through the book.

There are two objectives in describing them here (besides keeping the explanation in a single place): one is that you understand the structure of the data being used. The second, is allowing you to create your own data in the format of your choice: database, Excel file, and so on, excepting of course, when the data is used in a recipe that explain database steps, in which case the data should be in a database.

Book's data structure

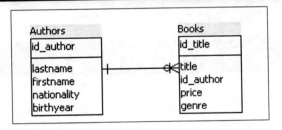

Books

Field	Description	Example
`id_title`	Identification for the book. It is a string with the format `CCC-CCC` (3 characters, a hyphen, and 3 more characters)	`123-456`
`title`	Title of the book	`The Tommyknockers`
`id_author`	Identification for the author of a book; it references to the author's data	`A00002`
`price`	Price for the book. It's a decimal value.	`39.00`
`genre`	Genre of the books	`Fiction.` Possible values are: `Fiction`, `Non-fiction`, `Business` or `Children`

Authors

Field	Description	Example
`id_author`	Identification for the author	`A00002`
`lastname`	Author's last name	`King`
`firstname`	Author's first name	`Stephen`
`nationality`	Author's nationality	`American`
`birthyear`	Year of author's birth. It's a numeric value.	`1947`

Museum's data structure

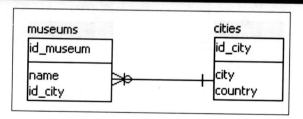

Museums

Field	Description	Example
id_museum	Identification for the museum	3
name	Museum's name	Museo de Arte Latinoamericano
id_city	Identification for the city; it references to the city's data	1

Cities

Field	Description	Example
id_city	Identification for the city	1
city	City's name	Buenos Aires
country	City's country	Argentina

Outdoor data structure

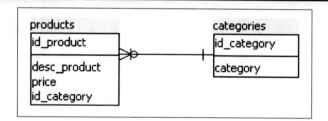

Products

Field	Description	Example
Id_product	Identification for the product	12
desc_product	Product's description	Kelty Grand Mesa 2-Person Tent (Ruby/Tan)
price	Product's price	$107.96
Id_category	Identification for the category; it references to the category's data	4

Categories

Field	Description	Example
Id_category	Identification for the category	4
category	Category's description	Tents

Steel Wheels structure

Some specific recipes use the Steel Wheels database included in Pentaho. This database represents the data for a fictional store named Steel Wheels. In the following diagram, you can see the tables used in the recipes and how they are related:

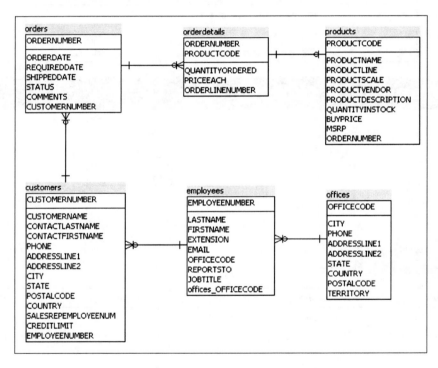

Index

internet
  data, searching over 173, 174
intranet
  data, searching over 173, 174

J

Janino library 253
jar file 10
Jaro algorithm 168
Jaro-Winkler algorithm 168
Java
  URL, for tutorials 299
JavaScript step
  executions, controlling 235
JDBC 252
JNDI data source 9
job, executing
  by setting parameters 217-219
  by setting parameters dynamically 220, 221
  by setting static arguments 217-219
  by setting static arguments
        dynamically 220, 221
  job name, determining at runtime 223-225
job part
  executing, for every row in dataset 225-228
  executing, until true condition 231-234
jobs
  copied row, accessing from 229, 230
  executing, by setting parameters 217-219
  executing, by setting static
        arguments 217-219
  job part, executing for every row
        in dataset 225-228
  launching 216
  log files, isolating for 292
  loops, implementing in 235
job XML nodes 312
Join Rows (Cartesian product) step 197
joins options
  about 200
  FULL OUTER join 200
  INNER join 200
  LEFT OUTER join 200
  RIGHT OUTER join 200
Json
  about 305
  URL, for info 307

Json files
  example 305
  reading, dynamically 307
  working with 306, 307
  writing 307, 308
Json input step 306
junk dimension tables 25

K

Kettle
  about 6, 8, 214, 249
  custom functionality, programming 293-299
  custom log file, generating 288-291
  e-mails, sending with attached files 284-286
  folders, comparing with files 141, 142
  jobs, launching 216
  process flow, creating 237-240
  rows, merging of two streams 184-187
  sample data, generating for testing
        purpose 302, 303
  transformations, launching 216
  unsupported database connection 10
KettleComponent inputs 265
Kettle Franchising Factory (KFF) 304
keywords 15
Kitchen documentation
  URL 217
kjb file 10
KJube 288, 304
ktr file 10, 225

L

last row
  identifying, in stream 210
LEFT OUTER join 200
Levenshtein algorithm 168
libext/JDBC directory 10
lib folder 257
location
  specifying, of transformation 265
log files
  about 63
  clean log file, creating 292
  filtering 292
  isolating, for different jobs 292
  isolating, for transformations 292

X

xls extension 126, 127
XML 93, 252
XML, as field 96
XML file
  validating, against DTD definitions 106-108
  validating, against XSD schema 108-111
XML file name, as field 96
XML Schema Definition. *See* **XSD schema**
XML structures
  fields, generating with 113, 114
XML transformation
  HTML page, generating with 121-123

XPath 100
XPath notation
  fields, specifying with 97-100
  multiple nodes, retrieving 102
  working 100
XSD schema
  XML file, validating against 108-111
XSL transformation
  HTML page, generating with 121-123

Z

ZIP files
  working with 145-147

Thank you for buying
Pentaho Data Integration 4 Cookbook

About Packt Publishing

Packt, pronounced 'packed', published its first book "*Mastering phpMyAdmin for Effective MySQL Management*" in April 2004 and subsequently continued to specialize in publishing highly focused books on specific technologies and solutions.

Our books and publications share the experiences of your fellow IT professionals in adapting and customizing today's systems, applications, and frameworks. Our solution based books give you the knowledge and power to customize the software and technologies you're using to get the job done. Packt books are more specific and less general than the IT books you have seen in the past. Our unique business model allows us to bring you more focused information, giving you more of what you need to know, and less of what you don't.

Packt is a modern, yet unique publishing company, which focuses on producing quality, cutting-edge books for communities of developers, administrators, and newbies alike. For more information, please visit our website: www.packtpub.com.

About Packt Open Source

In 2010, Packt launched two new brands, Packt Open Source and Packt Enterprise, in order to continue its focus on specialization. This book is part of the Packt Open Source brand, home to books published on software built around Open Source licences, and offering information to anybody from advanced developers to budding web designers. The Open Source brand also runs Packt's Open Source Royalty Scheme, by which Packt gives a royalty to each Open Source project about whose software a book is sold.

Writing for Packt

We welcome all inquiries from people who are interested in authoring. Book proposals should be sent to author@packtpub.com. If your book idea is still at an early stage and you would like to discuss it first before writing a formal book proposal, contact us; one of our commissioning editors will get in touch with you.

We're not just looking for published authors; if you have strong technical skills but no writing experience, our experienced editors can help you develop a writing career, or simply get some additional reward for your expertise.

Pentaho 3.2 Data Integration: Beginner's Guide

ISBN: 978-1-847199-54-6   Paperback: 492 pages

Explore, transform, validate, and integrate your data with ease

1. Get started with Pentaho Data Integration from scratch.

2. Enrich your data transformation operations by embedding Java and JavaScript code in PDI transformations.

3. Create a simple but complete Datamart Project that will cover all key features of PDI.

JasperReports 3.5 for Java Developers

ISBN: 978-1-847198-08-2   Paperback: 368 pages

Create, Design, Format, and Export Reports with the world's most popular Java reporting library

1. Create better, smarter, and more professional reports using comprehensive and proven methods

2. Group scattered data into meaningful reports, and make the reports appealing by adding charts and graphics

3. Discover techniques to integrate with Hibernate, Spring, JSF, and Struts, and to export to different file formats

Please check **www.PacktPub.com** for information on our titles

open source *
community experience distilled

PACKT
PUBLISHING

Pentaho Reporting 3.5 for Java Developers

ISBN: 978-1-847193-19-3   Paperback: 384 pages

Create advanced reports, including cross tabs, sub-reports, and charts that connect to practically any data source using open source Pentaho Reporting

1. Create great-looking enterprise reports in PDF, Excel, and HTML with Pentaho's Open Source Reporting Suite, and integrate report generation into your existing Java application with minimal hassle

2. Use data source options to develop advanced graphs, graphics, cross tabs, and sub-reports

3. Dive deeply into the Pentaho Reporting Engine's XML and Java APIs to create dynamic reports

JasperReports 3.6 Development Cookbook

ISBN: 978-1-849510-76-9   Paperback: 396 pages

Over 50 recipes to create next-generation reports using JasperReports

1. Create, size, and position the titles, headers, footers, and body of your report using JasperReports and iReport

2. Enhance the look and feel of your report using background images, watermarks, and other such features

3. Create multi-page and multi-column reports using multiple types of data in the same report

Please check **www.PacktPub.com** for information on our titles

Lightning Source UK Ltd.
Milton Keynes UK
UKOW020731070613

211896UK00004B/136/P